THE BOOK OF ART

THOMAS J. CRAUGHWELL

Tess Press

This edition published by Tess Press, an imprint of
Black Dog & Leventhal Publishers, Inc.
151 West 19th Street
New York, NY 10011

Manufactured in China

ISBN-13: 978-1-60376-038-6

h g f e d c b a

CONTENTS

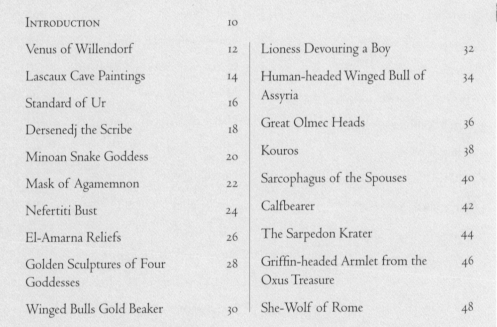

30,000 B.C.

Venus of Willendorf

ca. 2400 B.C.

Dersenedj the Scribe

ca. 1500 B.C.

Mask of Agamemnon

ca. 500 B.C.

She-Wolf of Rome

ca. 500 B.C.
Griffin-headed Armlet

ca. 460 B.C.
Poseidon of Artemision

ca. 211 B.C.

Terracotta Army of Xian

ca. 100 B.C.

Alexander Mosaic

ca. 80 B.C.

Venus de Milo

ca. 800

Book of Kells

ca. 1200

Muisca Raft

ca. 1330

Great Mongol
Shahnama

1431

Cantoria Panels

1445

Portrait of a Lady

1511

Creation of Adam

ca. 1512
Isenheim Alterpiece

ca. 1520
Ivory Pendant of Idia

1633
Storm of the Sea of Galillee

1665
Girl with a Pearl Earring

1759
Still Life with Fruit and a Glass

1778

Watson and the Shark

1856

Sudden Shower at the Atake Bridge

1861

Frederick Remington

1872

Piet Mondrian

ca. 1876

Prima Ballerina

1880
Pointillism

1886
The Kiss

1892
Erté

1898
Tamara de Lempicka

1913
Composition VII

Small Vase of Flowers

1916

Dadaism

1920

Socialist Realism

1931

My Uncle

1935

Ram's Head White Hollyhock and Little Hills

1991

INTRODUCTION

For many people fine art is as puzzling as Egyptian hieroglyphics. Yet in almost every case artists intend their paintings or sculptures to be accessible. If nobody can understand what the artist is doing, no one will look. Worse, no one will buy!

To be honest, much of the work of the last one hundred years, the period loosely covered by the term Modern Art, has only made the situation more difficult. Many artists of the 20th century rejected traditional notions of beauty and composition, opting for various cerebral approaches to painting and sculpture that left most viewers baffled, troubled, and sometimes offended. A notorious example took place in New York City in the 1980s. A government-sponsored arts organization commissioned Minimalist sculptor Richard Serra to create a sculpture for Federal Plaza in Lower Manhattan. Serra delivered a piece he called *Tilted Arc*, a massive rusting steel wall one-hundred-twenty-feet long and twelve-feet high. Employees at Federal Plaza, and even passers-by, found Serra's *Arc* alienating, intimidating, and utterly depressing. They petitioned—successfully—to have the rusty wall removed. Rarely do we encounter such a clear-cut example of the polarization of the artist and his audience. It reinforced a widespread notion among the public that modern artists regard ordinary people with contempt and confirmed a belief among artists that they were persecuted and misunderstood.

From the beginning, and for most of human history, art was not polarizing, nor was it the exclusive property of museums and connoisseurs—it appeared in everyday settings where everybody could see it, and in quite a few cases even own it (after all, it didn't cost much to buy a beautifully made pottery bowl, or a woodcut holy card). One of the main goals of this book, then, is to reassure our readers that in the vast majority of cases, art is viewer-friendly. And even those Serra-esque works of art that people find it hard to warm up to deserve at the very least to be understood. You don't have to like it, but it never hurts to learn the idea behind the style.

The Book of Art is arranged as a visual timeline, starting ca. 30,000 B.C. with a chubby clay figurine known as the Venus of Willendorf. It spotlights 250 masterpieces (*Mona Lisa* and *Starry Night*), artists (Mary Cassatt and Joshua Reynolds), movements (Baroque and Pop Art), and types of art (Bas Relief and Fresco). I've avoided the jargon of specialists, and tried to discuss each work of art in a straight-forward, down-to-earth manner. Since works of art are influenced by their times, I've told stories of political, social, and religious movements that are reflected in the painting or sculpture. If incidents from the artist's life were a factor, I tell those stories, too.

I've identified religious, mythological, and historical figures; explained symbolic elements; and pointed out the artwork's composition and the artist's technique. The objective of this book is to give viewers a way into the work of art, to help them understand not only why Giotto was a such a big deal in his day, but also what Andy Warhol was thinking when he painted a giant can of Campbell's Tomato Soup.

Venus of Willendorf

The traditional name for this little sculpture—Venus of Willendorf—has become a point of contention in recent years. Some archaeologists and art historians argue that the name "Venus" (which was given to the figurine and the dozens of others like it that have been found in prehistoric sites across Europe) is an ironic, even disparaging moniker since the woman represented is so obviously a departure from the classical ideal of what the goddess of love must look like. For these critics, the preferred name is "the Woman of Willendorf." There is no grand arbiter of such things, so viewers are free to call the little statue anything they like.

This sculpture was discovered in 1908 near the village of Willendorf in Austria by the archaeologist Josef Szombathy. The statuette is carved from limestone, stands 4.375 inches high, and once was painted with red ochre, traces of which can still be detected on the piece. Because the breasts are large and full and the belly is prominent it has always been believed that the woman depicted is pregnant and close to giving birth. Those details, combined with the way the sculptor emphasized the genitals, have led art historians to believe that this is a fertility figure. Some have even identified it as a representation of the Earth Mother, or Mother Goddess. We know so little about the religious beliefs of humans 30,000 years ago, however, that such ideas must be chalked up to pure speculation.

There are many intriguing details in this small sculpture. While the tight braids of the woman's hair are carefully carved, her face is blank—no features at all. The arms are thin, almost skeletal, and the figure has no feet. Exactly what these things mean is an ongoing subject of debate. For nonexperts the statue has an undeniable appeal—enigmatic, fascinating, even humorous.

Lascaux Cave Paintings

In the late 1930s, on a wooded hill above the village of Montignac, near the manor of Lascaux in France, a huge pine tree toppled over, revealing a narrow opening into an underground cavern. No one explored the cave until September 12, 1940, when four teenage boys with a taste for adventure squeezed through the crevice, scooted down a large pile of rocks, and entered a long underground chamber. As they swung their lantern around they saw painted on the walls images of bulls, stags, and horses. This chamber, known today as the Great Hall of the Bulls, led directly into a place even more wonderful—the Painted Gallery, a passageway about 90 feet long, almost completely covered with magnificent paintings of wild beasts, including aurochs, a kind of ox that has long been extinct. Art historians call the Painted Gallery "the Sistine Chapel of prehistoric art."

The unknown artists used paints derived from metal oxides, including iron oxide and manganese oxide. In other chambers, the figures of animals were incised into the stone face of the cave, probably using a sharp piece of flint. There is only one human figure in the Lascaux caves, in a room known as the Shaft of the Dead Man. The scene is dramatic: A man lies flat on the ground while above him is a huge bison, its head down, poised to gore the man. Off to one side, a figure of a rhinoceros is seen fleeing from the bison.

After the end of World War II, the Lascaux caves became a tourist destination, with about 1,200 visitors escorted through the chambers every day. By 1955 it was obvious to the caretakers of the caves that the tours were altering the atmosphere and the paintings were beginning to deteriorate. In 1963 the French Ministry of Cultural Affairs decided to close the caves to tourists. Since 1983, however, visitors have been able to explore Lascaux II, an exact reproduction of the Great Hall of the Bulls and the Painted Chamber.

THE STANDARD OF UR

ca. 2500 B.C.

In the 1920s, when English archaeologist Leonard Woolley uncovered this object, he wasn't entirely sure what he had found. He discovered it lying in a large tomb in the Royal Cemetery of Ur in southern Iraq, so he assumed it must be something of great significance. The "thing" was triangular in shape, approximately 19.5 inches long by 8.5 inches high. On one side were scenes of war, on the other scenes of peace. Woolley concluded he had found the national emblem or standard of the kings of ancient Sumeria, and so the object has been known as the Standard of Ur (Ur was the Sumerian capital). In fact, no one knows how the Sumerians used it; nonetheless, Woolley's name for the beautiful but mysterious object has stuck.

Sumer is one of the oldest civilizations in the world. The city of Ur was the home of Abraham before he set out for Canaan, and it is possible that Ur's ziggurats, a kind of pyramid-shaped temple that rises on a series of steplike platforms, were the inspiration for the biblical story of the Tower of Babel.

The Standard is two mosaic panels made of shell, red limestone, and the semi-precious blue stone, lapis lazuli. The War panel depicts the Sumerian army on the march, complete with chariots. The Sumerians skewer their enemies with spears, crush them beneath the wheels of their chariots, then strip and bind the prisoners of war and present them to the King of Sumeria. The Peace panel shows men herding flocks of goats, drinking at a banquet, and listening to a musician play the lyre.

Woolley brought his treasure home to England where it is displayed today in the British Museum in London.

DERSENEDJ THE SCRIBE

ca. 2400 B.C.

Nearly 27 inches tall, this almost life-size sculpture represents the Egyptian scribe Dersenedj. He was a bureaucrat who worked at one of the granaries of Egypt. He is shown here, carved in pink granite, doing his job—a papyrus scroll lies unrolled in his lap, and his fingers are in the position of holding a pen. This is not a portrait sculpture: There is nothing individualistic about the face, the body is barely carved at all, and the head shows faint lines to suggest the bands of plaited hair in Dersenedj's wig. Very likely the statue was carved for his tomb.

The sculpture dates from the period known as the Old Kingdom (ca. 2649–2150 B.C.). Typical of the Old Kingdom style, the Dersenedj statue portrays the scribe as heavily although indistinctly muscled (he is not "chiseled," in either the classical Greek or in the bodybuilding sense). His face is round and bland. There are no distinguishing features or characteristics to the figure because this sculpture is not intended to be a portrait; it is supposed to represent a type that will live on in the Egyptian afterlife. Later sculptures from the Old Kingdom period show a more refined, less lumpy approach to carving, but individuality is still absent.

The other important goal of Old Kingdom artists was to uphold the hierarchy of the kingdom. The pharaoh appears quasi-divine, or at least more than an ordinary man, because that is the role he plays in Egyptian society. Dersenedj is shown seated on the ground, his legs crossed, his hand ready to write. The pose tells us that he was a scribe, and while scribes were essential in a kingdom where very, very few people could read or write, they were still far from Egypt's upper strata. Consequently, Dersenedj appears dowdy rather than heroic.

Minoan Snake Goddess

Arthur Evans (1851–1941) was not the man who discovered the palace complex of Knossos on the island of Crete, but he did excavate the entire site. To ensure that his right to dig could not be challenged by any rival archaeologists, around the year 1900, he bought the entire area and then started digging in earnest. In 1903, Evans uncovered a remarkable artifact—a faience figurine (faience is a type of glazed ceramic), 13.5 inches high, of a woman in a long gown, with her breasts exposed, her arms raised, and holding a snake in each hand. Evans called it "the Votary," meaning a person dedicated to a god and sworn to serve in the god's temple. It was art historians who named the figure "the Snake Goddess." Unfortunately, after more than a century of digging all over the island, virtually no archaeological evidence has turned up to suggest that there was a serpent cult among the Minoans.

The figurine is elegant, graceful, dressed in the formal style of the Minoan court with multiple flounces falling from her waist to her feet. The snakes writhe in her hands, which gives the little statue an extra touch of animation. The figure is so famous and so appealing that there is always a large crowd around the case in which it is displayed in the Heraklion Archaeological Museum in Crete.

Since the identification of the figurine has never been definitively proven, art critics, anthropologists, students of religion, and fans continue to project their own interpretations on to the "Snake Goddess." She is said to be a fertility figure (because her breasts are large and exposed), or a malevolent goddess from the underworld (because she holds snakes), or a household goddess for women. In more recent times feminists and goddess worshippers have interpreted the figurine as a representation of the spiritual power of women.

Mask of Agamemnon

In 1876, Heinrich Schliemann (1822–1890), a German amateur archaeologist and treasure hunter, was excavating at Mycenae, the site of the ancient palace and fortress of Agamemnon, his queen Clytemnestra, and their children Orestes and Electra. Schliemann was obsessed with ancient Greek mythology, and was especially keen to prove that Homer's epic poem, the *Iliad*, was based on historical events.

At the bottom of a burial shaft, in what is known as Grave V, Schliemann found the remains of a warrior king, buried with his weapons, his face covered with this golden mask. According to an archaeological urban legend, Schliemann cabled the king of Greece (or a Greek newspaper—there are at least two versions of the story), "I have gazed on the face of Agamemnon." In fact, Schliemann did not say the mask covered the face of Agamemnon; since it is the finest of the golden masks found at Mycenae, it came to be attributed to the renowned king who had led the Greeks against Troy.

Unlike the other masks in the royal burial shafts, this one is three-dimensional (the others are flat). The eyebrows are arched and individual (most Mycenaean masks show a "unibrow"). The mouth is expressive, the nose and ears very prominent, and in addition to the triangular beard found in other Mycenaean masks, this man has a handlebar mustache. These features, which make the mask distinctive, have given rise to charges that it is a forgery, or a pastiche, or a mask from another, unknown ancient site that Schliemann used to "seed" the burial shaft. The argument continues to rage in archaeological journals. In the meantime, the curators of the National Archaeological Museum in Athens display the mask as one of their greatest treasures.

NEFERTITI BUST

ca. 1305 B.C.

A masterpiece of ancient Egyptian portrait sculpture, this bust of the queen Nefertiti is thought to have been carved by Thutmose, the master sculptor, because it was unearthed by German archaeologists in 1912 in the remains of his house and studio at El-Amarna. Under the circumstances, it is a logical assumption.

The bust is carved limestone and painted in multiple brilliant colors (a technique known as polychrome). The sculpture is wonderfully realistic, a product of a new style of art promoted by Nerfertiti's husband, Pharaoh Akhenaten. Previously, pharaohs, their families, and their entourage had been represented in a lovely but highly idealized manner. During the reign of Akhenaten, a new naturalistic style became fashionable. The pharaoh himself was depicted with a long face, thin arms and legs, a protruding belly, and big, broad hips. It is possible that Akhenaten insisted, for reasons that have not come down to us, upon accurate portraits of himself, in which case it stands to reason that Nefertiti's portrait is also a true likeness. (Her name, incidentally, means "a beautiful woman has arrived.")

Nefertiti is believed to have been the stepmother of the famous Tutankhamun, or "King Tut."

The portrait bust has been in the Egyptian Museum in Berlin, Germany, since 1913, but a squabble erupted around the sculpture in 2007. Zahi Hawass, head of Egypt's Supreme Council of Antiquities, claimed that Germany acquired the artifact illegally and demanded its return. Then Hawass declared he would settle for a temporary loan of the piece so the Egyptian people would have an opportunity to look upon the face of their queen. The museum curators in Berlin have insisted that Germany acquired the bust legally and have declined to lend it to Egypt, citing their anxiety that the statue might be damaged in transit.

EL-AMARNA RELIEFS

ca. 1360 B.C.

About 200 miles south of Cairo, on the eastern bank of the Nile, lie the ruins of El-Amarna, for a very brief time the capital of Egypt. Akhenaten is remembered as the pharaoh who turned his back on the gods of Egypt and urged his people to follow his example and worship only Aten, the god represented by the disk of the sun. As another sign of his break with Egypt's past, Akhenaten built a new royal city, El-Amarna, where there would be no temples except those dedicated to Aten, and where the pharaoh and his queen, the exquisitely lovely Nefertiti, would be the high priest and high priestess.

The pharaoh's interest extended beyond theology to art. He sponsored a new style that esteemed accuracy and naturalism, especially in depictions of people. In the place of the rigid, idealized figures of traditional Egyptian art, Akhenaten called for paintings, reliefs, and sculptures that would portray the love that exists between husbands and wives, parents and children. These lifelike works of art also showed human emotion, which was unprecedented in ancient Egypt.

The reliefs—and the paintings, too—from El-Amarna are a clear break with Egypt's artistic past. Men, women, and children are no longer perfect human specimens, the ancient world's equivalent of models. If they are skinny, chubby, or have oddly shaped heads, the artists of El-Amarna painted them that way. But the El-Amarna artists were just as honest if their subject was truly beautiful, as in the case of the queen, Nefertiti. The quality of the work at El-Amarna was superb, but after the death of Akhenaten, the city was abandoned, as were his ideas about one god and naturalism in art.

GOLDEN SCULPTURES OF FOUR GODDESSES

Part of the elaborate embalming process practiced in ancient Egypt was the removal of the deceased's lungs, liver, intestines, and stomach. Each of these organs was mummified, then sealed in separate jars (known as canopic jars), and each jar was placed in a separate compartment in a wooden box that was entombed with the body. In the case of the boy-pharaoh Tutankhamun, the process was much more impressive. Howard Carter (1874–1939), the English archaeologist who discovered the young king's intact tomb in 1922, found Tutankhamun's organs enshrined in a grand wooden chest, about 6 feet high, sheathed in gold. Standing around the chest were gilded images of four Egyptian goddesses: Isis, Selket, Nephthys, and Neith. The statues, all standing about 35.5 inches high, all carved from wood, then covered with thin sheets of gold, and their eyes and eyebrows delineated with thick lines of black paint, are perfectly identical—only the unique emblem each figure wears on its head distinguishes one goddess from another. Carter found the statues of the four goddesses standing, one on each side of the chest, each with its arms extended, protecting the sacred viscera of the king. The heads of the goddesses are turned and they look over their shoulders so they will not be surprised by any evil thing that may try to creep up behind them. On Isis' head is her traditional symbol: an empty throne, a reference to her murdered husband, the god Osiris.

Carter praised the statues, saying, "They represent the culminating power of Egyptian art in the Eighteenth Dynasty—they are tender in feeling and true to the idea." (The Eighteenth Dynasty, 1550–1292 B.C., saw a kind of artistic renaissance in Egypt, culminating in the expressive, realistic Amarna style sponsored by Pharaoh Akhenaten, the man who was probably Tutankhamun's father.)

Winged Bulls Gold Beaker

Imagine an entire cemetery filled with King Tut-type tombs. That is what archaeologists discovered in 1961 at Marlik in northern Iran—dozens of graves dating back more than 3,000 years, and none of them had been looted by grave robbers or treasure hunters. In less than a year, the excavators had retrieved thousands of precious artifacts, including hundreds of objects made of gold or silver. The beauty of these works of art stunned the archaeologists, but one in particular took everyone's breath away. This gold beaker, or cup, was covered with a sculpture in high relief of four winged bulls. These are mythical creatures, but the portrayal of the winged bulls is so intricate, so natural, that it seems within the realm of possibility that they might soar into the air.

The bulls stand in pairs on their hind legs, with their forelegs resting against the trunk of a palm tree. The detail of the feathers of the wings, the hide of the bulls, as well as their faces, is astonishing.

The cup, which stands a little over 7 inches high and is 5.5 inches across, was made from almost pure gold, a choice that made the metal very soft. Consequently, the beaker became crushed during its long centuries in the grave. Although the shape of the cup is not perfect, the artistry of the piece is not diminished in the least.

Tragically, in 1962, the government of Iran ordered the archaeologists to leave the site. In their absence, grave robbers looted the remaining artifacts at Marlik.

Lioness Devouring a Boy

Renowned British archaeologist Max Mallowan (he is also famous as the husband of the best-selling mystery writer, Agatha Christie) discovered this ivory carving in the bottom of a well at the palace of King Ashurnasirpal II (reigned 883–859 B.C.) in Nimrud, the capital city of the ancient Assyrians. It is one of a pair of carvings that probably adorned an elaborate piece of royal furniture, possibly a throne. When the Medes and the Babylonians conquered the city in 612 B.C., the palace was destroyed and many of its treasures smashed and scattered.

It is an interesting piece on several levels. In the first place, it is not Assyrian work—it was created by a Phoenician artist who probably worked somewhere in what is now Lebanon. Second, the scene is not Mesopotamian—the youth is African, probably from a noble family since he was portrayed originally wearing an armlet and a bracelet (the jewelry is gone, but the marks on the ivory show where they were attached to the figure). Furthermore, his pleated kilt is gilded, and so is his hair.

Above the sculpture is a pattern of stylized lilies and papyrus. This area was gilded, too, and set with carnelian and lapis lazuli. A bit of lapis lazuli was even embedded in the forehead of the lioness. This was, then, a very opulent piece of furniture.

It is a sensuous carving: The lioness has wrapped one of her forepaws around the boy, as if embracing him. And although she has sunk her teeth into his throat, his facial expression is serene—no trace of pain or even fear.

ca. 900 B.C.

HUMAN-HEADED WINGED BULL OF ASSYRIA

In 879 B.C., the king of Assyria, Ashurnasirpal II (reigned 883–859 B.C.), inaugurated his capital at Nimrud in what is now northern Iraq. It was an entirely new city, built from scratch, that covered an area of 900 acres. In the center of town Ashurnasirpal erected his palaces, temples, and offices for the administrators of the Assyrian Empire. And to ward off invaders, he surrounded the 5-mile circumference of his city with defensive walls 42 feet high. An inscription survives that tells us, in Ashurnasirpal's own words, how he decorated his palace. "Beasts of the mountains and the seas, which I had fashioned out of white limestone and alabaster, I had set up in its gates. I made it [the palace] fittingly imposing."

The technical name for these "fittingly imposing" sculptures (they stand over 10 feet tall) is *lamassu*. They represent divine spirits who guard the palace, the king, and the empire. The sweeping horns on the hat represent immortality, and the belt around the bull's loins is an emblem of power.

The bull also has five legs. It is a kind of early *trompe l'oeil*: Seen straight on from the front the bull appears to be standing rigidly at attention, like a palace guard. But seen from the side, the bull's legs are carved as if it were moving forward.

GREAT OLMEC HEADS

The Olmecs were the first great civilization of Mesoamerica. They lived in south-central Mexico, the area roughly equivalent to the modern states of Veracruz and Tabasco. This was a fertile region, well watered with rivers and streams. It was easy here to produce an abundant crop of maize, or corn, and with the essentials of life taken care of, the Olmecs had time for other pursuits: They produced the first writing system in the Americas, developed a compass, and created works of art of astonishing power and beauty. Among their most impressive works are the Great Heads. Seventeen have been found so far, and they measure in size from 4 feet, 9 inches to 11 feet high, and weigh on average 20 tons.

The heads are carved from single blocks of basalt, a volcano rock the Olmecs quarried in the Tuxtlas Mountains. They were carved in 850 to 700 B.C. in place at the quarry, then dragged or possibly floated on heavy-duty rafts to the Olmecs' ceremonial centers at La Venta, San Lorenzo, and other locations. Archaeologists have estimated that it would have taken a work crew of about 1,500 men three or four months to move a stone head from the quarry to its final destination.

The heads wear a helmet that is believed to be part of the gear Olmecs wore during the ritual ballgame that was part of religious life in Mesoamerica for 3,000 years. Since their name means "the rubber people," the Olmecs may have invented the ballgame.

Some viewers see African or Asian facial features in the colossal heads, which has led to theories that the great civilizations of Central and South America were founded by settlers from Africa and/or Asia. In the absence of any other evidence, no reputable historian believes such claims.

The heads were set up at ceremonial centers near tombs, monuments, platforms (which may have been the setting for religious dramas), and altarlike structures (which may have been used for sacrifice). The exact role the heads played in these places is unknown, but most historians assume the heads were erected as tributes to heroic chiefs.

ca. 850 B.C.

Kouros

"What is beautiful is loved," sang the fifth-century B.C. Greek poet Theognis. And the ancient Greeks loved physical beauty, especially when it was combined with nobility of character. During the Archaic Period (700–480 B.C.) in Greece, sculptors produced an endless stream of statues of young men (kouros) who were physically beautiful—although in a formal, stylized kind of way. These sculptures are not portraits of individuals; rather, they are representations of an ideal.

To contemporary eyes the kouros looks a bit stiff; the arms are locked at the figure's sides, the eyes look straight ahead, and on the lips is an enigmatic smile. The only sense of movement or animation is the left foot that is always shown taking a step forward.

Then there is the chiseled physique, which is not only a sign of physical perfection, but is also a tribute to geometrical symmetry. The musculature certainly flaunts a well-developed body, but look at it again and you'll see that the muscles are a series of flawlessly rendered patterns.

Kouros sculptures were usually commissioned by wealthy individuals who gave them as votive offerings at temples or shrines of the gods. The statue represented the giver—he could not stay perpetually at the shrine, worshipping the god, so the kouros served as his stand-in.

Viewers have noticed a similarity between the kouros sculptures and the full-length sculptures of pharaohs and court officials in Egypt. It is likely that those Egyptian works were the original inspiration for the kouros. But, typical of the ancient Greeks, they took someone else's idea and made it their own. Egyptian sculptures tended to be positioned against a wall or slab and were at least partially clothed; the Greek kouros is freestanding and nude. Since the kouros wears no clothing, no ornaments, and carries no object, it can't be tied to a time or place—it becomes a representation of eternal youth, of beauty that never fades.

Another Greek poet, Simonides, writing about 50 years after Theognis, praised the youths who were the models for these sculptures: "In hand and foot and mind alike—fashioned without flaw."

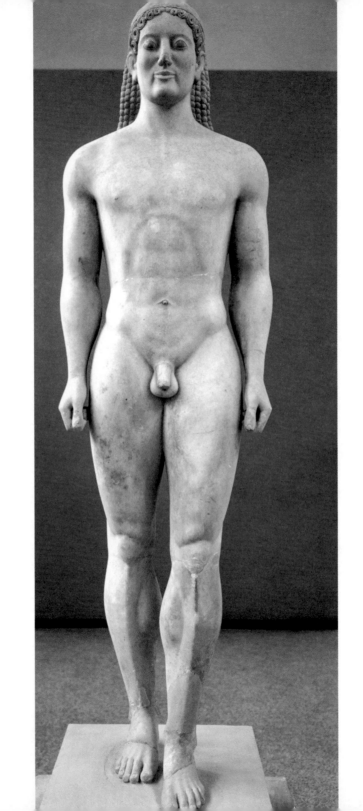

SARCOPHAGUS OF THE SPOUSES

This striking sculpture is the lid of a tomb of an Etruscan husband and wife. It was found in Cerveteri, a field north of Rome, where beginning in the ninth century B.C. the Etruscans constructed at least 1,000 elaborately decorated tombs. The bodies of the husband and wife would have been cremated and the ashes deposited within this sarcophagus.

Typically a sarcophagus was carved from stone—granite in Egypt, marble in Greece and Italy. But this sarcophagus is made of terracotta, a type of clay that, after it is fired, comes out of the kiln a brownish orange color. The sarcophagus would have been brightly painted, and some traces of the paint can still be seen.

To modern eyes it looks like the couple is propped up in bed. In fact, they are reclining on a couch at a banquet in the afterlife. Many ancient societies—the Greeks, Romans, Etruscans, and Israelites—dined while lounging on well-padded couches.

The figures' almond-shaped eyes, long braids of hair, and broad smiles—especially the smiles—are all characteristic of Etruscan art. So are the graceful gestures of the arms and hands.

What makes this piece exceptional is the subject matter—a loving couple displaying their affection for one another. The wife leans against her husband's chest; the husband, in a light embrace, rests his arm on his wife's shoulder. In general, Etruscan artists were strongly influenced by the artistic styles of the Greeks, but this Etruscan artist broke with Greek tradition by depicting such a tender, even intimate scene.

ca. 700 B.C.

CALFBEARER

ca. 570 B.C.

Sometime in the late sixth century B.C., Rhombos, a well-to-do citizen of Athens, commissioned a life-size portrait sculpture of himself bearing on his shoulders a calf he intended to offer in sacrifice to the goddess Athena. The statue remained on the Acropolis, in or near the Parthenon, and was discovered there in the nineteenth century—the top half in 1864 and the bottom half in 1887.

The style is Archaic Greek, an intermediate stage between the stiff, stylized sculpture of the kouros and the more fluid, lifelike sculpture of the Classical period. Unlike the somewhat artificial look of the kouros sculptures, the Calfbearer includes a few features intended to represent the man who offered the sculpture, such as his beard and his hairstyle with its row of tight curls framing his brow. And of course the Calfbearer is doing something—he has two of the calf's legs firmly gripped in his strong hands. It is not a complete break from the kouros style, however: The Calfbearer still wears the traditional, enigmatic smile, he steps forward with his left foot, and the pattern of his abdominal muscles as well as the muscles in the calf's leg are symmetrical and clearly delineated.

Originally, brightly colored stones would have been mounted in the long-empty eyeholes, and the statue would have been painted (traces of blue paint survive on the calf).

The Calfbearer statue is a variation on a classic motif from Greek sculpture—the Rambearer; the god Hermes was often depicted with a ram or occasionally a lamb over his shoulders. And this sculpture was the forerunner and inspiration for a later work, the image of Christ as the Good Shepherd.

THE SARPEDON KRATER

Thomas Hoving, the former director of the Metropolitan Museum of Art in New York City, has gone on record saying that the drawing on the Sarpedon Krater is on par with anything produced by Leonardo da Vinci, that the dramatic impact of the pot is equal to anything created by Rembrandt, that the shape of the krater is "Parthenonesque although on a much smaller scale," and in terms of innovation, that the artist was in the same class as Picasso. That is saying quite a lot about a Grecian urn, but Hoving is not exaggerating—the Sarpedon Krater is a gem.

It is signed by the potter, Euxitheos, and by the painter, Euphronios. Euphronios was the Michelangelo of sixth-century B.C. Greek kraters, and twenty-seven of his masterworks survive, although almost all of them are battered or in fragmentary condition. The Sarpedon Krater is the only one perfectly intact. It is a calyx krater, used to mix wine. In ancient Greece the wine tended to be extremely potent, so it was customary to mix it with water to dilute the alcohol. At parties, which the Greeks called symposia, the wine was mixed in large urns such as this—the Sarpedon Krater holds twelve gallons. It stands 39 inches high with a diameter of almost 22 inches. The krater's name comes from its primary scene—the death of Sarpedon, the young king of Lycia who fought with the Trojans and was killed by the Greek warrior Patroclus. The heroic king's body is shown being carried off the battlefield by Sleep and Death.

Red-on-black is typical for such pottery, but in the case of the Sarpedon Krater, Euphronios introduced a full palette of reds, ochres, browns, and even pink, which he used for the inscriptions. To acquire such a remarkable work, in 1972 the Met paid $1 million. Unhappily, it has been proven that the krater had been looted from a tomb near Cerveteri, Italy, in 1971. After 35 years of controversy, in 2006 the Metropolitan Museum agreed to return the Sarpedon Krater to Italy.

GRIFFIN-HEADED ARMLET FROM THE OXUS TREASURE

The Oxus Treasure, an extraordinary hoard of Persian gold and silver objects, suddenly turned up in the northern Afghan province of Tajikistan in 1877. According to the story, the Oxus River flooded that year; when the water receded, local villagers found pieces of the treasure sticking out of the sand. How many objects were collected originally is unknown as it is likely that the villagers kept some of them, probably breaking them up or melting them down.

In 1880 merchants from central Asia passed through the neighborhood on their way to India. The villagers realized another windfall when the merchants offered to buy the treasure. Unfortunately for the merchants, news of their purchase traveled faster than they did. Near Peshawar in Pakistan, bandits captured the merchants and seized their treasure. Before any harm could come to them the merchants were rescued by a British officer, Captain F. C. Burton, who drove off the bandits and recovered the treasure. As a souvenir of the adventure, Captain Burton purchased this griffin-headed armlet from the merchants. In Rawalpindi the merchants sold their hoard. Word of the sale reached A. W. Franks, an English antiquarian; he purchased the treasure from Indian dealers for the collection of the British Museum where it is displayed today, along with Captain Burton's griffin armlet.

The Greek writer Xenophon saw armlets such as this during his travels in Persia in the early fourth century; he tells us they were highly sought after at the royal court because the king of Persia gave armlets as a token of his personal esteem. Colored glass and semiprecious stones would have been set in what are now empty spaces in the filigree.

ca. 500 B.C.

SHE-WOLF OF ROME

According to the foundation myth of Rome, Mars, god of war, seduced a Vestal Virgin (a priestess who took a vow of perpetual chastity) named Rhea Silvia. Nine months later Rhea gave birth to twin sons. The king of this part of Italy was Rhea's brother; afraid that these sons of a god would grow up to seize his kingdom, he put the infants in a wooden trough and pushed it into the current of the Tiber River. When it came ashore a she-wolf discovered the babies—but instead of eating them she adopted them and nursed them as though they were her own wolf cubs. The boys, Romulus and Remus, did grow up to kill the uncle who tried to kill them, and later Romulus founded the town that became Rome.

This ancient bronze sculpture brings the myth to life. It was cast by an unknown Etruscan sculptor (the Etruscans, who occupied central Italy before the Romans, were especially fine artists). The wolf is nearly life-size and bears a fearsome expression. The figures of the twins were added much later, in the fifteenth century, by the Italian Renaissance artist Antonio del Pollaiolo.

In the days of Julius Caesar (100-44 B.C.) the statue was gilt (covered with thin sheets of gold) and stood on Rome's Capitoline Hill, the site of the city's great Temple of Jupiter, king of the gods. For this reason the statue is sometimes known as the Capitoline Wolf. The statue was considered one of the most sacred objects in Rome, and even after the Romans had converted to Christianity and the city was overrun by the Goths and then the Vandals, the She-Wolf was carefully preserved as an ancient emblem of Rome.

In the late 1920s, Benito Mussolini, the fascist dictator of Italy, tried to win the goodwill of the American government by sending copies of the She-Wolf to several American cities—including Rome, Georgia.

ca. 500 B.C.

POSEIDON OF ARTEMISION

This superb sculpture is often called "The God from the Sea," and understandably so. In 1926, a diver discovered this magnificent bronze statue of Poseidon, god of the sea, in the remains of an ancient ship that had gone down in the Aegean in the sixth century B.C. Because the sculpture was found near the cape of Artemision on the Greece's eastern coast, the sculpture is known as the Poseidon of Artemision, or simply the Artemision Bronze (because some art historians insist it is a statue of Zeus).

The sculpture is larger than life—truly godlike—standing a little over 82 inches tall. It shows Poseidon poised to throw his trident (or Zeus poised to throw a thunderbolt). The god's muscles are tensed for the exertion, but his facial expression is relaxed. The sculpture is perfectly balanced: Poseidon's left leg and his left arm are extended; his right leg and right arm are bent, ready to hurl his weapon. It is comparable to a snapshot of an Olympic athlete captured the instant before he makes a winning throw.

The god sports a magnificent full beard. His hair has been styled with perfect curls falling on his forehead, while a headband holds the rest of his hair in place.

The statue's eye sockets are empty, but originally they would have held "eyes," probably made of bone or ivory. The eyebrows would have been silver, and the lips and the nipples plated with copper. All of these final touches to the sculpture were lost during the 2,400 years it lay at the bottom of the sea.

Scythian Gold Pectoral

In 1971, archaeologist Boris Mozolevsky traveled out to the steppes of the Ukraine to a barrow near the town of Ordzhonikidze. He hoped the barrow, a mound of earth and stone raised over a grave, might contain a trove of ancient Scythian artifacts. It had happened before: For decades, archaeologists had been excavating Scythian barrow tombs and often had been rewarded with wonderful finds. But what Mozolevsky found at the Tovsta Mohyla Barrow took even him by surprise.

Draped over the chest of the dead man—undoubtedly a king—was a golden pectoral, or collar, that was clasped behind the neck and hung down on the wearer's chest. Many ancient societies had such jewelry, but none had anything to compare with the treasure Mozolevsky found.

The pectoral (the word comes from the Latin term for chest or breast) is comprised of three bands, with twisted ropes of gold separating the three tiers. The first and third bands depict scenes from daily life in Scythian villages and on the steppes: two men making a coat from a sheepskin; a lion and a leopard dragging down a stag; a colt nursing; a man milking a ewe. These figures are all three-dimensional and exquisitely detailed.

The central tier is solid and adorned with stylized flowers, birds, and geometric patterns (usually spirals), each of which were fashioned separately and then attached to the band.

The pectoral tapers toward the top where two lion heads each hold a ring in its mouth; here the pectoral was clasped or pinned to the wearer's clothes.

Writing of the pectoral later, Mozolevsky said, "The soul of the whole people [of Scythia] is embodied in it."

BAS RELIEF

Bas (pronounced *bah*) is French for *low*, and bas relief is a type of sculpture carved or etched from a flat stone. The bas reliefs found inside Egyptian tombs are very low indeed, the figures barely rising from the stone slab. But the reliefs carved in Greece during the fifth century B.C. are almost fully rounded and seem barely attached to the flat stone behind them (this style is known as "high relief").

Twenty thousand years ago, prehistoric artists were creating relief sculptures in caves, generally using the natural contour of the rock ceiling or wall as the base sculpture. The caves of Creswell Crags in Derbyshire, England, have a large collection of prehistoric bas reliefs. But the technique is found almost everywhere on the planet—from India and Southeast Asia to Egypt, from the Parthenon in Athens to the Christian catacombs of Rome. The largest bas relief in the world is found at Stone Mountain outside of Atlanta, Georgia. The carving, 90 feet high and 190 feet wide, portrays three heroes of the Confederacy: Jefferson Davis, Robert E. Lee, and Thomas "Stonewall" Jackson.

The undisputed masters of the art form were the ancient Greeks. The decorative sculptures (known as friezes) that they carved around the exterior of their buildings are very fine, but the finest work of all is the relief sculptures carved for the pediments of the temples and around the base of altars. Classic examples include the sculptures from the Pergamon Altar, and the Parthenon, or Elgin, Marbles.

During the Renaissance, the revival of interest in all things Greek or Roman revived the art of the relief, and it was even used in metal sculpture, such as Ghiberti's gilded bronze *Gates of Paradise* at the Baptistery of Florence's Duomo, or Cathedral.

Bas reliefs have also been made in porcelain and ceramic as decorative flourishes on the walls of the Forbidden City in Beijing or as cozy household ornaments during the Arts and Crafts movement of the late nineteenth/early twentieth centuries.

ca. 450 B.C.

Bas relief of a Mayan warrior from Chichen Itza, (ca. 900–ca. 1200)

THE PARTHENON SCULPTURES

By Phidias

Some art critics—Thomas Hoving, for example—regard Phidias' sculptures from the Parthenon as the pinnacle of the sculptor's art in the West. They are sublime, even in their battered state. (In the seventeenth century, the Parthenon was used to store gunpowder; during a bombardment of Athens the temple took a direct hit and almost all of the sculptures were damaged in the explosion.) Nonetheless, the Parthenon sculptures represent the Western ideal of humankind at its most noble and most beautiful.

The gods and goddesses, the heroes and ordinary citizens of Athens, and even the horses Phidias sculpted are the pinnacle of physical perfection, yet the carving is so lifelike that all the figures appear to be in motion.

Like all Greek artists, the human body enchanted Phidias. Consequently, even when he depicted figures that are clothed, their robes and gowns appear to be soaking wet—they cling to the figure, revealing every sensuous detail that lies just beneath the cloth.

The sculptures from the two pediments—the triangular space over the front and the rear of the temple—depict the birth of Athena and the contest between Athena and Poseidon to determine who would be the patron god of Athens. The frieze, a series of low sculptural reliefs that encircled the exterior of the temple, shows Athenians of all ranks of society participating in a religious procession in honor of Athena. The metopes, individual sculptural panels, portray scenes from Greek mythology, such as the war between the gods of Olympus and the Giants, and a battle between centaurs and men.

Approximately half of the Parthenon sculptures are displayed in the British Museum in London. Between 1801 and 1812, Thomas Bruce, the Earl of Elgin, had the sculptures removed with the permission of the Turkish authorities (Greece, at this time, was part of the Ottoman Empire). Elgin shipped the sculptures home to Britain where Parliament authorized their purchase. For many years the Greek government has lobbied to have the sculptures returned, but to date the British government has refused.

APOLLO BELVEDERE

In a lighthearted moment the art historians Mary Beard and John Henderson described the Apollo Belvedere as "the pin-up" of Classical sculpture. Apollo is said to have been the best-looking of the gods, and there is no doubting the beauty of this sculpture. It sent the eighteenth-century art critic Johann Winckelmann into raptures. "An eternal spring, such as reigned in the blessed Elysian fields," he wrote, "clothes the attractive manliness of full-blown maturity with delectable youth and plays about the majestic frame of his limbs with soft tenderness."

It is true of course that in the ancient world nudity was routine: Whether at the public baths or at the gymnasium, most people saw their neighbors nude, and if they went to an athletic event they would see the athletes competing buck naked. Nonetheless, the Apollo Belvedere is not an entirely nonchalant nude; there is a sensuous quality there that Winckelmann recognized, even if he did take his rhapsody a bit over the top.

The Apollo is probably a marble copy made by a Roman sculptor of a bronze sculpture cast around the year 320 B.C. by Leochares, an artist who received many commissions from Alexander the Great. Like the *Laocoon*, the popes acquired it and Michelangelo studied it—it was the inspiration for his fresco *The Creation of Adam* on the Sistine Chapel ceiling.

The statue was discovered in 1489 and purchased by Cardinal Giuliano della Rovere, who installed it in his garden. When Cardinal della Rovere was elected pope, taking the name Julius II, he brought his Apollo with him to the Vatican, setting it up in the Belvedere Courtyard along with the *Laocoon* (see p. 70). In later years a marble fig leaf was attached to the statue to cover Apollo's genitals (the fig leaf was removed in the twentieth century).

ALEXANDER SARCOPHAGUS

Alexander the Great was never buried in this magnificent sarcophagus. We know because it turned up in a necropolis, an ancient burial ground, near Sidon in Lebanon in 1887, and Alexander was entombed in Alexandria in Egypt.

It is known as the Alexander Sarcophagus because one of the four sculpted scenes depicts Alexander at the Battle of Issus where he crushed the army of Darius III and conquered the Persian Empire. Alexander is the figure on horseback, wearing a lion headdress, about to throw a spear. The Macedonian warrior on horseback near Alexander may be Hephaestion, Alexander's closest friend and said to have been his lover.

On the other side of the sarcophagus is another spectacular scene of Macedonians and Persians hunting together. The most dramatic element of the sculpture is the lion, its teeth sunk into the chest of a horse, while hunters and hunting dogs try to kill him.

The sarcophagus probably held the body of Abdalonymus, whom Alexander appointed King of Tyre (in what is now Lebanon) in 332 b.c.

The sarcophagus' superb lid has survived, and we see that the tomb is modeled on a Greek temple. Originally the entire piece would have been painted (traces of the paint can still be seen on the marble figures).

Dying Gaul

The poet Lord Byron was so struck by this sculpture when he saw it in Rome that he worked it into his epic poem, *Childe Harold*. Byron imagined it depicted a prisoner of war, captured by the Romans during their conquest of Gaul, who was hauled back to Rome to fight and die in the arena as part of Rome's victory celebration, "Butcher'd to make a Roman holiday," as Byron put it.

The statue's pedigree is a source of debate. The traditional interpretation states that this is a Roman copy of a Greek original that had been erected in the Greek city of Pergamon (in what is now Turkey) to commemorate a victory over the Galatians, a people who were ethnically related to the Gauls. It is possible, however, that this is a Roman original.

The unknown sculptor has managed to strike a balance between the heroic and the pathetic. The Gaul is naked, which is consistent with the historical record—Julius Caesar tells us that many Gallic warriors went into battle naked. The twisted torque around his neck is also accurate—archaeologists have turned up torques virtually identical to the one worn by the statue. Even the clumps of spiky hair are correct—the Gauls used a product to style their hair.

The statue was discovered in Rome in 1623 when workmen were digging the foundations of a new palace for the Ludovisi family, members of the Roman nobility. Pope Clement XII purchased the statue in 1737, and it became one of the "must-see" works of art for every traveler to Italy. Very fine copies were made of the sculpture for palaces and universities from Stockholm to Dublin to Prague. Perhaps the finest is a reproduction in black marble made for Syon House, the residence of the Duke of Northumberland. But less expensive copies were made for the tourist trade—including Dying Gaul paperweights.

ca. 275 B.C.

Ngoc Lu Drum

ca. 250 B.C.

Three thousand years ago, in the Red River Valley of northern Vietnam, the Dong Son culture flourished. The Dong Son people were fishermen, rice farmers, and kept herds of buffaloes and pigs. But they are most famous for their skill as bronze sculptors, particularly as creators of bronze drums. The largest Dong Son bronze drums stood 3 feet high and weighed 220 pounds. They were musical instruments, but they also served a religious purpose: They were beaten to bring rain, or an abundant harvest, or to pay tribute to the dead during funerals. The deep booming sound of the Dong Son drums also made them ideal on the battlefield where they intimidated the enemy.

The Ngoc Lu Drum was discovered accidentally in 1893 in Ha Nam Province, southeast of Hanoi. The surface of the drum is covered with intricate engravings of geometric patterns and scenes of deer, egrets, and hornbills.

Especially interesting are the engravings of humans participating in a festival or religious ritual. Arranged in a circular band around a central sunburst are musicians, including drummers, men wearing feathered headgear and bird masks, and a couple threshing rice with feather-decorated poles. Art historians and cultural anthropologists have yet to decipher the meaning of this scene.

Vietnam president Lee Duc Anh (left) presents a replica of the ancient Ngoc Lu Drum to United Nations Secretary General Boutros Boutros-Ghali at the United Nations General Assembly in New York.

Terracotta Army of Xian

In 1974, Chinese peasants in Xian, Shaanxi province, were digging a well when they struck bits of ancient pottery. When archaeologists came to inspect the site they found a treasure beyond anyone's wildest dreams: more than 8,000 terracotta soldiers, archers, cavalry horses, and chariots, all arranged in battle formation, with the infantry in the front and the chariots at the rear. The soldiers are larger than life (for the time, in any case), ranging from 6 feet to 6 feet, 5 inches; the tallest figures are thought to represent generals.

The army was created for and buried with Emperor Qin Shi Huangdi (reigned 247–210 B.C.), the emperor who unified China and began construction of the Great Wall.

Incredibly, the face of each human figure is unique, which has led to the suggestion that these figures are portraits of people who lived at the time. Each figure was also hand-painted. The artists who fashioned this army made the bodies, arms, legs, and heads separately, then assembled them and fired them in a kiln.

Each figure bears the identifying stamp of the terracotta workshop where it was created (many potters were called in to help complete the project). It is a source of wonder to art historians that workshops that, days earlier, had been turning out roof tiles were now creating terracotta sculptures of a very high caliber.

The army stands in the pits where it was originally buried 2,200 years ago.

Gundestrup Cauldron

As often happens with ancient artifacts, the Gundestrup Cauldron has an almost hypnotic quality, even if we aren't certain exactly what all the scenes and figures embossed on this grand silver pot mean. It was discovered in a peat bog in Denmark in 1891. At 27 inches in diameter and standing about 16.5 inches tall, this is the largest silver work of art to survive from this period of Celtic history. Twenty-two hundred years ago the Celts were not limited to Ireland—their civilization covered Europe from Hungary to France, from Switzerland to Denmark.

One panel shows armed horsemen and foot soldiers watching as a man is dunked headfirst into a barrel. This may be a warrior initiation ritual, not unlike Christian baptism.

The seated figure with antlers sprouting from his head is identified as Cernunnos, also known among the Celts as "the Horned God," and "the Lord of Wild Things." In this panel he is surrounded by animals, so it seems plausible that the figure is indeed Cernunnos.

There is also a scene of men with swords slaying bulls, which may be a religious sacrifice, or perhaps a bull hunt.

The identification of the woman flanked by six-spoked wheels and mythical beasts is problematic; so are the other figures represented with just heads and arms.

ca. 2000 B.C.

Laocoon

From the moment in 1506 when a farmer digging in his vineyard uncovered this great statue on the Esquiline Hill near Rome's Basilica of Santa Maria Maggiore, everyone knew what it represented: the death of the Trojan priest, Laocoon, and his two sons. According to the story in Virgil's *Aeneid*, moments after Laocoon warned the Trojans not to bring the Greeks' giant wooden horse into the city, Athena (who was on the side of the Greeks) sent two immense sea serpents to crush the life out of the priest and his innocent sons. The writhing bodies of the three men caught in the merciless twisting coils of the sea snakes mesmerized everyone who saw the sculpture. Pope Julius II snatched it up for the Vatican's collection, installing it in the Belvedere Courtyard where it is still displayed to awestruck crowds.

The Roman philosopher and naturalist, Pliny the Elder, wrote about a Laocoon sculpture that he said was carved by three Greek masters from the island of Rhodes—Hagesander, Polydorus, and Athenodorus. The finished statue was, in Pliny's opinion, "a work to be preferred above all others, whether paintings or bronzes." Art historians continue to debate if this is the *Laocoon* Pliny knew, or if it is a copy, or if it is a different *Laocoon* entirely. It scarcely matters; it is a magnificent work on its own merits, at once monumental and sensual. Michelangelo was only one of the Renaissance masters who studied it closely: Raphael, Titian, and El Greco were also fascinated by it.

When Napoleon conquered Italy in 1799 the *Laocoon* was one of the treasures he stole from the Vatican and installed in the Louvre museum. After the final defeat of Napoleon in 1816, the French were compelled to return the *Laocoon* to the pope.

ALEXANDER MOSAIC

ca. 100 B.C.

It is one of the most magnificent mosaics to survive from the Roman world—even with about a third of it missing. Archaeologists found it in 1831 amid the ruins of Pompeii in the mansion known as the House of the Faun. The scene is a theatrical tour de force: On the battlefield Darius, king of Persia, has come face-to-face with his nemesis, Alexander the Great. While Alexander skewers a Persian soldier with his spear to get to Darius, the Persian king's driver has already turned the chariot's horses—Darius is ready to flee. It is a spectacular scene that captures the whirl and chaos of battle, and it does so in tiny cubes of colored stone known as tesserae.

The mosaic measures approximately 10 feet by 19 feet. The density of the tesserae varies throughout the mosaic, but on average the artist used about 15–30 cubes in every four-tenths of an inch, which means about four million cubes were used to create this masterpiece.

Although the mosaic is named for Alexander, it is Darius who commands the viewer's attention first. His bright white breastplate draws the eye to the figure of the king. Then we follow his body language: His eyes are wide with fear (the whites of them as easy to see as the white of his armor); his arm is thrown out in surprise, directing our gaze now across the scene to the damaged figure of Alexander. But if Darius is a vision of panic, Alexander is firm, determined, confident, unstoppable. The unknown artist has captured a decisive moment in the lives of two kings and two empires—disaster for Darius and the Persians, glory for Alexander and the Greeks.

How the mosaic came to be in a rich man's house in Pompeii is a source of contention. Some art historians argue that the Romans carried it off as plunder from a conquered Greek province; others insist that Greek artists were employed by the Roman owner of the House of the Faun to create the mosaic on-site—which does seem to be the more plausible explanation.

Fayum Mummy Portraits

Well-to-do Roman families commissioned sculptors to carve marble portraits of themselves in life, but it is also possible that families ordered postmortem portraits of a loved one based on wax death masks taken directly from the corpse. In Roman Egypt, in and around area known today as Fayum (in ancient times the city bore the unforgettable name of Crocodilopolis), a custom arose of painting exquisitely life-like portraits of the dead and mounting them on the deceased's mummy. Since the population of Fayum was ethnically diverse with Egyptians and Greek and Roman colonists intermarrying, the custom combined traditional Egyptian mummification with the Roman (and to some degree Greek) interest in accurate portraiture. Sometimes the portraits were painted directly onto the mummy's cloth wrappings, but it was more common to paint the portrait on a thin wooden board.

Like marble busts, the Fayum paintings depict the head with only a bit of the chest and shoulders. The faces are wonderfully expressive, displaying a technical skill that would not be seen again until the sixteenth century. It is possible that these portraits were made during the individual's lifetime and were displayed in his or her home; at the time of death the paintings were given to the embalmers to be incorporated into the mummy wrappings. CAT scans of a cross-sample of Fayum mummies have shown that the age of the mummy within the wrappings corresponds to a rough estimate of the age of the individual depicted in the portrait. Since many of these individuals are young—early twenties and thirties, and quite a few are children—the Fayum mummies also represent a tragic record of just how short life expectancy was in Egypt 2,000 years ago.

Venus de Milo

The Venus de Milo stands in Paris today because of a French-won brawl between French and Turkish soldiers over possession of the statue.

The sculpture was found in pieces in 1820 on the Aegean island of Melos. Once the pieces had been roughly reassembled on the Melos beach, everyone who saw it realized they were looking at a masterpiece of ancient Greek sculpture. Such treasures were at a premium in Europe at this time: Britain's Lord Elgin had just purchased the sculptures from the Parthenon, and the crown prince of Bavaria had entered the market with his purchase of the sculptures from the Temple of Aphaia. France wanted her share of the treasures of the classical world, but the Turks, who still occupied Greece, were not always willing to let such valuable works of art leave their empire—hence the fistfight on the beach.

The loveliness of the sculpture sent the Romantics, who dominated the arts at the time of Venus' discovery, into raptures. Years later sculptor Auguste Rodin was still under its spell, praising the sculpture as "voluptuousness regulated by restraint—the joy of life cadenced, moderated by reason."

The statue's missing arms, however, troubled some people, and would-be art historians of the nineteenth century put forward a host of ideas on how Venus should be restored. One version had her arranging her hair; another would have placed an enormous mirror in her hands in which she studied her beautiful reflection; yet another possibility imagined her with her right hand raised in a "keep-your-distance" pose.

In one respect, however, we can imagine what the statue looked like 2,000 years ago. The Greeks painted their sculptures and adorned them with jewelry. No trace of the ancient paint survives, but we can still see the small holes bored into the marble for earrings, arm bands, a necklace, and a crown.

ca. 80 B.C.

VILLA OF THE MYSTERIES FRESCOES

The violent eruption of Mount Vesuvius on August 24, 79 A.D., both destroyed and preserved the Roman city of Pompeii. The volcanic ash that buried the ancient town proved to be a great preservative, not only of bronze sculptures, but also of 2,000-year-old wall paintings. Many of the homes and businesses in Pompeii were decorated with frescoes, and almost all of them survived.

One of the most enigmatic series of frescoes is found in what has come to be known as the Villa of the Mysteries, located in a suburb just outside of Pompeii. All four walls of one of the villa's larger rooms are covered with frescoes depicting almost life-size figures of women, gods, and satyrs—but no men. They all seem to be participating in a festival or perhaps a religious ritual. Exactly what everyone in the painting is doing remains elusive, and has been a subject of lively debate for at least one hundred years (the villa was excavated early in the twentieth century). The frescoes are so animated that many visitors who have entered this room feel as if they are intruding, and in fact several of the figures in the frescoes look directly at the viewers.

Many of the scenes are intimate: The god Dionysus reclines in the lap of his human lover Ariadne; a female satyr suckles a goat; a kneeling woman fondles some object beneath a cloth; a nude dancer turns her back to the viewer, while at her feet a half-naked woman is whipped by a winged figure.

The entire series is set against a deep red background; the other dominant colors are purple, gold, and yellow. It is a marvelous group of paintings, even if we're not sure what is going on.

90 B.C.

Prima Porta Augustus

When it comes to portraits of Caesar Augustus we encounter an embarrassment of riches. Art historians estimate that at least 25,000 portraits of Rome's first emperor were created during his 41-year reign (27 B.C.–14 A.D.). Examples have turned up in every corner of the empire. The most famous of these is the full-length, slightly larger-than-life (the statue stands 6 feet, 6 inches tall) marble sculpture known as the Prima Porta Augustus.

Excavators discovered the statue in 1863 in the ruins of the Villa of Livia at Prima Porta, a suburb of Rome where Livia, Augustus' wife, retired after his death. Today the statue is displayed in the Vatican Museums.

The sculpture portrays Augustus as commander-in-chief of Rome's legions. He wears an elaborately decorated cuirass, or breastplate, depicting Mars, the god of war, and personifications of the lands Augustus has conquered—Hispania, Gaul, and Germania. The breastplate also bears the figure of Parthia (modern-day Iran) and that is the success in which every Roman at the time took special pride. About 33 years earlier a Roman commander had lost the standards of his legions in a battle against the Parthians. The Romans regarded the standards with almost religious awe; to have them fall into the hands of barbarians was not only sacrilegious, it implied that the gods were displeased with Rome. Yet through skillful diplomacy and without the loss of a single Roman soldier, Augustus recovered the standards.

The garment wrapped around his waist and draped over his left arm is not a military cloak, but a toga, the symbol of Augustus' role as the First Citizen, the title Augustus preferred because traditionally Romans were uncomfortable with anyone who called himself "king" or "emperor." The little figure at his feet is a representation of Cupid, an allusion to Augustus' descent from the goddess of love, Venus (Cupid was her son).

That this portrait was found in Livia's villa suggests that she and Augustus approved of the statue. It was popular with other Romans as well—it was copied at least 148 times.

20 B.C.

Gemma Augustea Cameo

The *Gemma Augustea*, Latin for "the Gem of Augustus," depicts an idealized portrait of Augustus Caesar (shown in the upper half of the jewel, seated and bare-chested, with a wreath of oak leaves held over his head) attended by gods and members of his family.

The cameo is cut from Arabian onyx, the figures appearing in milky white against a dark bluish brown background. The gold setting dates from the seventeenth century when the cameo was in the possession of the Holy Roman Emperor. It is a large piece—7.5 inches tall, 9 inches wide, and about half an inch thick. Many art historians believe this to be the work of Augustus' favorite gem cutter, Dioscurides, who also fashioned Augustus' personal seal.

Holding the wreath above Augustus is Oikoumene, a personification of the civilized world. The woman seated beside Augustus wearing a helmet and holding a spear is Roma, the patron goddess of Rome and the Empire. The bearded figure behind Augustus is Oceanus or Neptune; the woman holding the cornucopia is Gaia—together, they represent Augustus' dominion over sea and land. The figure in the chariot is Victoria, the Roman version of Nika, the Greek goddess of victory.

The figures in the lower half of the cameo are harder to identify. The group at the far left and far right are captives taken in war, Celts or Germans. The other figures in military dress appear to be Roman soldiers raising a trophy of victory and preparing the captives for a triumphal parade. There is another interpretation that they are the gods Mars and Hermes participating in Rome's triumph over these barbarians.

The point is less about precise identifications than the overall message of the cameo: It displays the power and glory of Augustus, suggesting that he is as invincible as the gods who attend him.

ca. 10 A.D.

Galloping Horse Treading on a Flying Swallow

This bronze sculpture stands nearly 18 inches tall and weighs about 17.5 pounds, yet it is balanced on a single hoof. That hoof, by the way, is trampling on a sparrow. The sculpture was created by an artist who possessed great gifts, including an unerring sense of where his statue's center of gravity was located.

The Chinese of the Han Dynasty were "horse people," who had an almost cult-like devotion to these animals. The sculpture depicts a legend current during the Han era, that a truly swift horse could outrun a swallow in flight. As the horse's hoof strikes, the bird looks up in shock. The horse itself, sensing that it has stepped on something out of the ordinary, neighs and begins to twist its head toward its rear leg to see what is happening.

The sculpture was discovered in 1969 in the Leitai Tomb, the burial place of a Chinese general, in Wuwei County in southwestern China. The green patina is the result of nearly 2,000 years of oxidation. Since it was unearthed, the *Galloping Horse* has been praised as one of the finest examples of ancient bronze sculpture. It has achieved the status in China of a national treasure, and it has become an instantly recognized icon of the Han Dynasty. Many Chinese see the horse as an emblem of their own society: Dynamic, spirited, and outpacing their rivals.

ca. 25

ILLUMINATED MANUSCRIPTS

Technically a manuscript may be described as "illuminated" only if its illustrations are embellished with gold or silver leaf. Pedantry notwithstanding, in common usage any book from the Late Classical or medieval period embellished with hand-painted illustrations and decorative motifs is known as an illuminated manuscript.

In ancient Egypt, it was not unusual for papyrus scrolls to be embellished with illustrations or some decorative device to mark off blocks of text. Ancient Roman manuscripts often featured a painted portrait of the author on the first page. But it was Christian monks and scribes who began the tradition (which lasted more than 1,000 years) of filling borders, and even the initial letters of paragraphs with exquisite miniature paintings. The motivation for these decorative schemes was twofold: reverence for the text in the case of the Bible or the Missal (the book which contained the prayers for Mass) and high regard for books in general. In the age before the printing press, when every copy of every book had to be copied out laboriously by hand, a book was regarded as a precious item. The natural response in *scriptoria*, the chambers in a monastery or convent where books were copied, was to make the volume even more valuable by lavishing decoration on each page.

The first masters of this art were the Irish monks who, around the year 600, developed a dazzlingly intricate style. Monks in England and Scotland adopted the Irish manner of manuscript illumination, and kings and abbots on the Continent tried to lure these artists away from their monasteries in Ireland or Britain.

By the fourteenth century, Jewish artists were illuminating their own manuscripts, particularly copies of the Passover Haggadah. By the fifteenth century, aristocrats and wealthy merchants were commissioning artists to illustrate their personal prayer books, known as Books of the Hours. These small, handheld volumes became highly prized, one-of-a-kind works of art. Book lovers' attachment to these illustrations was so strong that when Johannes Gutenberg printed his Bible, he added hand-painted flourishes in the borders and decorated initial letters to make his innovation more appealing.

Tree of Jesse from the Arundel Psalter, ca. 1310

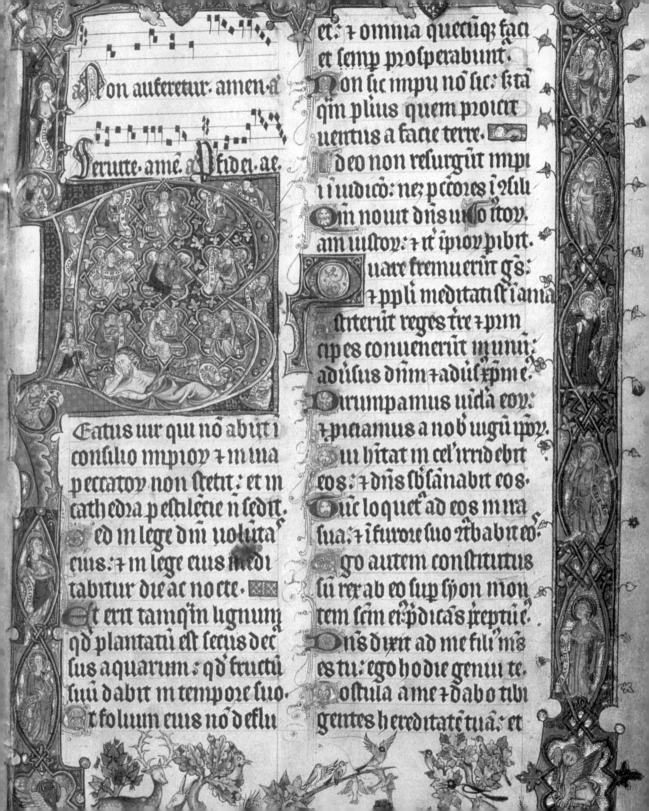

Non auferetur. amen a...

ferutte ame. Pfidei ae.

Eatus uir qui no abiit i
consilio impiou z in uia
peccatou non stetit: et in
cathedra pestilecie n sedit.
ed in lege dni uoluta
eius: z in lege eius medi
tabitur die ac nocte.
Et erit tamqin lignum
qd plantatu est secus dec
sus aquarium: qd fructu
suu dabit in tempore suo.
Et foliuu eius no deflu

et: z omnia quecuq; faci
et semp prosperabunt.
Non sic impu no sic: s; ta
qin pluis quem proicit
uentus a facie terre.
Ideo non resurgut impi
ii iudicio: nez peccores i cosili
Qm nouit dns uia iusto itoy.
am iustoy: z it ipiou pibit.
uare fremuerut gs.
z ppli meditati st i ania
stiteriit reges tre z prin
cipes conueneriit in unu:
adusus dnm z adus xpm e.
Dirumpamus uicla eoy.
z pietamus a nob iugu ipoy.
u hitat in cel irridebit
eos: z dns sbsanabit eos.
uc loquet ad eos in ira
sua: z i furore suo ctbabit eo
go autem constitutus
su rex ab eo sup sion mon
tem scm ei: pdicas preptu e.
Dns dixit ad me fili ms
es tu: ego hodie genui te.
ostula a me z dabo tibi
gentes hereditate tua: et

Moche Portrait Vase

Like the ancient Greeks, the Moche people of Peru were master potters. These portrait vases probably represented important individuals in Moche society. It is possible that every time one of these men achieved a landmark moment in his life, a new pottery portrait of him was made.

There is no doubt among art historians that the vases or pots were meant to be portraits: Look at a collection of such ceramicware and you will see distinctive facial features, and even facial expressions.

The portrait pottery was shaped as vases, jugs, even bowls, and was probably used to carry liquid such as *chichi,* a kind of beer made from maize. Almost all Moche pottery used only two colors—creamy yellow and deep red. And virtually all of them had semicircular handles with a tube or spout attached through which liquid was poured into the pot, or was poured out.

Moche potters were the finest in ancient America, and they were flexible about their techniques. Sometimes they molded the clay, other times they sculpted it. They even used the method known as coiling, in which long strands of wet clay were twisted like a rope, then laid one on top of another to create the desired shape. Such pots were not only visually interesting, but the assembling of the coils was done so precisely that the pot was watertight.

Recently, anthropologist Christopher Donnan has argued that many Moche portrait pottery represent victorious warriors or captives whose likenesses were made just before they were executed or sacrificed.

ca. 500

Reliquary Statue of St. Foy

St. Foy, also known as St. Faith, was an adolescent Christian girl, perhaps as young as twelve, who was martyred in 303 during the last great wave of anti-Christian persecution to sweep across the Roman Empire. She died in her hometown, Agen, in France. In the fifth century, an anonymous artist crafted a golden bust of St. Foy to hold the martyr's skull.

In 866, a monk from the nearby Abbey of Conques stole the golden reliquary bust and a few other bones of St. Foy and spirited them back to his congregation. A century later, an unnamed goldsmith carved a wooden statue of the saint, plated it with gold, studded the surface with jewels and antique Roman cameos, then mounted the fifth-century head on his golden statue. The statue of St. Foy has been the chief treasure of Conques ever since.

The famous English art historian Sir Kenneth Clark once described the statue as "a golden idol," which he found ironic since St. Foy laid down her life rather than worship idols of the Roman gods. Sir Kenneth points to the impassive face and the large, expressionless eyes to support his opinion. He is being a bit unfair. By the fifth century, the style that has come to be called Byzantine, characterized by emotionless faces, was spreading across Christian Europe. In fact, the saint is dressed and crowned like a Byzantine empress.

During the Middle Ages, crowds of pilgrims came to Conques to pray before the reliquary of St. Foy, begging her intercession. It was said she was especially effective in freeing prisoners taken captive by the Moors in Spain and restoring sight to the blind.

Barberini Ivory

Pagan and Christian motifs are combined in this splendid ivory sculpture made in honor of Emperor Anastasius I (ca. 430–518). The piece is an assemblage of five panels, with the central panel of the triumphant emperor on horseback dominating the work. The winged figure in the upper corner of the panel is not an angel, but Nika, the Greek goddess of victory, who is extending a crown to Anastasius (sadly, both the crown and Nika's arm have broken off). The bearded fellow in the pointed cap is a Phrygian, who represents the barbarian nations the emperor has subdued. The female figure supporting the emperor's foot is probably Gaia, goddess of the earth, which suggests that Anastasius has dominion over the world.

To the emperor's right is a Roman consul. The empty panel probably displayed a consul, too, since they served in pairs. Below are emissaries of the Goths (on the left) and Indians (on the right) bringing tribute to Anastasius. At the top is Christ, beardless, youthful, and handsome like Apollo. Were he not holding a cross, it would be easy to mistake him for the sun god. The Lord, depicted in low relief, is almost an afterthought in this piece. Anastasius is the star of the show.

The emperor's face is distinctive, and it clearly was meant to be a true-to-life portrait.

The emblems of pagan Rome included in this ivory carving are not a coded message about Anastasius' religious convictions. He was a Christian; almost all the inhabitants of his capital, Constantinople, were Christians. The appearance of Nika, Gaia, the Phrygian, and the consuls are meant to convey that Anastasius rules with the full authority exercised by the caesars of old.

ca. 500

San Vitale Mosaics

The exteriors of the churches, shrines, and tombs built in the sixth century in the Italian port town of Ravenna are misleading. The dull brownish red bricks give no sense of the glories to be found inside. Cross the threshold, however, and you find yourself inside a jewel box.

During the late fifth and early sixth centuries, the finest mosaic artists from Constantinople came to Ravenna to cover the walls and ceilings of these holy places with dazzling visions of Christ, the Virgin Mary, and the saints. In the octagonal Church of San Vitale are two mosaics unlike all the others: They are portraits of the Byzantine Emperor and Empress, Justinian and Theodora, with their attendants, stopping momentarily as if someone had called their names just as they were about to go into the church. In fact, in the Theodora mosaic, one of the gentlemen of her entourage is pushing aside the curtain at the entrance to the sanctuary.

Looking at Theodora, resplendent in her imperial robes and heavy jewelry, and even sporting a halo, no one would suspect her upbringing. She was the daughter of a bear-keeper who arranged animal acts for the Hippodrome in Constantinople, and Theodora started life as an actress, performing in the lewd farces Romans and Byzantines loved. In spite of her low rank in society, her marriage to Justinian was a love match.

At the edge of Theodora's robe are three figures—the Three Magi bringing gifts to the Christ Child. The border decoration echoes what Theodora herself is doing—she carries in her hands a chalice, her offering to God and a gift for the Church of San Vitale.

Portraiture is very rare in Byzantine art, which preferred idealized depictions of human beings. The five female attendants at the far right are perfect examples of the typical Byzantine style—their faces are interchangeable. But Theodora and the two women closest to her, her friend Antonina and Antonina's daughter Joannina, show signs of individuality.

PALENQUE SCULPTURES

The Maya, one of the great civilizations of America before the arrival of the Europeans, produced sculpture almost exclusively to celebrate the king and his nobles, the chief women of the royal family and the aristocratic families, and their favored servants—musicians and artists particularly. Living as they did in the dank rain forests of southern Mexico and Guatemala, the Mayans' wood carvings rotted, and their paintings developed mold. But stone sculptures lasted for centuries.

When jungle explorers of the nineteenth century sent home to Europe the first sketches of Mayan art, the art critics described the Mayan sculptures as "baroque." Certainly, Mayan sculpture can be complicated, with so many flourishes and embellishments that it can be hard at first to make out the subject of the relief (and almost all Mayan sculpture is carved in relief). Once one gets past the stylistic twists and knots of Mayan motifs, however, the viewer finds that Mayan sculptors delighted in portraying elaborate headdresses, intricately patterned fabrics—anything, in fact, that was complex and ornate.

The sculptures of Palenque were created in the Late Classic period (550–900), a time when Mayan society was fabulously wealthy and the upper classes spent lavishly on fine art and grand architecture. In the seventh century, some of the most innovative and technically sophisticated sculpture emerged at Palenque. One stunning example is the sarcophagus lid of King Hanab Pakal, who died when he was in his eighties, but was depicted on the slab as a young man. The sculpture shows him falling on his back, the traditional pose of a victim of human sacrifice, but in this case the "victim" is falling into the jaws of death.

Palenque sculptors usually carved in limestone because it could be polished, which removed all traces of chisel marks, giving the work a finished look the Maya admired.

ca. 600

TANG DYNASTY HORSE

By the sixth century, the Chinese had elevated porcelain to an art form. It reached a new level of excellence during the Tang Dynasty (618–906) when porcelain artists developed figures with fluid lines and correct physical proportions. But many of these Tang porcelain sculptures were never displayed in a Chinese home—Tang porcelain makers turned out a vast number of figurines of courtiers, soldiers, musicians, dancers, as well as animals such as camels and horses, to be buried with the emperor or high officials within his government. When the soul of the deceased arrived in heaven, these porcelain figurines would come to life, as it were, as immortal attendants. The larger the number of figurines, the more likely the departed would be regarded in the afterlife as a person of great prestige.

During the Tang period, potters developed *sancai*, or the three glazes. This does not mean they only used three colors. In fact, the Tang potters had a full palette with many colors and shades of lead-based glazes from which to choose. But on an individual figurine they would use only three colors.

This ceramic sculpture comes from the collection of the Victoria and Albert Museum in London. The horse stands 28 inches high and is 31 inches long. The saddle and the leaf decorations were made separately and applied to the figure of the horse. This example, like most Tang horses, was discovered in a tomb.

ca. 704

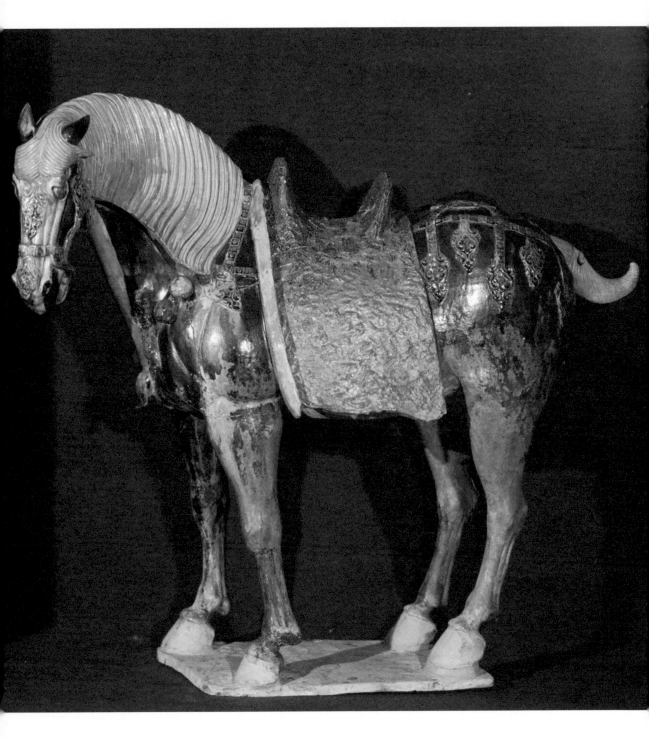

ARDAGH CHALICE

In 1868, Jimmy Quin and Paddy Flanagan were digging up potatoes in a field near the village of Ardagh, County Donegal, Ireland. As they turned over a spade full of earth they discovered a treasure: a small bronze chalice, four elaborately decorated brooches, and a magnificent silver chalice known today as the Ardagh Chalice. The treasure was not wrapped, or locked away in a chest, it was just lying together in a hole. Perhaps monks had buried it hastily in the ninth or tenth century to hide it from Viking raiders. No one knows for certain.

The chalice is a large silver bowl connected by a gold pedestal to a smaller silver base. Just below the rim of the cup is a band of gold filigree studded with small enamel medallions of red and blue. And engraved upon the cup below the gold band are the names of the Twelve Apostles. Even the underside of the base of the chalice is decorated, with a large gold roundel carved with Celtic knots and spirals, and sporting a large rock crystal in its center. Around the bottom rim of the base more filigreed work is engraved and set with eight semiprecious stones.

The chalice would have been used at Mass to hold the wine the priest would consecrate for Holy Communion. Because the bowl of the cup is so large—9.5 inches in diameter—and to prevent any of the consecrated wine from spilling when the priest lifted it to drink, the master silversmith who made the chalice added two splendid handles, each of them embellished with gold and enamelwork.

The Ardagh Chalice is a masterpiece of Celtic Christian art, the finest example of eighth-century metalwork yet found. Created in the workshop of a monastery, it gives us a tantalizing glimpse of the marvels that were being produced in Ireland before the devastation of the Viking invasions.

ca. 725

Temple of the Murals, Bonampak

Inside a rather mundane Mayan building at Bonampak near the Mexico-Guatemala border are the finest surviving examples of Mayan wall paintings. The building is called the Temple of the Murals, and the paintings cover the walls of three rooms.

The first room depicts the ceremony in which a child is recognized as the heir of a noble Mayan family. As part of the celebration, musicians have been called in, and we see them playing their drums, and trumpets, and other instruments, while a band of Mayan noblemen huddle together in conversation.

The paintings in the second room are set during a time of war. We see the warriors of Bonampak in battle, taking prisoners, and then presenting their captives to the Lord of Bonampak. The prisoners are bleeding from the fingers, perhaps a ritual sign that they are destined for human sacrifice.

The murals in the third room depict dancers at a festival. Members of the city's ruling family make an offering to the gods of their own blood by piercing their tongues with needles.

Thanks to inscriptions incorporated into the painting, we can date it accurately to 790.

The paintings were done in fresco. Since there are no seams in the paintings, it is clear that the master artist and his assistants plastered the room and painted it quickly, all in one session, before the wet plaster dried.

The colors are vivid red, blue, yellow, green, purple, sepia, and mauve, with each figure outlined in black. Each figure and scene is shown in such detail as to give us an intimate glimpse of Mayan rituals, warfare, and festivals.

Book of Kells

ca. 800

One of the greatest treasures of Christian Celtic art is the *Book of Kells,* a collection of the four gospels written on vellum (calfskin) and lavishly illustrated. The art historian Francoise Henry detected the distinct styles of at least three separate artists—one who did the portraits of the four evangelists, another who painted such dramatic full-page scenes as "The Arrest of Christ," and a third who created the elaborate ornamental, sometimes known as carpet, pages. The manuscript is 680 pages long, and all but two of those pages are richly decorated. At least 60 pages, however, are missing, lost over the centuries during Ireland's turbulent history.

The book was probably produced at the monastery on the island of Iona off the western coast of Scotland. This monastery had been founded by an Irish monk, St. Columba, also known as Columcille, in the sixth century. Isolated and unprotected, Iona became a repeated target of Viking raiders. In 878, the monks took the relics of St. Columba and various other treasures—including the precious manuscript—to Ireland for safety. Perhaps as early as the ninth century, the book found its way to the abbey at Kells in County Meath. In 1006, disaster struck—thieves stole the book, pried off its golden cover studded with precious stones, and discarded the manuscript. Months later, as if by a miracle, it was found under lumps of turf in a peat bog. By another miracle the *Book of Kells* survived destruction during the Reformation, passing into the hands of a Protestant bishop, James Ussher. In 1660 Ussher donated the book to the library of Trinity College in Dublin, where it has remained ever since.

The full-page illustrations are the true marvel of the *Book of Kells,* with their dazzling colors and intricate interlacing patterns, delicate spirals, and fantastic images of real and mythical beasts. When Gerald of Wales paged through the book in the twelfth century he delighted in the designs that are "so delicate and so subtle, so full of knots and links, with colors so fresh and vivid, that you might say that all this were the work of an angel, and not of a man."

Oseberg Ship Figurehead

ca. 800

In 1903, while digging on his land, a Norwegian farmer named Knut Rom uncovered part of a Viking ship. Rom traveled to Oslo to report his find to Professor Gabriel Gustafson at the University Museum of Antiquities. Two days later Gustafson arrived at the Rom farm and confirmed that the partially excavated artifact was indeed a Viking ship. In addition to a nearly perfectly preserved ship from the ninth century, Gustafson found a treasure trove of Viking artifacts, including a superb ship's figurehead.

Animals were the most common motifs in Viking art, especially serpents, dragons, and horses. Serpents and dragons were the most fearsome beasts, and so they were the most likely choice as figureheads on Viking warships—so much so that the people of Western Europe who were victims of Viking raids referred to the raiders' vessels as "dragon ships."

Interlacing patterns as well as coils and spirals were typical embellishments on Viking animal art: They showcased the skill of the artists but also suggested movement of the creature portrayed. These writhing patterns were especially well suited, of course, for snakes and dragons. The Oseberg figurehead is a classic, dynamic example of Viking art. The beast has opened its jaws wide, its nostrils flare, its eyes bulge—the viewer can almost hear the terrible roar.

But if the Viking style of art was fearsome, it was also a tour de force. Of all the people the Vikings raided and conquered, the English and Irish were particularly taken with the style of tight interlaced patterns and fabulous beasts and monsters. The monks who illustrated (the word they used was "illuminated") Irish and English manuscripts filled whole pages with such intricate designs, and stone carvers adopted the Viking style to decorate the doorways of castles and churches.

RAMAYANA FRIEZE AT PRAMBANAN

The Prambanan temple complex is the most spectacular Hindu shrine in Indonesia. There are eight main temples surrounded by 250 small temples, many of which, sadly, have crumbled into ruins. Each one is crowned with many-pointed spires, and the exteriors of the temples are covered with sculptured reliefs. The three largest temples are dedicated to Brahma, Shiva, and Vishnu, the three most important gods of the Hindu pantheon. Shiva's temple is the tallest at Prambanan, standing 154 feet high.

The three main temples are covered with dramatic carvings of scenes from the *Ramayana*, a sacred epic poem that follows the adventures of a prince, Rama, who is an incarnation of the god Vishnu, and his wife, Sita, who is an incarnation of the goddess Lakshmi, Vishnu's consort. The epic provides artists with an inexhaustible source for memorable scenes—abductions, battles between humans and demons, trials of strength and valor, and seductions. The result is tens of thousands of figures representing everything from the deepest human emotions to the most frightening images from the Hindu underworld, to the most homey scenes of daily life. One of the most astonishing reliefs tells the story of Sita being carried off by a wicked ogre, and her rescue by Rama, King Hanuman, and an army of monkeys.

The sculptures at Prambanan are so numerous, so varied, and of such high quality that a legend about them arose among the people of the region. A princess agreed to marry a certain prince on one condition: He must build a temple with 1,000 statues between sundown and sunrise. An army of supernatural builders and stone carvers appeared to help the prince. When it appeared obvious to the princess that he would make the dawn deadline, she tricked him: She built a fire, which a rooster mistook for the rising sun. The cock crowed, the helpers vanished, and the prince lost the challenge. He avenged himself by turning the faithless princess into stone—and her sculpture is the loveliest at Prambanan.

MUIREDACH'S CROSS

Irish monks erected hundreds, perhaps thousands, of stone High Crosses before their churches and monasteries. Some were plain and simple, and others were richly carved with figures of saints and scenes from the Bible. Unfortunately, many were destroyed by the English during the Reformation. The finest surviving cross is Muiredach's Cross in Monasterboice, north of the town of Drogheda, the site of a monastery founded in the late fifth century.

At the base of the cross, intertwined around sculptures of cats, is an inscription that begs the reader to pray for the soul of Muiredach; historians have come to believe that the man in question is the abbot of Monasterboice, Muiredach mac Domhnaill, who died in 923.

The cross stands nearly 18 feet tall and is carved from a single block of stone. Every inch of the cross is covered with sculptures or geometric patterns. At the center of the cross on the west side is the Crucifixion of Christ; on the east side the center shows Christ returning to earth for the Last Judgment. Running up and down the shaft and arms of the cross are scenes from famous Bible stories, each in its own frame: Eve tempting Adam with the apple; Cain slaying Abel; Moses drawing water from a rock; the Magi bringing gifts to the Christ Child; soldiers, their swords drawn, arresting Christ in the garden of Gethsemane; and Doubting Thomas, his hand extended, ready to probe the wound in the risen Christ's side.

More than 1,000 years of exposure to the weather, not to mention the destructive rage of iconoclasts, have left many High Crosses in sad condition, yet Muiredach's Cross is an exception: Most of the figures are still sharp and the details are clear.

Harbaville Triptych

In the tenth century, ivory carving had achieved a very high level in Constantinople, and this superb example is one of the best. It is a triptych, meaning that when the doors of this small (it measures 11 inches wide, 9 inches tall when closed) portable shrine are opened, there is a central panel flanked by two wings. Although the figures are carved in very high relief, the ivory background has been pared away until the ivory is so thin as to be translucent in spots.

The composition is elegant and balanced, while the carvings of the individual figures are richly detailed—Christ's throne, for example, and the uniforms of the soldier saints.

Christ, enthroned like a Byzantine emperor, is flanked by the Virgin Mary and St. John the Baptist. In the panel below are five apostles: from left to right, St. James, St. John, St. Peter, St. Paul, and St. Andrew. St. John and St. Paul each carry a fat book rather than a scroll because they were prolific writers who contributed a significant portion of New Testament texts.

The saints depicted in the wings are a mixed collection of martyrs, which suggest that the triptych may have been a commissioned piece and the patron listed the saints he or she wanted depicted. Since four of the saints are military men—St. Theodore the Recruit, St. Theodore the General, St. George, and St. Eustace—it's possible the triptych was made for a member of the Byzantine army.

ca. 950

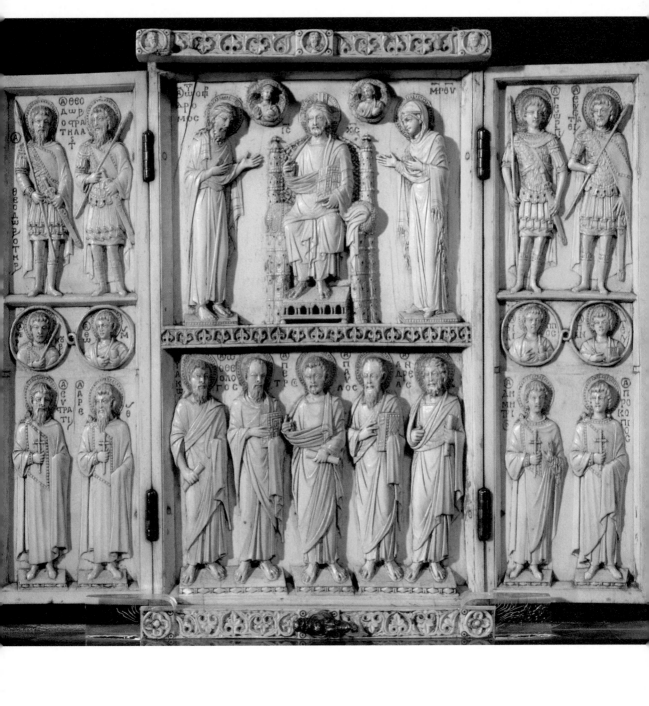

MIMBRES BOWL

For nearly 1,100 years, New Mexico's Mogollon Mountains were home to the Mogollon people, a tribe that erected impressive apartment-building-style dwellings beside the mountain cliffs. After 1300, the Mogollon vanished. No one knows why. Perhaps they were driven out by drought or famine, or they were decimated by war or disease. The ruins of their high-rise homes survive, and beneath the floor of these houses are the graves of the Mogollon dead: Tradition demanded that the departed be buried inside their homes, the body bent in the fetal position, a pottery bowl placed over the deceased's head. Before the bowl was set in place, it was ritually "killed" by having a small hole knocked through it. For this reason, virtually all Mogollon or Mimbres bowls have a hole in them. (*Mimbres* is a term for a late period of Mogollon pottery, fashioned after 1000.)

Mimbres potters painted black on white, employing a geometric style reminiscent of the Cubists of the early twentieth century. The quail is a recurring image or motif in Mimbres pottery, although what it represented in Mogollon culture is not known. Some bowls show humans morphing into animals, or animals becoming humans. Other pots depict fantastic beasts such as a mammal with the tail of a fish or the wings of a bird. Some anthropologists have suggested that since the Mogollon used hallucinogenic plants, the strange images on the bowls may be illustrations of drug-induced visions.

The Mimbres potters did not have pottery wheels. They made their bowls by arranging twisted coils of wet clay, one on top of another, then smoothing them with a gourd. Only the interior of the bowl was painted, using brushes made from the fibers of the yucca plant. Mimbres bowls are considered among the best—and most collectible—of all prehistoric American pottery.

BAYEUX TAPESTRY

Like a 230-foot-long cartoon strip, the Bayeux Tapestry gives us a visual record of the Norman conquest of England in 1066. No documents survive to tell us who made the tapestry, or who commissioned it, although it's likely that the work was ordered by Bishop Odo of Bayeux, the half brother of William the Conqueror. Odo participated in the battle and actually appears in the tapestry wearing a helmet and chain mail armor and swinging a club (it's said he declined to carry a sword because, as a bishop, he did not want to shed Christian blood). It is certain that for many centuries the tapestry was among the treasures of Bayeux Cathedral. It was almost destroyed during the French Revolution—part of it, in fact, was ripped or cut off—but the major part of the tapestry was saved.

Technically, this is not tapestry. The scenes are not woven into the cloth, they have been embroidered. It is also a work of art with a point of view: It portrays Harold, Earl of Wessex, an oath-breaker who failed to support William, Duke of Normandy's claim to the English throne. God punished Harold by sending the Normans to conquer England, and at the Battle of Hastings, the place where the Normans first came ashore, Harold was killed.

The figures in the tapestry appear stiff to us, yet look again and you see remarkable liveliness of action, gesture, and facial expressions. War horses charge across the battlefield; along the tapestry's border, hunting dogs pursue a deer; and townsfolk watch with dismay as Halley's Comet streaks across the sky.

As a social document the tapestry is remarkable. It is a glimpse of life in England and Normandy 1,000 years ago, providing us with details of clothing, interiors of buildings, and familiar scenes such as banquets and even a royal funeral.

ca. 1077

Moai Statues of Easter Island

The island of Rapa Nui lies 1,400 miles west of South America and more than 1,000 miles from the islands of Eastern Polynesia. It acquired the name Easter Island in 1722 when the Dutch explorer Jacob Roggeveen came upon the island on Easter Sunday.

The giant stone figures known as *moai* are the most famous works of Polynesian art. There are 900 of them on Easter Island. The sculptures represent powerful ancient chiefs of the Polynesians. Because these men were descended from the gods, their spirits possess supernatural powers. By erecting these statues the people of Rapa Nui secured the blessings and protection of these chiefs.

All of the statues were carved from tufa, a soft volcanic stone found in the crater of Rano Raraku, an extinct volcano on the island. Men used picks with basalt blades to hack out large rectangular blocks of the tufa. Master carvers sculpted the heads on-site at the Rano Raraku quarry, then a work crew, using ropes and levers, eased the unfinished sculpture down the slope of the volcano. From there a second crew of about 40 men raised the block onto a wooden sled or perhaps rollers and moved it to its intended location. Once the stone was raised, carvers added the final details.

On average, a moai weighs 10 to 13 metric tons, and stands about 13 feet high. At the quarry there is an unfinished moai lying flat on the ground—it measures 70 feet long.

Some moai were set up on stone platforms, such as the row of moai at the Ahu Akivi Temple. Others are crowned with hats carved from red stone. The hats may represent ceremonial headgear, or they could represent an aristocratic hairstyle.

ca. 1100

EVE

By Gislebertus

This sinuous sculpture of Eve once adorned the North Portal of the Cathedral of St. Lazare in Autun, France. It was carved by Gislebertus, arguably the finest sculptor in twelfth-century Europe, a man whose energy matched his talent: It is very likely that he carved personally all the sculptures over the cathedral's doors as well as all the sculptures that decorate the sixty capitals in the church's interior. They are marvelous works of art, especially the *Suicide of Judas* and the *Dream of the Magi*. Art historians have praised the expressiveness of his sculptures, particularly scenes from the infancy of Jesus, and in Gislebertus' carvings of demons they see the birth of Surrealism. But *Eve* is one-of-a-kind—this is the first large-scale sculpture of a nude female since the collapse of the Roman Empire more than 600 years earlier.

Gislebertus depicts Eve reclining, her left arm reaching back for the forbidden fruit while her right hand appears to be cupped as if she were calling Adam to come and share her folly. It is a daring sculpture for a cathedral, but Gislebertus' prudent placement of a shrub eliminated any chance of the carving being smashed by prudes, or Gislebertus himself called up on charges of public lewdness.

The artist must have been proud (and justly so) of his work, because he did what very, very few artists of the twelfth century dared to do—he signed his work. On the lintel through which worshippers would pass, just beneath the feet of a statue of Christ, he carved, "GISLEBERTUS HOC FECIT," which is Latin for GISLEBERTUS MADE THIS.

Suryavarman II Holding Court, at Angkor Wat

ca. 1130

This elegant relief carving depicts the founder of Angkor Wat: King Suryavarman II (reigned 1113–1150) of the Khmer realm, the land known today as Cambodia. This relief is unique in Southeast Asian art as it is the first portrait of a Khmer king.

Viewers tend to notice that the proportions are off—Suryavarman is larger than everyone else in the scene. This is a convention of royal portraiture that is found in virtually every society—by representing the king as larger-than-life, his authority and status are emphasized.

Even in low relief, closer to an engraved stone than a sculpture, this inaugural royal portrait is especially lovely. Suryavarman reclines in a graceful pose against the arm of his throne. His legs are folded beneath him. He gestures toward his court, holding what appears to be a small snake in his outstretched hand (the significance of the snake is unknown). His clothing is minimal, but he is well adorned with jewelry: necklaces, earrings, armlets, bracelets, anklets, and a fine pointed crown. Seated on the floor at his feet are court officials, a scribe, and several servants waving large fans to cool the king.

Unlike previous Khmer kings, Suryavarman's favorite god was Vishnu rather than Shiva. It is likely that he built the temple complex of Angkor Wat in honor of his patron god, since it faces west, which in Hindu theology is the direction associated with Vishnu. Even his throne in the carving expresses his devotion: The chair is decorated with *nagas,* hooded cobras, which are an emblem of Vishnu.

CHRIST PANTOCRATOR OF MONREALE

With its stark stone walls and main portal guarded by two towers that look more like battlements than belfrys, the Cathedral of the Assumption of the Virgin Mary in Monreale, Sicily, bears a strong resemble to a fortress. Inside, however, is one of the wonders of the medieval world. Covering the cathedral's interior walls, arches, and part of the ceiling is 68,243 square feet of mosaics, the work of Greek masters brought here from the Byzantine Empire by King Roger II to decorate his church.

The church's long aisle (it runs 334 feet) focuses the visitor's attention on one image—a huge mosaic half-length portrait of Christ that fills the apse, the half-dome, above the altar. In the language of Byzantine icons, this image is known as "Christ Pantocrator," meaning Christ, the Ruler of All.

Typical of Byzantine iconography, there is virtually no variation in depictions of Christ Pantocrator because every element of the image has a meaning and conveys a message. The gospel book in the Lord's left hand is the book of Christ's law. His right hand is raised in blessing, because even when he sits in judgment Christ still loves all humankind. He has a high forehead—a sign of wisdom. His nose is long and narrow—a sign of dignity.

The artist who designed the Monreale Christ Pantocrator varied the image just a bit, but it is a significant difference. He extended the arms of Christ so that they reach out and fill the curve of the apse. This gives the appearance that he has opened his arms to embrace the faithful, an especially human gesture, but one that is drawn from the Byzantine liturgy in which the priest often invokes Christ as "O Lover of Mankind!"

PORTRAIT OF MINAMOTO NO YORITOMO

By Fujiwara no Takanobu

Minamoto no Yoritomo (1147–1199) founded the Kamakura Shogunate, a military dictatorship that he ruled from his capital city southwest of present-day Tokyo. He was related to the emperor of Japan through his father and was a member of the distinguished Fujiwara clan through his mother. During the political upheavals of the 1160s in Japan, some of Yoritomo's relatives were executed, and he was banished from the imperial court. This portrait of Yoritomo was made while he was in exile.

The year after the painting was completed, Yoritomo and all his family rose up against their enemies, the Taira clan, who had sent Yoritomo into exile. The rebellion succeeded: Yoritomo's clan installed a new emperor, but real political and military power was exercised by Yoritomo.

Fujiwara no Takanobu (1142–1205), who was probably related to Yoritomo, was a well-respected master of "likeness drawing," the Japanese term for portraiture. He painted this portrait of Yoritomo on a silk scroll.

The sharp angles of Yoritomo's severe black robe have reminded many viewers of twentieth-century abstract painting, and perhaps even origami, the Japanese art of paper folding. Yoritomo wears the traditional court headdress, and holds a wooden scepter as an emblem of his rank among the emperor's retainers. The gold hilt of his sword is a striking splash of color against the black.

There is nothing abstract about Yoritomo's face, however. It is a natural, realistic painting of a Japanese aristocrat who may be in exile, but has lost none of his composure or dignity.

Sun Temple of Konark

ca. 1200

There is nothing in the world to compare with this astonishing temple overlooking the Bay of Bengal in Orissa, India. It is built in the shape of the chariot of the sun god, supported by twelve pairs of wheels and drawn by a team of twelve pairs of horses. The decoration of the temple ranges from tiny details incised in the stone with a jeweler's precision, to grand larger-than-life sculptures. There are other chariot temples in India, but the one at Konark is the finest.

The carvings include humans, animals, gods, demons, mythical creatures, lush plants, and meticulous geometric patterns. They are all lovely, a feast for the eye, yet the sculptures every visitor—tourist or art critic—remembers are the erotic ones. They are found everywhere on the exterior of the Sun Temple, and while they were a conventional element in Hindu temple decoration in thirteenth-century India, they still come as a surprise, even a shock, to modern-day visitors. The bewitching sculptures of nude women appear tame beside the explicit sculptural groups of men and women engaging in a variety of sexual adventures.

Erotic sculpture appears on Jain and Buddhist temples from the period, too, but the purpose of such lascivious scenes is a subject of ongoing debate among art historians. Some argue that these scenes of pleasure were meant as a warning to worshippers that earthly happiness is transitory. Others argue that the sight of copulating couples drove away demons, while other scholars believe that the carvings reveal a kind of mania in India 700 years ago for the erotic.

Muisca Raft

In 1537, a Spanish conquistador, Gonsalvo Jimenez de Quesada, encountered the Muisca people in the mountains of central Colombia. From that time a legend developed, based on an actual custom of the Muisca when a new chief or king was about to take office. On the day of coronation, the priests stripped the king naked, covered his body with a sticky substance, then blew gold dust until he was powdered with it from head to toe. At this point the king stepped aboard a raft and was rowed out to the center of Lake Guatavita, the Muisca's sacred lake, where he threw gold and emeralds into the water as an offering to the goddess who lived there. The Spanish name for the gold-dust-covered king was El Dorado, the Golden Man. The story fired the imaginations, not to mention stirred up the greed, of the Spanish, who mounted one expedition after another throughout South America in search of the legendary character and his gold-and-emerald-laden kingdom.

In fact, the legend was close to the truth, as this extraordinary artifact proves. In 1969, inside a small cave south of Bogota, three peasants discovered a large ceramic bowl shaped like an obese man sitting and thinking; inside was the golden raft. Before it could be purchased by a private collector or a foreign museum, the Gold Museum, located in Bogota's Banco de la Republica, acquired the piece.

The raft is 7.5 inches long, 3.75 inches wide, and 4 inches high. It was cast as a single piece of almost pure gold, strengthened with a little silver and copper.

The tall central figure is the king, the Spaniards' El Dorado, and accompanying him on the raft are his attendants. Some carry banners, others wear jaguar masks, still others bear wizard maracas on their wrists. True to the legend, the king has set sail for the center of the sacred lake where he will toss gold and emeralds into the water.

In 1580, the Spanish tried to drain Lake Guatavita in hopes of reclaiming the gold and jewels at the bottom. The attempt was partially successful, yielding a large cache of gold and emeralds.

ca. 1200

BAMBERG HORSEMAN

This is the first life-size equestrian statue since the collapse of the Roman Empire 800 years earlier. The identity of the sculptor is unknown. The inspiration for the sculpture is unknown. Even whom the sculpture is supposed to represent is unknown.

The statue stands in Bamberg Cathedral in Bavaria. It is in its original location, where it was installed sometime between 1225 and 1237. The crown tells us it is a figure of a king or a prince. Some historians have suggested that this is a portrait sculpture of St. Henry II (973–1024)—the statue is looking toward the saint's tomb. But Henry was Holy Roman Emperor, and the statue bears none of the emblems of an emperor. Another possibility is that the figure is St. Stephen of Hungary (975–1038), Henry's brother-in-law. Recently, a German history professor, Hannes Moehring, has suggested that this is a statue of Christ as described in the Book of Revelation, "Behold, a white horse! He who sat upon it is called Faithful and True, and in righteousness he judges and makes war" (Rev. 19:11).

Aside from being the first equestrian statue in centuries, there is another interesting detail about the Bamberg Horseman: It is the first equestrian statue to depict the animal wearing horseshoes.

ca. 1230

CRUCIFIX OF SAN DOMENICO, AREZZO

By Cimabue

Florence, the city that has produced more than its fair share of great artists, was the birthplace of the painter who took the first steps toward the Renaissance style. Cimabue's (ca. 1240–ca. 1302) figures look a bit stiff and formal to us, not much of a departure from the rigid Byzantine style. Yet in his own day, the innovations Cimabue introduced stunned viewers. He moved away from the flat depictions of people characteristic of Byzantine icons and gave his Madonnas, and saints, and angels a touch of three-dimensionality.

Cimabue's Crucifix (or Crucifixes—he painted at least two) is his masterpiece. Before Cimabue, the convention had been to show Christ stripped to a loincloth and nailed to the cross but not even to hint at the physical agony he must have endured. By this formula, Christ was not suffering and dying on the cross; he was reigning from it. Cimabue broke with this tradition, portraying Christ with his body twisted in pain, his head fallen onto his shoulder, his face a mask of anguish, his eyes tightly shut—perhaps in death. Such a crucifix was new in Italy, and it caused a sensation. After he had painted one for the Church of San Domenico in Arezzo, the Franciscan friars at the Church of Santa Croce in Florence, Cimabue's hometown, commissioned a crucifix, too; it was virtually identical to the one in Arezzo.

Tragically, in 1966 the River Arno flooded its banks and raged through the historic city. The water was 22 feet deep in the neighborhood around the Church of Santa Croce. It reached Cimabue's Crucifix, washing away much of the paint from the body and face of Christ.

FRESCO

Fresco comes from the Italian word for "fresh" because the artist always painted on a layer of fresh wet plaster. That is the secret of fresco: An assistant would spread a layer about one-half-inch thick of wet lime-and-sand plaster on the surface, then the artist would paint while the plaster was still wet. The wet plaster absorbed the paint, and when it dried the painting was literally part of the wall or ceiling. All the binding agents—egg yolks, glue, beeswax—that artists of this period needed when painting on wooden boards or stone were unnecessary when painting a fresco. They just mixed their pigments with plain water.

Painters in ancient Crete, Egypt, Rome, and Mexico all used the fresco technique, but fresco has become most closely associated with the late medieval and Renaissance periods of painting. The technique has barely changed in 3,500 years.

The trick was judging how long the plaster would remain wet and how fast the artists could paint. In hot weather wet plaster would be dry in about 12 hours; in damp weather the plaster might stay moist as long as 24 hours. Experienced fresco artists knew how much space they could paint in one *giornata*, or day's work, and learned to calculate how long it would take to finish a job by measuring the square footage of the wall or ceiling. In 1485, when the painter Domenico Ghirlandaio was commissioned to fresco the Tournabouni Chapel in Florence's Church of Santa Maria Novella, he estimated that it would take him 250 *giornate*. Working with his pupils and assistants, Ghirlandaio managed to paint a 4-by-5 feet patch of wet plaster in one day.

Copy of a medieval original depicting April, from the *Occupations of the Months* fresco, Chapelle de Pritz, Laval.

FRESCOES IN THE CHURCH OF ST. CLEMENT, OHRID

Late in the thirteenth century, two young Macedonian artists named Michael and Eutychius set off a renaissance in fresco painting in their homeland. Icon painting, whether on a small wooden panel or on a church wall, was governed by strict, unvarying rules on everything from the composition of a sacred scene to the colors of the saints' clothes. But like other masters of the art of the icon, Michael and Eutychius found novel ways to work within these guidelines.

In the Church of St. Clement (also known as the Church of St. Bogorodica Perivlepta, or St. Mary-Who-Is-All-Perceiving), the artists were commissioned to paint ten large frescoes. The clergy requested the usual scenes found inside any Orthodox church such as Christ Pantocrator and the Last Supper. But Michael and Eutychius brought a fresh approach to these traditional subjects.

To emphasize the spiritual over the sensual, figures in icons were supposed to be flat, with only limited attention paid to actual human anatomy. Michael and Eutychius rounded out their figures, giving them a touch of three-dimensionality.

They also had a flair for the theatrical. For example, in their fresco *Lamentation Over the Dead Christ*, they assembled a crowd of mourners, most of them women, who tear their hair, throw up their arms in grief, turn to one another for comfort, or gesture pathetically toward the lifeless body of the Lord. It looks like a real funeral.

That same flair for the dramatic dominates the *Dormition of the Virgin.* At the bottom of the painting lies the figure of the Virgin Mary, who has just died (or "fallen asleep," which is what dormition means). This should be the focus of the viewer's attention, but our eyes drift up to the host of angels who surge out of the gates of Heaven and are funneled down a narrow street in Jerusalem to the deathbed of the Mother of Christ.

LAMENTATION OVER THE DEAD CHRIST

By Giotto

You can almost hear the wails of grief—not only from Christ's mother and friends, but also from the heartbroken angels hovering overhead. The gospels tell how, at the moment Christ died, darkness blotted out the sun, lightning split the sky, the earth quaked, and spirits of the dead wandered through the streets of Jerusalem. Giotto sidesteps such high drama for a more intimate scene of family and friends bewailing the cruel death of a loved one. Of course, he does not ignore the cosmic implications of this death, as grief-stricken angels descend from heaven to join the human mourners.

We are so accustomed to naturalistic art that Giotto barely makes an impression on us. But 700 years ago, the first people to see Giotto's frescoes would have been shaken by "the shock of the new." This was the first time since the Roman era that an artist had given his figures mass, tried to convey real human emotions, and set his scene in a true-to-life landscape. And the *Lamentation* is just one scene among dozens in Padua's Arena Chapel, which Giotto covered completely, walls and ceiling, with his groundbreaking frescoes. We can scarcely imagine the visual, emotional, and intellectual wallop the first viewers of the chapel frescoes must have experienced.

Giotto di Bondone (1267–1337) was the son of peasants who lived outside Florence. As a boy, Giotto's job was to watch the family's flock of sheep. A legend that dates back at least to the sixteenth century says that one day the shepherd boy amused himself by making a chalk sketch of a sheep on a rock. The artist Cimabue happened by and was so impressed by the lifelike drawing he begged Giotto's father to let him train the boy as an artist.

Cimabue was already moving away from the Byzantine style that dominated art in Italy, but in terms of artistic innovation, Giotto far surpassed his teacher. He was the precursor, even the father, of the Italian Renaissance.

GOLDEN HAGGADAH OF BARCELONA

A Haggadah is a collection of prayers and sacred texts recited and read aloud at the seder, the ritual meal that celebrates the Jewish festival of Passover. During the twelfth century, wealthy Jews commissioned artists to create lavish editions of the Haggadah as a token of their piety. This magnificent volume, created for a Spanish Jew who lived in or near Barcelona, must have created a sensation the first time it was brought to the table to be read from during the seder.

Haggadah is the Hebrew word for "narration": It tells the story of how God delivered the Jews from slavery in Egypt to freedom in the Promised Land. Because the pharaoh refused to free his Jewish slaves, God afflicted Egypt with ten plagues that ranged from the water of the Nile turning to blood, to the angel of death taking the life of the firstborn son in every Egyptian family.

Two unknown artists worked on the Golden Haggadah. One painted squat human figures, giving them overdone facial expressions. The second artist painted more elongated, elegant figures. Although they worked in Spain, their work was influenced by the French Gothic style of painting, which was fashionable at the time. And although the artists were probably Jews, and illuminating a Jewish text for a Jewish audience, the way they portray biblical scenes is virtually indistinguishable from the technique of their Christian counterparts.

In 1492, Ferdinand and Isabella of Spain banished all Jews from their kingdom. The owner of the Golden Haggadah took his (or her) treasure to Italy where it passed through a succession of Jewish families until it was acquired sometime in the nineteenth century by a Hebrew poet and rare-book collector, Giuseppe Almanzi. In 1865, the British Museum Library purchased Almanzi's entire collection, including the Golden Haggadah, for a paltry £1,000. Almanzi's private library became the basis for the British Library's collection of Hebrew manuscripts.

Great Mongol *Shahnama*

The *Shahnama*, the Book of Kings, is the masterwork of the Persian poet Firdausi, who wrote it about the year 1000. It is an epic collection of stories about the heroes and kings of ancient Persia (now Iran) in the centuries before the coming of Islam. Sometime in the 1330s the vizier, Ghiyath al-Din (?–1336), commissioned a luxurious copy of the *Shahnama* for his own private library.

We do not know the names of the artists and calligraphers who worked on this masterpiece. According to an educated guess by art historians, the work was probably bound in two volumes totaling about 280 folio pages, each measuring about 9.75 inches by 7.75 inches; the finished work probably had 190 illustrations.

Early in the twentieth century, a rare-book dealer in Paris, Georges Demotte, acquired the bound volumes of the *Shahnama* and took them apart so he could sell the pages, especially the illustrations, individually. As a result, the surviving pages of the book are scattered in a host of art museums and private collections around the globe.

The painted pages of the manuscript are full of barely contained energy. Routinely, the artist paints trees and battle standards that break out of the tidy frame of the picture. The artist also blended a variety of styles: Although the stories are set in ancient Persia, he paints them as if they were happening in the Mongol court (Persia in the fourteenth century was under Mongol rule). Since the Mongols had invaded from China, the artist dresses his figures in Chinese clothing, and even represents landscapes in the style of Chinese scroll paintings.

ANDREI RUBLEV

(ca. 1360–ca. 1430)

A monk at the monastery of the Holy Trinity and St. Sergius, Andrei Rublev is the undisputed master of icon painting in medieval Russia. He was the student of Theophanes the Greek, a Byzantine artist who left his home in Constantinople to decorate the churches and monasteries in and around Moscow. All icon painters, even to this day, pray and meditate on the sacred mystery they are about to portray before they pick up their brushes. However, it is said that Theophanes was particularly saintly, with a touch of a mystic about him, an artist who attempted to paint, as one of his biographers put it, "the spiritual beauty that his spiritual eyes perceived."

Icon painting is bound by a set of canons, or regulations, intended to preserve the spiritual continuity of the images and limit freewheeling innovations that are the products of an artist's imagination. The clothing styles of the figures in the icon, the gestures, even the colors are fixed so that the faithful who look at an icon, whether it was made on Mount Sinai 1,500 years ago or in the United States last week, will be able to recognize the scene and the figures instantly.

Working within this tradition, Rublev developed a personal style characterized by elegant lines and graceful and serene figures. From Theophanes, Rublev appears to have picked up the palette of cool, harmonious colors that the Greek master preferred. About the year 1411, he produced his most famous and most highly praised work, an icon of the Trinity in which the Father, the Son, and the Holy Spirit are depicted in the traditional Byzantine style as three angels. About the year 1409, St. Nikon of Radonezh, abbot of Trinity and St. Sergius Monastery, began to rebuild the Holy Trinity Church, which the Tartars had destroyed. Rublev painted his icon of the Trinity for the new church; today it is displayed at the Tretyakov Gallery in Moscow.

In 1988 the Russian Orthodox Church canonized Andrei Rublev. His feast day is July 4.

GENTILE DA FABRIANO

(ca. 1370–1427)

By age ten Gentile da Fabriano was essentially an orphan: His mother had died, and his grief-stricken father had entered a monastery. The details of where Gentile went or who took care of him have not survived. It is likely that his father, before taking his vows as a monk, apprenticed his son to an artist who would have provided Gentile with room and board.

By 1408 he was in Venice, accepting important commissions, including the decoration of a large council chamber in the Doge's Palace. Before 1420 he was in Tuscany, painting in Florence, Siena, and Orvieto.

Gentile painted in the International Gothic style that admired scenes crowded with opulently dressed figures, exotic people and animals, bright colors, and flowing lines. The best surviving example of Gentile's approach to International Gothic is his *Adoration of the Magi*, painted for the Church of the Santissima Trinita in Florence and exhibited today in Florence's Uffizi Gallery. The main scene of the Three Kings presenting their gifts to the Christ Child gets the attention of most viewers—and understandably so: The kings wear splendid garments and dazzling jewels, and they have come to Bethlehem accompanied by a huge entourage that includes camels, monkeys, and even a leopard. But in the upper portion of the painting, just below the curved arches of the frame, are the earlier incidents in the story of the journey of the Magi. At the far left the kings meet on the seashore and spot the star that will lead them to the manger. In the central scene they follow a road up a hill to Jerusalem to seek advice from King Herod about the likely location of the newborn King of the Jews. And in the scene on the right the kings are about to enter the little walled town of Bethlehem.

Go back to the far left side of the painting for an especially delightful detail: Standing behind the Virgin Mary are two women, her handmaidens, who are inspecting the gift just offered by the elderly king.

THE GUILD OF ST. LUKE

Guilds are commonly compared to modern labor unions, but a guild was much more complicated. Initially, membership in the Guild of St. Luke was restricted to painters, sculptors, and other artists who had demonstrated their skill. By the seventeenth century, the chapters of the guild in Belgium and the Netherlands admitted promising amateurs as well as art lovers and connoisseurs. The guild's primary function was to set the standards for works of art; artists who did shoddy work or used inferior materials risked expulsion from the guild. And the guild served another purpose—it arbitrated any disputes that arose between artist and client.

The first written reference to a Guild of St. Luke dates from 1382: In the city of Antwerp, artists formed an association under the auspices of St. Luke the Evangelist, the patron saint of painters. According to legend, St. Luke was an artist who painted a portrait of the Virgin Mary and the Christ Child. This story became a popular subject among artists in northern Europe; Rogier van der Weyden is just one of the masters who painted St. Luke painting Jesus and Mary.

The guild was still flourishing in the Low Countries in the seventeenth century when artists such as Vermeer and Frans Hals were members.

Something similar existed in Italy, although it was known as The Company of St. Luke, or the Academy of St. Luke. Leonardo da Vinci and Raphael are just two of the Renaissance masters who were members. The organization survives today as the National Academy of St. Luke; based in Rome, the academy promotes painting, sculpture, and architecture.

St. Luke Painting the Virgin by Rogier van der Weyden, ca. 1430

Wilton Diptych

A diptych is two panels connected by hinges so it can be opened or closed like a book. Typically diptychs are of modest size (each panel of the Wilton Diptych measures only 22.4 inches by 11.5 inches) because they were intended for a little altar or shrine in a private home.

Few English religious paintings from the Middle Ages survive—during the Reformation in the sixteenth century virtually every sacred image in the country was destroyed. The handful that escaped the first wave of iconoclasm were destroyed by the Puritans in the first half of the seventeenth century. Yet the Wilton Diptych is not only intact, the condition of the painting is exceptional: The gold background shimmers, the vivid blue of the robes of the Blessed Virgin and the angels is rich and resplendent.

The painting was commissioned by England's King Richard II (reigned 1377–1399), seen kneeling as three saints present him to the Virgin and Child. The saints are St. Edmund the King, who was shot to death with arrows by the Vikings; St. Edward the Confessor, who lived in chastity with his wife, rebuilt Westminster Abbey, and was generous to the poor; and St. John the Baptist, who, the gospels tell us, pointed out Christ to a crowd, saying, "Behold the Lamb of God."

Richard was a man of exquisite taste, perhaps the first art collector of the English royal family. The scene is King Richard's vision of Heaven. One of the angels carries the Banner of St. George, the flag of England; and all of the angels wear a little image of a white hart with a crown around its neck—Richard's personal emblem and a clear sign of whose side the angels are on.

WELL OF MOSES

By Claus Sluter

Late in the fourteenth century, a sublime style of Gothic art emerged that was embraced all across Christian Europe—from England to Bohemia, from the Low Countries to Italy. Its prosaic name is the International Style, but it is also known, understandably, as the Beautiful Style. The anonymous genius who painted the Wilton Diptych, and the Limbourg Brothers, who created such splendid illuminated manuscripts for the Duke of Berry, were members of this school of art. Among sculptors from this period, Claus Sluter (ca. 1340–1406) of the Netherlands was the finest.

Sluter worked almost exclusively for Philip II, Duke of Burgundy. Today Burgundy is a province in France, but during the Middle Ages it was in essence a distinct kingdom, fabulously wealthy, notoriously influential in European politics, and blessed with a long line of dukes and duchesses who had discriminating taste.

Philip commissioned Sluter to carve an elaborate Calvary for his favorite monastery, the Charterhouse of Champmol. Calvaries in the late Middle Ages were complicated, even extravagant affairs, with dozens of figures gathered around the foot of Christ on the cross. As the pedestal for the crucifix, Sluter designed a six-sided base with near-life-size statues of Moses, David, Jeremiah, Isaiah, Daniel, and Zechariah, all of whom had prophesied the coming of Christ.

The facial expressions, the hand gestures, and the poses of the figures are utterly natural, and the folds of their voluminous robes look completely realistic. The sculpture of Moses is the most theatrical with his huge beard cascading down his chest as he holds the tablets of the Ten Commandments in one hand and the unrolled scroll of the Torah in the other. The short lumpy horns on his head, by the way, are the result of a mistranslation of the biblical text at the time, which read "horns of light" coming from Moses' head instead of the correct "rays of light."

The Bellini Family

For many years the Renaissance style was not welcome in Venice. The Doge and the Patriarch, the nobles, the heads of the religious orders, and the wealthy merchants—in other words, the people who commissioned works of art—preferred the Byzantine and Gothic styles. Paintings and mosaics with golden backgrounds looked more opulent—a quality everyone in this wealthy city admired. And the elongated, austere depiction of Christ and the saints was infinitely more spiritual than the fleshy, sensual realism typical of Renaissance paintings and sculptures in Florence and Rome. Some of the great Renaissance masters visited and worked in Venice—Donatello, Uccello, Ghiberti—but barely made an impression on the Venetians' taste. It took a local family of artists, the Bellinis, to make the Renaissance palatable to the Venetians.

The father, Jacopo Bellini (ca. 1396–ca. 1470), was a tinsmith's son who had been apprenticed to Gentile da Fabriano in Florence. From there he studied in Rome, and in these two centers of the Renaissance he became enchanted with the new style. Sadly, few of his paintings have survived, but one that has, *Madonna and Child Blessing*, suggests that he swayed the Venetians by giving them a combination of the fresh and the familiar. The Christ Child is pure Renaissance—a robust, curly-haired, adorable little boy. The Virgin Mary, on the other hand, has the long face, the narrow eyes, and the impassive expression of a typical Byzantine icon.

Gentile Bellini (ca. 1429–1507), named for his father's teacher, kept up his father's campaign by painting grand works that depicted familiar scenes in Venice and portraits of some of its most important citizens.

The finest painter in the family was Giovanni Bellini (ca. 1430–1516). He adopted the rich, vibrant colors of Byzantium that Venice loved and used them to paint marvelously lifelike images of the Madonna. He had started with egg tempera paints, but found the colors too flat. He switched to the then-newfangled oil paints, which gave his colors depth and a shimmering effect that reminded the Venetians of their beloved Byzantine mosaics in St. Mark's Basilica.

Christ Carrying the Cross, by Giovanni Bellini, ca. 1505-10

THE GATES OF PARADISE

Michelangelo gave them their name—*The Gates of Paradise*—because if Heaven ever needed physical doors, these massive gilt bronze masterpieces, standing 20 feet tall and weighing 3 tons, would be ideal.

The bronze doors were the result of a competition hosted by Florence's Baptistery of St. John. The winner was a twenty-year-old goldsmith and sculptor, Lorenzo Ghiberti (ca. 1381–1455). His winning design was comprised of ten panels, each of which measures 31.5 inches by 31.5 inches; the scenes depicted all came from the Old Testament. Ghiberti worked on these doors from 1403 to 1424, and as soon as he finished, he received a commission to create a second pair of doors, also for the Baptistery. This second pair was not completed until 1452.

Look at the two sets of doors and you will notice a marked difference immediately. The first set is still in the medieval style, with all the figures fitting tightly together inside a compact Gothic frame. By the year 1424, however, when Ghiberti received his second commission, the new Renaissance style with its interest in landscape, the science of perspective, and the art of classical Greece and Rome dominated the Florence art world. Consequently, in the second set of doors the constricting frame is gone and the Bible stories take place amid hills and valleys and groves of trees; the figures of people and animals are shown in perspective to convey a sense of distance; and the inspiration for some of the figures come directly from ancient Roman sculptures. With his second set of *Gates of Paradise*, Ghiberti not only advanced Renaissance sculpture, he made medieval art look cramped and old-fashioned.

TRES RICHES HEURES

By Paul, Jean, and Herman Limbourg

Even now, monks and nuns gather in their chapels at prescribed hours several times a day to chant prayers, psalms, and hymns. Each of these sessions has its own name—matins, lauds, vespers, compline—and in the parlance of the Middle Ages, the monks and nuns were said to "chant the hours." Consequently, the prayer book used by the monks and nuns became known as "the Book of the Hours." By the fourteenth century it was popular among laypeople—men and women—to offer an abbreviated form of "the hours" prayer in their own private oratories or chapels. This led to a small industry for artists who created exquisite copies of these prayer books for private individuals.

There were many masters of this art, and among the best were a trio of brothers, Paul, Jean, and Herman Limbourg (ca. 1370s–1416), whose superb sense of color and design won them several commissions from one of the connoisseurs of the age, Jean, Duke of Berry (1340–1416). A man with a taste for the best and the income of a prince, the duke kept a small army of goldsmiths, jewelers, artists, sculptors, even tailors, busy creating glorious objects that he could admire, collect, eat off of, or wear. The Limbourgs, for example, had been trained as goldsmiths (which shows in the decorative motifs of the books that are always rich in gold leaf), but made the shift to painting after they found that Paul was a brilliant draftsman.

Many artists of Books of the Hours tried to fill every inch of every margin of every page with fanciful foliage and mythical beasts. The Limbourgs considered this to be overkill. To focus the reader's attention on the page's single, carefully composed illustration, they left their margins empty, or perhaps added an understated filigree pattern.

The *Tres Riches Heures* ran to over 400 pages, about half of which were full-page paintings. Tragically, shortly after the Limbourg brothers completed their commission, they and the duke all died in 1416, probably in an epidemic.

EXPULSION FROM EDEN

By Masaccio

His nickname, Masaccio, is Italian for "Big Ugly Tom." The artist's real name was Tommaso de Ser Giovanni (1401–1428). He came from a small town near Florence, and by the time he was twenty-one years old, he was already receiving commissions from well-to-do Florentines and members of the city's religious orders.

Masaccio's *Expulsion from Eden,* painted at the end of his brief life, is in the Brancacci Chapel in Florence's Church of Santa Maria del Carmine. The Brancacci family hired Masaccio and another artist, Masolino, to fresco their private chapel with episodes from the life of the apostle St. Peter. Perhaps on their own initiative or at the direction of the Brancaccis, the two artists also created a matched pair of frescoes at the chapel entrance: Masolino painted Adam and Eve plucking the forbidden fruit, while Masaccio painted them as they were being driven out of the Garden of Eden.

Masolino's painting is cool, rational—the First Couple look detached even as they commit the original sin. Masaccio's Adam and Eve, on the other hand, are positively heartrending. Adam, ashamed, buries his face in his hands and sobs, while Eve throws back her head and wails. Behind them is the tall, elegant, lovely gate of Eden, a hint of what they and their descendants have lost forever. The landscape they find themselves in now is harsh and barren, recalling God's verdict, "Cursed is the ground because of you; in toil you shall eat of it all the days of your life" (Gen. 3.17). And to make sure they don't try to come back, there is the angel with the sword.

Genesis says God took pity on Adam and Eve and gave them garments of animal skins to wear when they left Eden, but Masaccio, good humanist that he is, shows them naked. On the one hand it makes them more pitiable, going into the world entirely exposed; on the other it gives Masaccio an excuse to showcase his skill in rendering the human body and natural movement.

Cantoria Panels

By Luca della Robbia

The clergy of the Duomo, or cathedral, of Florence commissioned Luca della Robbia (1400–1482) to sculpt ten panels to adorn the cantoria, or choir loft. Della Robbia is most famous for his large glazed terracotta relief sculptures, but for the Duomo job he carved in marble.

The sculpture series is inspired by Psalm 150, in which the psalmist calls for trumpets, lutes, harps, timbrels, stringed instruments, pipes, cymbals, singers, and dancers to praise the Lord. "Let everything that breathes," he exclaims, "praise the Lord!" The panels illustrate the psalm, with children, some little more than toddlers, joyfully celebrating the glory of God.

Although the panels illustrate a Hebrew hymn and were intended for a Catholic cathedral, della Robbia depicts his young singers, dancers, and musicians as ancient Romans in classical dress, some wearing laurel crowns or draped in floral garlands as if they were decked out to attend a triumphal parade in honor of a conquering hero. As with his terracotta works, della Robbia carved almost all of the figures in very high relief—some are almost fully rounded sculptures. It was not just a matter of technique; it was a necessity if the panels were to have any visual impact on the congregation, because they would be mounted in a choir loft more than 30 feet above the church floor.

In 1688, to make way for an elaborate new decorative design in honor of the marriage of the Duke de' Medici, the Cantoria panels were removed from the choir loft. Today, della Robbia's panels are displayed all together in the Museum of the Works of the Duomo in Florence—although now they are mounted at eye level, so visitors can appreciate them.

ARNOLFINI PORTRAIT

By Jan van Eyck

Many feel that this double portrait of Giovanni Arnolfini and his wife (her name may have been Giovanna) portrays their wedding and reveals that when the couple exchanged vows, Giovanna was already far along in pregnancy. The curators of the National Gallery in London, where the picture is one of the treasures, insist that this is not a wedding picture, and Giovanna Arnolfini is not expecting a child; she is just holding up her voluminous gown in the manner fashionable at the time.

Dead center in the painting, on the wall behind the couple, is an elaborate calligraphy signature in Latin that reads, "Jan van Eyck was here 1434." Below the signature is a mirror in which can be seen two individuals, one of whom may be van Eyck. Giovanni Arnolfini's hand, then, is not raised because he is taking a vow, but is raised in greeting.

The painting is done in oil, still a new technique in 1434 (there is a long-standing belief that van Eyck invented oil painting). Painters in what is now Belgium and the Netherlands took to the new medium with enthusiasm because it brought to colors a level of clarity and brilliance not possible in tempera paints. And oil paints had another advantage—they let the artist portray delicate effects of light, as van Eyck did with the gleaming brass chandelier in this painting.

A great deal of ink has been spilled trying to interpret what some scholars take to be symbols within the room. For example, critics who believe this depicts a wedding ceremony argue that the single candle in the chandelier represents the presence of Christ, the Light of the World; the cast-off clogs suggests that the couple is standing, metaphorically, on holy ground. Critics who believe the lady is pregnant point to an image of St. Margaret of Antioch carved on the chair against the rear wall: St. Margaret is the patron of women in childbirth. This is a case of overinterpretation. The best that can be said at this date is that the painting shows a well-to-do couple in a room of their well-furnished home. As for the significance of the cast-off clogs, that may have to remain an unsolved mystery.

ANNUNCIATION

By Fra Angelico

You'll find this painting in Cortona, the Italian town that commissioned it almost six hundred years ago. Fra Angelico set the scene in a loggia overlooking a garden. The Archangel Gabriel is in the act of genuflecting before the Mother of God; the Virgin Mary, seated on a bench, bows slightly to hear the angel's greeting, "Hail, full of grace! The Lord is with thee."

This is a Renaissance painting that has not forgotten its medieval roots: Fra Angelico uses repeating Roman arches to give the scene perspective—one of the great discoveries of Renaissance painting—but like the masters of the Middle Ages, he frames the Virgin and the angel each in their own arch, recalling the niches found in churches. About the same time, Fra Angelico's fellow Florentine, Donatello, was creating a bronze sculpture of the Annunciation in which Mary and Gabriel occupy the same space. It is a much more intimate depiction of the scene, but Donatello was an innovator while Fra Angelico tended to be more traditional.

As his name suggests, Fra Angelico was a Dominican friar (his title, "Fra," means "friar" or "brother"). Most of his commissions came from churches and patrons in Florence or from nearby towns. From 1447 to 1449, however, he was at the Vatican painting fresco cycles in a tiny chapel for Pope Nicholas V.

Back home at his monastery of San Marco, Fra Angelico painted a fresco in the cell, or private room, of every friar. They are all in the style of this lovely *Annunciation*—elegant and a bit austere as befits a community of religious men who have taken a vow of poverty. In the friars' cells there is none of the gold and lapis lazuli that Fra Angelico used when painting for wealthy patrons. Instead of grandeur he gave each of his little frescoes tender religious emotion.

ca. 1440

DAVID

By Donatello

Donatello's *David* is one of those works of art that is discussed in every class on Renaissance art because it represents a landmark moment in the history of sculpture. It was the first freestanding bronze sculpture cast during the Renaissance period; it was the first freestanding statue of a male nude since the end of the Roman Empire about 1,000 years earlier; and unlike earlier sculptures, which were placed against a wall or tucked inside a niche, Donatello intended his *David* to stand upon a pedestal so viewers could walk around and view it from every angle.

The Renaissance was a period of renewed interest in the classical world of ancient Greece and Rome and in this bronze, Donatello found an ingenious way to suggest both the biblical story of David and Goliath while also alluding to classical mythology. David is nude except for boots and a helmet: The helmet refers to the biblical account of David and Goliath, found in I Samuel, in which King Saul tries to persuade David to wear armor before going into battle against the giant Goliath. But in pagan mythology the helmet was also a symbol of the god Hermes.

Donatello depicts David as very young, barely in his teens, with a kind of girlish prettiness to him. In contrast to the heavily armored Goliath, David is nude. In this way Donatello suggests the traditional Jewish and Christian interpretation of the story—that David, young, weak, and virtually defenseless in the eyes of the world, defeated and killed the giant because he relied upon the power of God rather than his own strength.

The sculpture was commissioned by Cosimo de Medici, the banking tycoon whose family became the power brokers of fifteenth-century Florence. In an age when kings and emperors ruled, the city of Florence and its surrounding territory was one of those rare places that had a republic. The people of Florence liked to think of themselves as a political David pitted against a host of royal Goliaths.

BATTLE OF SAN ROMANO

By Paolo Uccello

Paolo Uccello's wife used to complain to the neighbors that her husband stayed up all night working out, mathematically, the perfect vanishing point for perspective in his paintings. On those occasions when Signora Uccello lost her patience and demanded that her husband put out the light and come to bed, he would call back, "Oh, what a lovely thing this perspective is!"

We see this mathematically precise rendering of perspective in Uccello's most dramatic work, *Battle of San Romano*. Uccello painted the battle on three large panels, each measuring 71 inches by 126 inches. It is likely that the Medicis, the wealthiest, most politically influential family in Florence, commissioned the paintings. Since then the panels have been scattered: One is in the Uffizi in Florence, another is in the National Gallery in London, and the third is in the Louvre in Paris.

As the paintings suggest, the battle, fought between Florence and Siena in 1432, was a series of cavalry charges. The rearing horses, the very long lances, and the vibrant contrasting colors give the scene a theatrical flair. It looks more like a pageant or a tournament than a blood-and-guts battle. (In fact, it is reported that no soldier was killed at San Romano, although each side took a few hundred captives.)

Not only are the paintings a textbook study in perspective, they also go by the book in the arrangement of color. In his book, *Della pittura* (*Concerning Painting*), considered at the time to be the definitive work on the subject, Leon Battista Alberti (1404–1472) laid out the proper technique for artists. "The picture will have charm when each color is very unlike the one next to it," Alberti wrote. "When red is next to green or blue, they render each other more handsome and vivid...Dark colors among light ones look handsome, and so light ones look pretty among dark ones." In *Battle of San Romano*, Uccello followed Alberti's precepts to the letter.

ca. 1440

PORTRAIT OF A LADY

By Rogier van der Weyden

ca. 1445

For nearly one thousand years, portraiture was virtually dead in Western Europe. Individuals might appear worshipping Christ, venerating a saint, or witnessing an event from sacred history, but these were not portraits, they were archetypes—the noble and devout queen, merchant, or bishop. An effort to create an accurate image of how the individual truly looked in life was not a consideration, so long as he or she looked as a great queen/merchant/bishop should.

The first portrait in our sense of the word—a good likeness of a person made for its own sake—was painted by an anonymous artist around the year 1350. It is a portrait in profile of the French king, John the Good (Jean le Bon).

The timing of this precedent was excellent—the Renaissance, with its renewed interest in "man, the measure of all things," made portraiture both acceptable and fashionable. By the first decades of the fifteenth century there was a large demand for portraits in France, Burgundy, and the Low Countries—the region where John the Good sat for his portrait.

Artists of the Northern Renaissance such as Rogier van der Weyden (ca. 1399–1464) and Jan van Eyck earned well-deserved reputations for producing true-to-life portraits, although with enough flattering touches to keep the client happy.

We do not know the identity of the sitter in van der Weyden's *Portrait of a Lady*. She is probably the wife of a wealthy merchant or city official. She is stylishly but soberly attired. And since this is a secular work, her hands are folded gracefully, not in prayer. She is serene, sophisticated, genteel—exactly how a woman of her rank ought to appear in society.

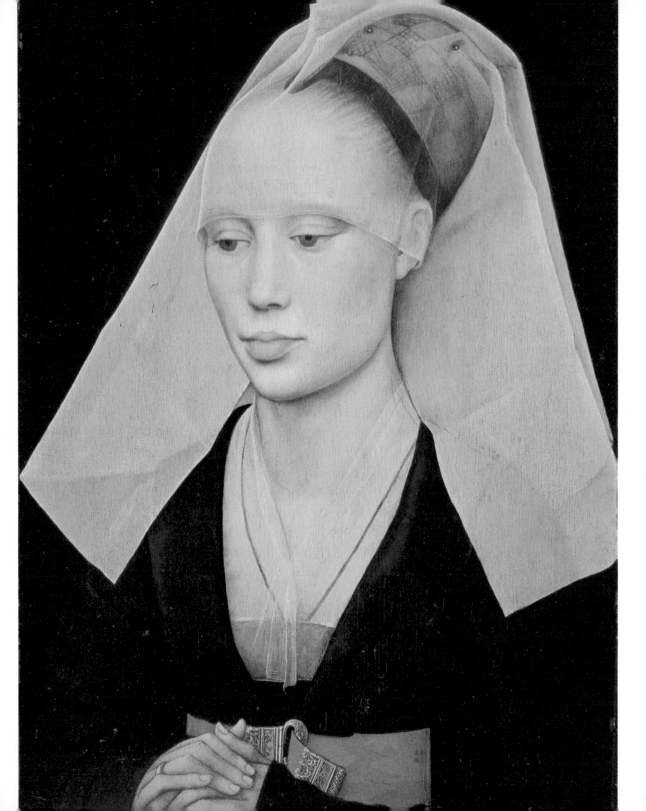

FLAGELLATION OF CHRIST

By Piero della Francesca

One of the most mysterious, most vigorously debated paintings of the Renaissance era, the *Flagellation of Christ* has an otherworldly quality that fascinates viewers, even when they don't understand everything in the painting.

It is a small picture, approximately 23 inches by 31 inches, which makes it too small for an altarpiece, but too big for a predella (one of those small pictures that ran like a cartoon strip along the base of a much larger painting).

The scene on the left half of the painting is straightforward enough—Christ bound to a column and scourged as a prelude to his crucifixion. The interior where the whipping takes place is beautiful in a cool, cerebral kind of way. No one in the scene seems emotionally involved—not Pontius Pilate in the judge's seat, nor the torturers; even Christ, bound to the pillar and waiting for the first blow to fall, appears aloof.

Things get even more puzzling outside Pilate's judgment hall. Who are these three men, and what are they doing in this painting? Art historian Bruce Cole has observed that they probably aren't portraits of actual people since the same faces or ones very similar appear in crowd scenes of other works by Piero della Francesca (ca. 1415–1492). So, they are not the donors of the painting, nor are they bystanders come to abuse Jesus. And why are they in the foreground, dominating the picture, while the torment of Christ is in the background?

One thing that is not perplexing is the harmony and symmetry of the composition. Della Francesca was a mathematician who specialized in geometry, so he brought to his paintings an unerring sense of perspective and balance.

ca. 1455

Tilman Riemenschneider

(ca. 1460–1531)

Adept at carving limewood or marble, at ease with sacred or secular themes, Tilman Riemenschneider was one of the greatest sculptors of the late Middle Ages. At the time, painting and gilding statues in bright colors (a technique known as polychrome) was still enormously popular; Riemenschneider was among the first to break with this tradition, displaying the bare wood or bare marble of his work.

Although most of his statues were set in a niche or against a wall, Riemenschneider nonetheless carved each freestanding figure carefully, as if they would be seen from every angle. Later in his career he made the shift to carving low reliefs. He is best known as a wood sculptor, and he preferred to carve limewood or linden—they were easier to sculpt than oak or other hardwoods, and the finished product had a lovely texture that over time took on a warm golden brown tone.

All of his altarpieces were grand, architectural works with multiple carved panels as well as three-dimensional sculptures. Over the centuries most of these have been broken up and the pieces scattered to various art collections throughout the world.

In 1499, he received a very prestigious commission from the clergy of Bamberg Cathedral: to carve a new shrine tomb for the relics of the emperor St. Henry II and his empress, St. Kunigunde. It took Riemenschneider fourteen years to complete the project.

During the Peasants' Revolt of 1525, Riemenschneider sided with the rebels against their lord, Prince-Bishop Konrad von Thüngen of Wurzburg. After the nobles crushed the rebellion, Riemenschneider pleaded with the bishop for forgiveness, but Konrad was not in a merciful mood. He ordered the sculptor arrested and tortured in case he possessed information about rebels in hiding, or knew of some plot for a follow-up uprising. Eventually Riemenschneider was released, although not before the bishop had seized a chunk of his property. From that time, Riemenschneider's commissions dwindled to almost nothing.

Tomb of Henry II and his wife Kunigunde, detail of the *Death of the Emperor*, 1499–1513
Bamberg Cathedral, Bavaria, Germany

The Cranach Family

In the decades immediately following Johannes Gutenberg's invention of the printing press in 1456, a large market opened up for inexpensive woodcuts and engravings, particularly of religious scenes. Lucas Cranach the Elder (1472–1553) from Franconia in what is now northern Bavaria made a tidy living churning out extremely fine woodcuts of Christ's sufferings and death, and the martyrdoms of various saints. But the market in Germany for religious art was about to change.

In 1517, Martin Luther, a priest of the Augustinian religious order, began to question the authority of the pope and the teachings of the Catholic Church. By 1520, Luther and Cranach had become friends, and when Luther finally broke with the Catholic Church completely, Cranach did, too. Now the artist used his talents to chronicle the Protestant Reformation. He painted portraits of Luther; Luther's mother and father; his wife, Katherina von Bora (a runaway nun); Luther's colleague, Philip Melanchthon; and Luther's protector and champion, John Frederick I of Saxony. As a portrait painter he had no interest in flattering his subjects: John Frederick's paunch, Katherina Luther's large nose, Philip Melanchthon's scarecrow appearance are all faithfully executed.

His son, Lucas Cranach the Younger (1515–1586), continued in his father's footsteps as chief painter of the Reformation. Cranach the Younger turned out a new type of religious work—paintings that advanced the Protestant point of view. His *Martin Luther in the Pulpit* shows a church interior stripped of all sacred art except for a life-size crucifix. Luther stands in a pulpit while the congregation listens attentively as he expounds the Word of God.

Some of the young Cranach's works are almost polemical cartoons. The 1582 painting *The Vineyard* shows Luther and his fellow Protestant ministers, all of them dressed in sober black, tending a beautiful vineyard. Just across the garden path is a hapless band of overdressed Catholic priests and bishops trying to salvage a few grapes from stunted, withering vines.

Portrait of Hans Luther by Lucas Cranach the Elder ca. 16th century

THE BIRTH OF VENUS

By Sandro Botticelli

We are lucky to have *The Birth of Venus* at all. Four years after Sandro Botticelli (1444/45–1510) completed this sexy masterpiece, Dominican friar Girolamo Savonarola (1452–1498) began preaching hair-raising sermons against the moral laxity of the Florentines and warning them of the wrath of God that would come upon them. In 1497, he urged the people of Florence to demonstrate their repentance by throwing on an enormous bonfire their mirrors, cosmetics, chess boards, musical instruments, books by pagan authors, and lewd paintings and sculptures. Tradition claims that some of Botticelli's paintings were consumed in Savonarola's Bonfire of the Vanities.

The painting is unabashedly pagan, exactly the type of work Savonarola used to rail against. According to Greco-Roman mythology, when the Titan, Cronus, emasculated the god of the sky, Uranus, he threw the god's testicles into the sea. Uranus' testicles fertilized the sea foam, and from it Venus emerged, fully grown and completely naked.

Botticelli shows her standing in a lovely scallop shell, ready to step ashore on the island of Cyprus (the place where Cronus and Uranus fought). Propelling Venus across the waves are two Zephyrs, gods of the winds, while one of the Horae, goddesses of the seasons, prepares to wrap Venus in a flowered cloak.

With her alabaster skin and billowing golden hair, standing on the delicate shell amid cascading pink flowers, Venus is the epitome of the feminine and the erotic. The painting was probably commissioned by Lorenzo the Magnificent (1449–1492), one of the Renaissance era's greatest patrons of the arts; he had commissioned work from Leonardo da Vinci, Filippo Lippi, Andrea del Verrocchio, Domenico Ghirlandaio, and he was so taken by Michelangelo that he invited the young man to live in his palace as a member of the family. Venus' pose in the painting recalls an ancient sculpture Lorenzo had in his private collection, known as the *Venus de Medici*.

CHRIST AND ST. THOMAS

By Andrea del Verrocchio

There's nothing remotely interesting about the Church of Orsanmichele in Florence: It is a solid, square, stone block of a structure. But beginning in the early fifteenth century the city's guilds—the hotelkeepers, the bankers, the butchers, among others—commissioned some of the greatest sculptors of the day to create bronze statues of the patron saints of their professions to be installed in niches built into the exterior walls of the church. Visually dull Orsanmichele was about to become an outdoor gallery of Renaissance art. The Merchant's Guild commissioned Andrea del Verrocchio to sculpt in bronze their patron, St. Thomas the Apostle, better known as "Doubting Thomas," at the moment when he realizes Christ has truly risen from the dead. It was an act of one-upmanship on the merchants' part: The other guilds had been happy with a static statue of their saint, but the merchants wanted a representation of one of the most dramatic moments in the gospel narrative.

The scene comes from St. John's gospel (John 20:24–29). Thomas is not with the other apostles the day the risen Christ reveals himself, and when they try to convince him that the Lord is alive again, Thomas refuses to believe it. Before he commits himself, he says, he wants to probe the nail wounds in Christ's hands and put his hand in the lance wound in Christ's side. The next time Christ appears before his apostles, Thomas is present. Del Verrocchio portrays the moment after Christ invites Thomas, "Put out your hand, and place it in my side." Christ exposes the gaping wound and waits as Thomas steps forward with his hand extended. Yet there is obvious tension between the two statues. Thomas's upper body is pulled back, not advancing; he is hesitating, ready to make his confession of faith. And Christ's arm is raised over his doubting apostle's head, ready to forgive and bless him.

St. Ursula Shrine

By Hans Memling

Part saint's life, part fairy tale, the legend of St. Ursula was extremely popular in the Middle Ages. According to the story, Ursula, a British princess, postponed her marriage to a handsome prince so she and her 11,000 virgin ladies-in-waiting could make a pilgrimage to Rome. On their way back to Britain they stopped at Cologne—just as the Huns attacked the city. Ursula and all 11,000 of her companions were slaughtered by the barbarians.

The nuns of the Hospital of St. John in Bruges, Belgium, possessed a few bones of St. Ursula. To pay homage to the martyr, the sisters commissioned Hans Memling (ca. 1430–1494) to create a portable chest to contain the relics. Memling designed a wooden reliquary—approximately 34 inches long, 36 inches high, and 13 inches wide—carved to resemble a Gothic chapel and gilded. For the two sides of the chest, he painted six scenes from Ursula's story. At the two ends of the chest he painted two panels: one, an image of St. Ursula in glory, with eleven maidens (representing the 11,000) huddled beneath her cloak; the other, an image of the Virgin and Child, with two nuns of the hospital kneeling at the Virgin's feet.

The panels based on the Ursula legend gave Memling an opportunity to showcase his talents as he portrayed harbor scenes, cityscapes, the Huns' camp, and action shots of the Huns picking off the 11,000 virgins while they were still on their ships. Painted late in the career of the last of the great Northern Renaissance masters, the Shrine of St. Ursula is enchanting.

The Hospital of St. John still stands in Bruges, although today it is a museum of the paintings of Hans Memling. Displayed among his other great works is the Shrine of St. Ursula.

THE DEAD CHRIST

By Andrea Mantegna

One of the child prodigies of the Italian Renaissance (by the time he was seventeen, he had his own artist's studio), Andrea Mantegna (1431–1506) favored a sharp, linear style of draftsmanship and enjoyed experimenting with perspective. One of his most daring yet successful efforts is this *The Dead Christ*. The technique he employed is called foreshortening, a kind of optical illusion that compresses a long figure—in this case the body of Jesus—into a space too short for it. The trick (which Mantegna pulled off perfectly) is to keep the image from appearing distorted.

Mantegna painted this as if the viewer were kneeling at the foot of the tomb slab—that is the intended perspective of the picture. The puncture wounds made by the nails in Christ's feet and hands are so sharp it seems strange that we can't see clear through them. And the feet themselves, which hang over the edge of the slab, also appear to project out of the canvas.

The wrinkles in the face of the elderly, weeping Virgin Mary echo the veins in the pink marble of the slab and the veins in the black stone ointment box beside the pillow that cushions the Lord's head.

The skin is taut over Christ's muscles, just as the shroud that covers the lower half of his body clings to his limbs, as if the cloth were wet.

It appears that Mantegna painted this for himself, out of religious devotion or perhaps to test his skill at foreshortening. When the artist died, this *The Dead Christ* was displayed at the head of his bier, and his son, Ludovico, inherited the painting.

ca. 1490

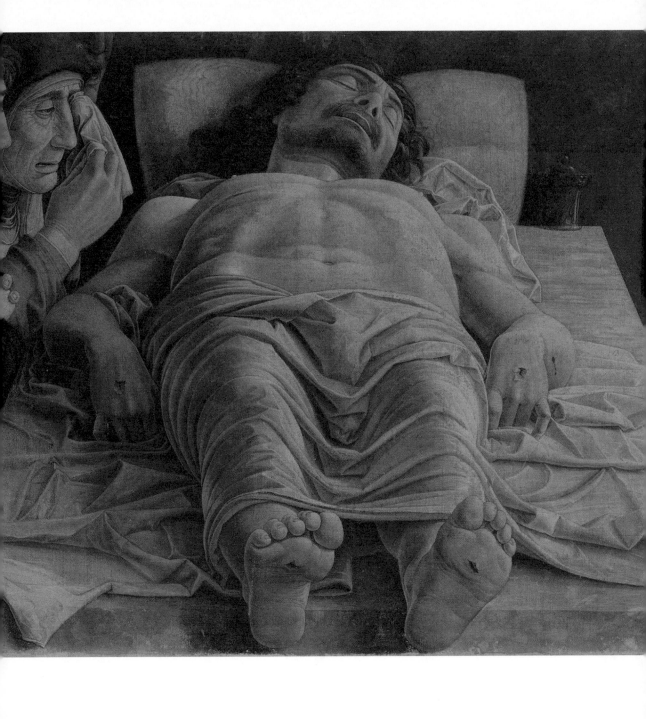

The Lady and the Unicorn Tapestry

In the 1830s, French historian and archaeologist Prosper Mérimée (1803–1870) traveled throughout France seeking to discover, recover, or restore works of art and cultural monuments that had been hidden or damaged during the violent upheavals of the French Revolution. In 1841, he discovered six late-fifteenth-century tapestries packed away and forgotten in Boussac Castle.

The tapestries depict a noble lady, always accompanied by a unicorn and a lion, acting out the five senses—taste, touch, sight, smell, and hearing. The subject of the sixth tapestry is proclaimed in an inscription embroidered above the entrance to the lady's pavilion, "A Mon Seul Desir," or "To My Only Desire." The meaning of this tapestry has sparked a lively debate. Since the lady is portrayed removing and putting away her jewelry, it has been suggested that she is renouncing worldly vanities. Since a popular preacher of the fifteenth century, Jean Gerson, taught that understanding is the sixth sense, it is possible that wisdom is the lady's "only desire." According to medieval lore, a unicorn could only be touched by a virgin, so perhaps the preservation of her chastity is what the lady desires above all else.

The tapestries were woven of wool and silk in Flanders (northern Belgium). Obviously the setting is not meant to represent an actual landscape; instead, this backdrop, dominated by a variety of flowers, is known as *mille fleurs*, or a thousand flowers. Recognized immediately as one of the great works of art of the medieval era, since the 1880s the six tapestries have been displayed together at the Museum of the Middle Ages in Paris.

MOSAIC MASK
OF QUEZTZALCOATL

About the year 1521, the Aztec emperor Montezuma presented a mask like this to Hernan Cortés, the Spanish conqueror of Mexico. It represents the Aztec god Queztzalcoatl, also known as the Feathered Serpent. Look closely and you will see two serpents, one made of green turquoise, the other of blue, snaking around the eyes and mouth of the mask. Initially, Montezuma took Cortés as an incarnation of Queztzalcoatl, since Aztec mythology taught that the god would come to Mexico over the eastern ocean and in the form of a bearded, pale-skinned man.

Thanks to a description from a Spanish Franciscan priest, Bernardino da Sahagun, we know that this mask is but a shadow of its original magnificence. Father Bernardino tells us that the mask was always worn with an elaborate headdress of long tail feathers of the quetzal, a bird of the rain forest. The iridescent green and blue of the bird feathers would have rivaled the beauty of the turquoise.

The base of the mask is carved wood, and the turquoise mosaic tiles are fixed to it with resin.

Although the mask resembles a human skull, Queztzalcoatl was not one of the Aztec gods placated by human sacrifice. The skull probably represents Queztzalcoatl in one of his other manifestations—as the god of death and resurrection.

Mona Lisa

By Leonardo da Vinci

Her first name was not Mona. "Mona" is a contraction of the Italian title "Madonna," which means *madame;* in other words, it is the Italian version of the English contraction "Ma'am."

The identity of the woman in what may be the most famous portrait in the world has been debated for centuries. In January 2008, the issue was settled decisively when Armin Schlechter of the University of Heidelberg in Germany announced that he had found a note in the margins of a copy of the works of Cicero. Dated 1503, Agostino Vespucci wrote that Leonardo da Vinci was painting a portrait of Lisa del Giocondo. This Mona Lisa was the wife of a well-to-do merchant in Florence, Francesco del Giocondo. Historians had long regarded Lisa del Giocondo as the front-runner in the quest to identify Mona Lisa, but now her identity is certain.

The Giocondos, however, never got to hang the portrait in their palazzo because da Vinci could never relinquish it. He worked on it for at least three years, perhaps as long as seven. And when he moved to France to serve as court artist of King Francis I, he took the *Mona Lisa* with him.

Giorgio Vasari, the pupil of Michelangelo and biographer of the masters of the Renaissance, tells us that Lisa del Giocondo loved music, so at each sitting da Vinci hired musicians to play and sing as he painted. This accounts, as Vasari put it, for the "smile, so pleasing, that it [is] a thing more divine than human to behold."

Da Vinci was the master of *sfumato*, a technique of using meticulous, tiny brush-strokes to give a hazy play of light and color to a landscape. The scene behind the sitter is a fantasy landscape rather than a true portrait of any corner of Italy. However, it has such depth and such beauty that viewers who can get past Mona Lisa's smile tend to get lost in the loveliness of that landscape.

GARDEN OF EARTHLY DELIGHTS

By Hieronymus Bosch

For anyone who has not seen the painting, Hieronymus Bosch's (ca. 1450–1516) title creates the impression of an idyllic scene of a golden age when people were content with simple pleasures. Alas, Bosch had something else in mind. So far as this Dutch master was concerned, human kind was going to hell in a handbasket—and to reinforce his point he devoted one panel of his triptych to a panoramic view of the nightmarish torments in a terrifying surreal underworld that awaits all sinners. It is a huge painting, 7 feet high and 12 feet wide, so it is easy to study the details.

The painting reads from left to right: In Eden, God introduces Eve to Adam, and all is peace and loveliness because the First Couple have not yet disobeyed God, and sin has not entered the world; the central panel depicts a bizarre orgy with men and women indulging in some very odd "delights;" while the final panel, of course, is Hell, and the horrific fate that awaits the lovely, heedless young things in the central panel who thought more about physical sensation than the salvation of their souls.

This much of Bosch anyone can make out; it is decoding the details of the paintings that has stumped generations of art historians. Some bits of the painting seem clearer than others. For example, in Eden the fruit, the trees, and the animals are all their normal size, and everything lives peaceably together. In the central panel there is giant fruit (a symbol of overindulgence in pleasures of the flesh), oversized birds and humans riding pigs and bears and lions (suggesting that the natural order is out of whack). Humankind's punishment for overindulgence and corrupting the world is eternity in Hell, where a sow wearing the veil of a nun takes a man as her lover, humans are food for monstrous birds, and musical instruments are instruments of torture. In other words, whatever sinners found most pleasant in this world is what will torment them in the next.

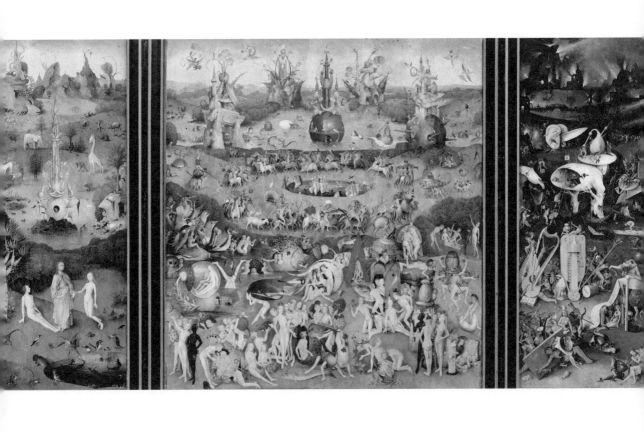

THE TEMPEST

By Giorgione

Ignore for a moment the barely dressed nursing mother and the young man with the staff, and focus instead on the bolt of lightning in the background. That little slash of light is the first time in the history of Western art that a thunderbolt appears in a painting.

That fact about the lightning is one of the tiny handful of certainties we possess regarding this picture. The artist, a Venetian named Giorgione (ca. 1477–1510), was the student of Giovanni Bellini and the teacher of Titian. Within fifty years of Giorgione's death, *The Tempest* already had artists and critics mystified. Even Giorgio Vasari, the tireless biographer of the Renaissance masters, had no clue what the picture portrayed or what it meant. Some critics claim it represents the Virgin and Child with St. George. If so, this is an extraordinary, even scandalous, representation of the Mother of God. Another suggestion is that it represents a soldier and gypsy. The two stubby broken columns and the wall with blind arcades that ends abruptly also bewilder the historians.

Perhaps the human figures have distracted us. The dominant image of the scene is the landscape and the approaching storm. Yet landscape painting was at least a century away when Giorgione painted *The Tempest*. As every artist going back as least as far as Giotto knew, they could only pursue an interest in landscape if they made it the backdrop to a religious or mythological scene.

In *The Tempest,* Giorgione disdains to tell a story. His painting summons up a sense of anticipation as the blue summer day darkens, storm clouds gather, and the first flash of lightning slashes across the sky. Perhaps the trouble has been our attempts to read Giorgione's painting from the Renaissance perspective, when man was "the measure of all things." If we put that aside and look it as a seventeenth-century Dutch landscape painter would have seen it, then the human figures become incidental and the scenery and the weather take center stage.

SCHOOL OF ATHENS

By Raphael

The Stanza della Segnatura in the Vatican Palace held the private library of Pope Julius II (reigned 1503–1513). Raphael Sanzio (1483–1520) designed four frescoes for the room that would illustrate the harmony between Christian theology and ancient Greek philosophy, a subject dear to the hearts and minds of the men and women of the Renaissance.

The scene, of course, is imaginary—the philosophers, mathematicians, and artists assembled in this lofty hall lived in different centuries. Raphael modeled at least three of the figures in the fresco on living artists: Plato, the bearded fellow with his finger pointing upward, situated dead center in the painting, is Leonardo da Vinci; Heraclitus, the melancholy philosopher, seated on a step just below Plato, with his cheek resting on his hand, is the dour Michelangelo; and the second figure to Heraclitus' right, the handsome young man in white, is Raphael as the Greek artist Apelles.

The "schoolroom" where these great minds have met is thought to be based on the architect Donato Bramante's plans for the new St. Peter's Basilica. The gigantic sculpture on the left is Apollo, the god of light, beauty, and truth; the one on the right is Athena, the goddess of wisdom. The setting delivers the message that the inklings of truth and wisdom that God granted to the ancient Greeks was brought to fulfillment with the coming of Christ into the world.

This is a very active school—the various individuals and groups are involved in debate, discussion, teaching, learning, and pondering. On the lower right Euclid, bending over, teaches a group of students the principles of geometry. On the left the Greek mathematician Pythagoras writes while the Arab mathematician Averroes (in a turban) looks over his shoulder. Walking with Plato/Leonardo is Aristotle. And the bearded man in the greenish brown robe above Raphael is thought to be Socrates, posing his usual thought-provoking questions to a group of young men.

CREATION OF ADAM

By Michelangelo Buonarroti

In summer 1511, Michelangelo was reluctant to continue painting the Sistine Chapel ceiling. Julius II, the pope who had commissioned the work, was seriously ill; everyone agreed that he was likely to die. If Julius died, there was a better-than-even chance that the next pope would cancel the contract for the ceiling, and if Michelangelo was not going to be paid, why should he continue to paint? Besides, he would have to clear out of the Sistine Chapel anyway so the cardinals could meet there to elect a new pontiff. And so while the papal physicians fretted over their patient, and the pope's enemies schemed how they would reassert their power after his death, the great artist dawdled.

But Pope Julius did not die. His physicians sighed with relief, his enemies fled from Rome, and Michelangelo moved his scaffolding in preparation for his next and most remarkable panel on the Sistine ceiling—*The Creation of Adam.*

For centuries theologians had assured Christians that Adam had been the summit of physical perfection—"his body [was] most glorious, subtle, agile and immortal," wrote St. Bonaventure in the thirteenth century. And that is the Adam of Michelangelo, the perfect work of God, with a nod to the Greeks' notions of idealized male beauty. As for the figure of God, Michelangelo broke with tradition. The convention was to portray God as elderly and serene, standing upright in Eden, his hand raised in blessing over the newly created Adam. Michelangelo has God billowing out of a whirlwind, and bringing Adam to life by touching with his index finger the outstretched finger of the first man. This scene, unique in its time, has become one of the world's most recognized iconic images. But it is no longer entirely the work of Michelangelo.

Shortly after Michelangelo's death in 1564, cracks appeared in the Sistine's plaster ceiling, and the hand of Adam required repair. Pope Pius IV gave the job to a painter from Modena. The famous finger of Adam, then, as it exists today is not by Michelangelo but by Domenico Carnevale. That finger is Carnevale's best work.

Isenheim Altarpiece

By Matthias Grünewald

Not until the twentieth century would art lovers see anything as graphic, distorted, and grotesque as the Crucifixion panel of the Isenheim Altarpiece. Explicit paintings and sculptures of Christ's sufferings were ubiquitous in the Middle Ages, reminding the faithful that it was because of their sins that the Lord suffered so dreadfully. But none compared with Matthias Grünewald's (ca. 1470–1528) nightmarish, expressionistic painting. Christ's arms are stretched to an unnatural length, his fingers becoming claws as rigor mortis claims the body. His face is hideous in death, and his flesh is not only torn from the whip, but studded with thorns, as if he had been lashed with brambles.

Flanking the Crucifixion are panels depicting two saints: St. Anthony the Abbot, sporting a flowing white beard, and St. Sebastian. St. Anthony is the patron of the monastery hospital in Isenheim for which Grünewald painted the altarpiece, and St. Sebastian was invoked against plague.

This is only one portion of the painting. Grünewald designed an elaborate polyptych, or multipaneled altarpiece that included nine painted panels and an interior shrine of three wooden sculptures. Two themes dominate the work: how the world was saved and the life of St. Anthony.

When the panels are closed one sees the Crucifixion and Sts. Anthony and Sebastian. Open the panel doors and the scene changes to the Annunciation, a choir of angels serenading the Virgin and Child, and the Resurrection. Open the doors one final time and one sees a statue of St. Anthony enthroned, flanked by statues of St. Augustine and St. Jerome. The painted panels depict Anthony visiting St. Paul the Hermit and Anthony being attacked by demons.

By turns disturbing and comforting, depending on which panels are open, this is the most original paintings of the Renaissance period.

ca. 1512

MELANCHOLY I

By Albrecht Dürer

There is no agreement on how to title this engraving (it can be found in art books listed as *Melencolia I* or *Melancholia I* or *Melancholy I*), or how to interpret it. It is one of the most intensely studied engravings in the history of art. In 1991, Peter-Klaus Schuster, general director of the State Museums in Berlin and director of Germany's National Gallery, published a two-volume study of *Melancholy I*.

Thanks to the invention of the printing press, artists discovered that woodcuts and engravings could generate a steady stream of income while they waited for the next big commission to come their way. In the course of his career Albrecht Dürer (1471–1528) of Nuremberg would create approximately 350 woodcuts and 130 engravings. Most of these engravings were straightforward affairs: Episodes from the life of the Virgin Mary, or from the Passion of Christ, or from the Apocalypse. *Melancholy I* is something different—mysterious, enigmatic, and a bit depressing.

The title for the piece probably comes from the first type of melancholy as diagnosed by Dürer's contemporary, Heinrich Cornelius Agrippa von Nettesheim, who said that this variety of melancholy is caused when a creative individual lets his or her imagination run wild, without reason to restrain and focus it.

The seated figure has wings to soar, but is not going anywhere. The little cherub perched beside her is the spirit of Genius, but with his inspiration rejected he has nothing to do. Scattered all around are tools that represent the satisfaction of doing something constructive—but the tools lie idle.

Above the seated figure are scales, an hourglass, and a bell that could strike at any moment—all symbols of the passage of time. And these objects may be the key to the picture. Against the relentlessness of time, all human effort to do and produce seems futile.

Mannerism

Once the great artists of the Renaissance mastered perspective, composition, and color, they began to experiment; some might even say that having perfected the basics, they began breaking the rules.

Mannerist paintings and sculptures have an artificial quality: The perspective appears off; the poses seem odd and unnatural; the bodies have been elongated in a way unknown in the real world; and the faces are not just chiseled but are sharply angular.

Typical of Mannerist paintings is the *Madonna of the Long Neck* by Parmigianino (1503–1540). The title gives away the painting's most famous feature—the Virgin Mary's excessively long neck. But there is another Mannerist feature to the painting—the grotesquely oversized Infant Jesus whom Mary holds so lightly and at such a precarious angle that the baby appears to be tumbling off his mother's lap.

Michelangelo's sculptures for the Medici Chapel are excellent examples of Mannerism in marble. He was commissioned to carve tombs for several members of Florence's wealthy, distinguished, and politically powerful Medici family (the family that had been among the artist's early patrons). Michelangelo did not bother to make the portrait sculptures look anything like the deceased Medicis he was supposed to immortalize. Other sculptures are so roughly carved they appear to be unfinished. And still others are twisting in ways that appear to be painful if not anatomically impossible.

Arguably the most famous and most extreme practitioner of the Mannerist style was El Greco. It is a rare painting by El Greco that does not showcase his penchant for elongated figures, but he took his preference to a new extreme in the *Fifth Seal of the Apocalypse*, an almost hallucinogenic scene of stretched-out saints, raising their distorted arms to heaven.

Madonna with the Long Neck, by Parmigianino (Francesco Mazzola) ca. 1534-40

IVORY PENDANT OF IDIA

This ivory pendant, almost 10 inches long, was worn from the waist by the Oba Esigie (ca. 1504–ca. 1550), king of Benin (now in southern Nigeria), when he led religious rituals in honor of his late mother, Idia. The bearded heads she wears as a kind of crown in her hair represent Portuguese explorers and traders because it was said that the people of Benin had their first encounter with the Europeans during the reign of Esigie. This handsomely modeled face is one of the finest examples of Benin ivory carving and conveys the strength of Idia's character. After her husband's death, she defended on the battlefield her son Esigie's right to succeed. At one point, she sided with Esigie against her younger son, Arhuaran, who had tried to seize the kingship for himself.

The Oba, or king, had a virtual monopoly on ivory. He was given a tusk from every elephant that hunters killed, and he had the option to purchase the second tusk as well. The ivory ornaments the Oba had carved for him were restricted to the royal family and the nobles. The elite of Benin wore or carried ivory bracelets, pendants, staffs, swords, and scepters when they walked in processions on religious or state occasions. During the rest of the time, the ivory objects were displayed upon family altars erected in honor of their ancestors. Sometimes an elephant tusk was not cut up for small carvings, but was incised over its entire surface with scenes of life in the royal court.

Ivory-carvers belonged to a guild that was closely linked to the king. Almost all of their commissions came from the royal family; usually, they lived in the palace like other members of the king's household. In addition to giving them living accommodations and even their daily meals, the king also presented his artists with wives and slaves. The artists were, in fact, almost completely dependent on the king for their livelihood. Generations of experience had taught the ivory-carvers that not all kings were great patrons of the arts. Consequently, most had farms outside the capital to support themselves and their families during lean years.

Portrait of Thomas More

By Hans Holbein

We are fortunate that during the momentous reign of Henry VIII, one of history's finest portrait artists was living and working in England. The English career of Hans Holbein the Younger (ca. 1497–ca. 1543), originally from Augsburg in southern Germany, began in 1526 when he arrived in Henry's realm with a letter of introduction addressed to Sir Thomas More (1478–1535). As a respected statesman, closely connected with Henry, Queen Catherine of Aragon, and the king's chancellor, Cardinal Thomas Wolsey, More was in an excellent position to help Holbein win commissions in the royal household. And he did. Between his arrival in England in 1526 and his death in or about the year 1543, Holbein painted or sketched at least thirty-nine portraits of Henry, his succession of wives, and members of the English aristocracy.

Holbein's portrait sketch of his first patron, Thomas More and his family, is typical of his style and his genius. More is dressed as a great counselor, a trusted advisor to his king: He wears a robe trimmed with a wide border of fur. Around his neck is a gold chain of office from which hangs a golden Tudor rose, the symbol of Henry VIII's dynasty. The elderly man on More's right is his father, Judge John More. More's wife, Alice, is seated at the far right beneath a lit candle. The rest of the group is the More children and step-children. This is a portrait of an upwardly mobile family at the pinnacle of their success.

Although he is forty-nine years old in this portrait, More shows no signs of his age, which is surprising since the average life span for an adult male in sixteenth-century England was forty-seven.

GIUSEPPE ARCIMBOLDO

(1527–1593)

Giuseppe Arcimboldo may have been the first surrealist painter. He did composite "portraits" of men using animals, fish, plants, vegetables, fruits, even tree roots. Bizarre, whimsical, or deeply disturbing—depending on your point of view—Arcimboldo's offbeat artwork appealed to his employer, Holy Roman Emperor Rudolf II. Arcimboldo even took a chance and painted a portrait of the emperor using peaches for his cheeks, a pear for his nose, gourds for his neck, and a pumpkin for his chest. Rudolf added the oddball portrait to his private art collection, along with Arcimboldo's other produce-inspired paintings.

Arcimboldo was born in Milan where his artist-father, Biagio, was employed by the clergy of the Duomo, or cathedral, to do occasional paintings or to touch up existing works of art. Through his father, Arcimboldo received one of his earliest commissions, to design a stained glass window with scenes from the life of the early Christian martyr, St. Catherine of Alexandria. He went on to paint frescoes for the cathedral in Monza and to design a large tapestry that portrayed the death of the Virgin Mary (the tapestry is still part of the treasury of the cathedral at Como).

In 1562, Holy Roman Emperor Ferdinand I brought Arcimboldo to Prague to serve as court portraitist. In the centuries before photography, copies of portraits of the emperor and other members of the imperial family and the court had to be done by hand. Arcimboldo spent long days reproducing portraits that could be sent as gifts to monarchs and high-ranking churchmen; it was tedious, but at least it ensured him of a steady cash flow. The emperor also employed Arcimboldo as a designer of scenery for pageants and theatricals at court, as well as for celebrations such as weddings, births, and coronations.

Two years later Ferdinand died, but his heir, Maximilian II, kept Arcimboldo on. For Maximilian, Arcimboldo also designed fantastic costumes for people and animals—one of his most successful efforts was creating dragon costumes worn by the emperor's horses.

In 1587, Arcimboldo retired as court painter and returned home to Milan. His eccentric optical illusion paintings remained in the imperial collection. When Prague was captured by Protestant forces during the Thirty Years' War, Arcimboldo's paintings were carried off to Sweden as a prize of war.

Spring by Giuseppe Arcimboldo, 1573

Eleonora of Toledo and Her Son

By Agnolo Bronzino

By the mid-sixteenth century, the Medici family had become the absolute rulers of Florence. True to their ancestral roots, however, the Medici remained avid collectors of art and artists, and so Duke Cosimo de' Medici appointed Agnolo Bronzino (1503–1572) his court painter.

Bronzino received many commissions from Cosimo, one of the most celebrated being this double portrait of the duke's wife, Eleonora of Toledo, and their young son Giovanni. Bronzino has captured perfectly the duchess' hauteur, but also the charm and innocence of the little boy who has not yet learned how to appear aloof. By the standards of her day, Eleonora had every reason to be proud: She was descended from the kings of Castile and was related to the Hapsburgs, the family that had produced (and would continue to produce into the nineteenth century) a long line of Holy Roman Emperors. This made her an especially desirable bride for the Medicis, whose dukedom was very new—unlike Eleonora, they were not the offspring of kings, but of bankers.

Bronzino's portraits of Cosimo, Eleonora, and their family became the prototype for royal portraiture for the next 100 years. Monarchs admired Bronzino's ability to convey self-assurance, self-sufficiency, and absolute confidence in their right to rule.

Today we also admire Bronzino's skill as a draftsman. His meticulous portrayal of Eleonora's elaborately patterned gown is a tour de force. It is so carefully rendered that it is almost the star of the painting. If she had not draped her arm around her little boy, thereby drawing him close and directing the viewer's attention to him as a secondary focal point, it's a matter of conjecture if we would notice the child at all.

Perseus and Medusa

By Benvenuto Cellini

As a goldsmith, Benvenuto Cellini (1500–1571) would have been accustomed to working with small objects such as jewelry, or perhaps serving pieces for banquet tables. Yet judging from this bronze sculpture of the Greek hero Perseus, one would believe that Cellini had been working on a monumental scale all his life. The statue stands 18 feet high.

Cellini has Perseus trampling underfoot the corpse of the gorgon, Medusa, and holding up her severed head as a trophy. (According to the Greek myth, Medusa was a monstrous creature whose hair was a tangle of live, writhing snakes. Anyone who looked at her turned to stone.) Although blood gushes from Medusa's trunk as well as from her head, there is no sense of violence, or horror, or even drama to the sculpture. Triumphant Perseus appears impassive. Medusa betrays no sign of emotion. As a result, a statue that should be grotesque strikes most viewers as beautiful.

By 1996, the statue, which had stood outdoors in Florence for 400 years, was pitted and streaked with grime and bird droppings. *Perseus and Medusa* was removed to the Uffizi where the museum's staff of technicians cleaned and restored the sculpture. In 2000, it was returned to its traditional spot in the Loggia, the covered walkway, of the Piazza della Signoria.

Cellini signed his work on the band that runs across Perseus' chest—probably in deliberate imitation of Michelangelo, who years earlier had carved his name on the band that runs across the chest of the Virgin Mary in his sculpture, the *Pietá*.

Illustration from the *Falnama*

By Aqa Mirak

Only twenty-nine pages of the *Falnama*, a masterwork of Persian manuscript painting, have been found—the book was broken up and the painted pages sold off by art dealers decades ago. Most of the surviving pages show episodes from the lives of the Old Testament prophets, Jesus Christ, and Muhammed (all of whom are revered as prophets in Islam, with Muhammed regarded as the last and greatest prophet of all). On the back of the paintings are notes regarding the holy men depicted and predictions regarding the fate of Shah Tahmasp (reigned 1524–1576) of Tabriz, the owner of the book. The *Falnama* was a book of divination that told the owner when to marry, when to go to war, when to make a business deal, and so on. These books tended to be very large, so that several individuals could consult them simultaneously.

The page shown here is a scene inside a mosque. The brown X in the center of the picture is a bookstand used to support the Koran, the sacred text of Islam. Flanking the bookstand are huge, elaborately decorated feet that represent the sacred footprints of Muhammed, said to be preserved in Constantinople (modern Istanbul).

The artist who created the *Falnama* is Aqa Mirak (ca. 1520–ca. 1575). He was a popular artist among the Persian ruling class, and during his career took on large-scale projects such as murals for palaces. He was best known, however, for his manuscript paintings, and he produced many fine books for his royal patrons. Shah Tahmasp became so fond of the artist's company, that he made him a member of his inner circle of friends, and gave him a position in the palace that would provide him with a more regular source of income than painting.

ca. 1550

RAPE OF EUROPA

By Titian

First, a word about the word "rape." In the Middle Ages and the Renaissance the Latin term *raptus* meant an abduction, a kidnapping, or a carrying off, rather than a violent nonconsensual sexual assault. And that is the scene Titian has portrayed here.

According to Greek mythology, Zeus, king of the gods, became enamored with Europa, a Phoenician princess. Taking the shape of a magnificent white bull, he mixed in with the royal herd of cattle. One day, when Europa and her attendants came to the pasture to collect flowers, the white bull caught her attention. Since he appeared to be tame, Europa climbed on his back; at once the bull plunged into the sea and swam for the island of Crete. There he revealed his true form, took Europa as his lover, and fathered children with her. Through her descendants the continent known as Europe (named in her honor) was inhabited.

Titian was seventy-seven years old when he painted this masterpiece, and it shows the old master's transition from the clean, classic lines and cool shades of the High Renaissance to the twisting bodies, splashes of vibrant colors, and strong brush-strokes of the baroque.

The painting shows the moment of no return. The bull has plunged into the sea, the shore is far away, and the two little cherubs swirling overhead, each one a cupid, foreshadows the romance that is to come when Europa and her bull land at Crete. Art critics have noticed that the way Europa writhes on the bull's back seems to anticipate a night of ecstasy with the god.

1562

CRUCIFIXION

By Jacopo Comin Tintoretto

In the fifteenth century, a group of Venetian men formed a confraternity, a religious organization, dedicated to the care of victims of the plague. They placed their organization under the protection of St. Roch (in Italian, San Rocco), the patron of plague victims. In time, the confraternity became very wealthy and built a private church for their group, as well as an adjacent assembly hall known as the Scuola di San Rocco. "Scuola" is generally translated as "school," but "institute" is closer to the old Venetian use of the word.

In 1560, the gentlemen of the confraternity resolved to fill the walls and ceilings of their scuola with paintings of episodes from the life of Christ and of St. Roch. Five artists, including Jacopo Tintoretto (1518–1594), were invited to submit sketches. Tintoretto left his competitors in the dust by completing a painting and having it installed in the scuola. The other artists cried foul, but the confraternity was dazzled. Tintoretto got the job.

For the next twenty-three years Tintoretto labored assiduously, painting fifty-six canvases that were affixed to the walls and ceilings of the scuola. In 1565, he unveiled his *Crucifixion*, a monumental painting approximately 40 feet long and 17 feet high. Nailed to a very high cross, Christ looks down to his grieving mother, but also appears to be leaning forward, off the wall, out of the canvas, toward the viewer. The effect is hypnotic, and many visitors walk away remembering nothing else about this painting except the dramatic optical illusion, which is unfortunate because the painting is filled with extraordinary details. Especially worth attention is the raising of the cross of the Good Thief mentioned in St. Luke's gospel. It takes six men to heave up the heavy cross. There is tremendous tension in this scene, as muscles and rope strain to lift the cross, but the thief's attention is not on the agonizing death he is about to endure; it is fixed on Jesus: Already, the thief is ready to repent.

Peasant Dance

By Pieter Bruegel the Elder

There's no denying that this scene is lively and earthy, but that doesn't mean the artist viewed himself as "a man of the people." Pieter Bruegel (ca. 1525–1569) was a town-dweller, educated and sophisticated, and he looked on the peasants in this jolly scene as yokels. The clumsy footwork of the dancers and the even clumsier romancing of the couples, who have had a few ales too many, deliver the message that this village festival (the long, pointed red banner being the images of two saints tells us the peasants are celebrating a holiday) may be picturesque, but it is no place for respectable people. It is an early example of genre painting, a work of art that takes a scene from everyday life as its subject rather than more elevated subjects such as an episode from the Bible, classical mythology, or the life of a saint.

By making the peasants look oafish, Bruegel was putting some distance between the rustics and himself—he was the son of peasant. Of course, Bruegel had scrambled up a few rungs of the social ladder, and now felt he could afford to poke fun at his own people.

In one respect Bruegel stayed close to his origins: His paintings never had the polish or the formality of Italian works of the same period. He even distanced himself from the exquisite compositions of his fellow Flemish masters, Rogier van der Weyden and Jan van Eyck. His subjects are down-to-earth, his colors are largely earth tones, and his scenes are unsentimentalized depictions of hunts, meals, and farm life. He was a skillful observer of day-to-day life in what is now Belgium and the Netherlands, and if he didn't always approve of what he saw, at least he rendered it accurately.

FEAST IN THE HOUSE OF LEVI

By Paolo Veronese

It was the dogs, dwarves, German mercenaries, and buffoons that got Paolo Veronese (1528–1588) into trouble with the Inquisition. The Dominican friars of the monastery of Santi Giovanni e Paolo in Venice had commissioned him to paint a grand *Last Supper*. He delivered this opulent but decidedly unconventional version of the classic scene. Veronese tried to mollify the tribunal by claiming, "my art is joyous and praises God in light and color," but the judges weren't buying it. The Catholic Mass, the most solemn act of divine worship, had been instituted by Christ at his Last Supper. For Veronese to fill up the scene with lewd and vulgar people, not to mention those German mercenaries who had wrought so much death and destruction during their sack of Rome back in 1527, was unforgivable. Veronese was in a tight corner, but he had a flash of inspiration. He changed the name of the painting from the *Last Supper* to the *Feast in the House of Levi*. According to the gospels, after Levi (also known as Matthew) was converted and became one of Christ's Twelve Apostles, he threw a splendid feast to celebrate. That banquet had no sacramental implications, so dogs and dwarves and other colorful types would not be out of place. The name change saved Veronese from a prison sentence.

In the painting Veronese transported the characters of the gospel story from Judea to Venice. The house is a Venetian palazzo built to imitate the ancient Roman style. Through the triple arcades is a classical city rather than Jerusalem. And the sky has the misty look of Venice rather than the harsh, hot, flat sunlight of the Holy Land. And crowding in to attend the banquet is the cream of Venetian society, fashionably dressed in silks and velvets.

Brass Plaque of Two Warriors

Brass was one of the favorite materials of Benin artists, but how or when brass-casting came to Benin remains a mystery. Beginning in 1897, anthropologists and art historians, even colonial officials, attempted to collect oral traditions regarding the origins of brass sculpture in Benin, but they had very little success. One story claims that the fifth king of Benin, Oba Oguola, admired the brass sculptures of the Ife people. Around the year 1280 he sent a delegation to the Ife king asking him to send one of his master sculptors to Benin to teach the art of brass-casting; the Ife king sent an artist named Iguegha. The story is plausible. So far, archaeologists have excavated only a few sites in Benin that date from the period prior to the arrival of the Europeans, but these digs suggest that brass-casting was being practiced in Benin by the thirteenth century.

The warriors in this brass sculpture are leopard hunters. The people of Benin regarded the leopard (not the lion) as the king of the forest, and as such the leopard was a manifestation of the king. Hunter-warriors such as these captured leopards alive and brought them back to the king, who would bring them out on state occasions and eventually sacrifice them.

About 1,000 brass plaques have survived. They all portray either individuals or events from the history of Benin, but whether the people in the plaques are meant to be portraits or just types—the valiant warrior, the wise king—is a subject of debate.

Actions by the British exacerbated the problem of understanding Benin art. In 1897, when they conquered Benin City, British troops carried off thousands of works of art from the palace and the city. Ripped out of their context, it is difficult for art historians to know the role of these works of art in Benin society.

ca. 1580

Burial of the Count of Orgaz

By El Greco

Domenicos Theotokopoulos was born in Heraklion on the island of Crete in 1541. When he was thirty-six years old, he moved to Madrid and spent the rest of his life in Spain, where he acquired the nickname "El Greco," the Greek. He settled in Toledo and did much of his best work there, including his greatest masterpiece, *Burial of the Count of Orgaz*, for the Church of Santo Tome.

Although the event in the painting occurred in 1312, El Greco did not let historical details trouble him: He dressed all the figures in the fashion of the late 1580s. The painting's subject is a miracle said to have taken place at the Count of Orgaz's funeral. A devout and charitable man, the count had funded the construction of the Augustinian monastery of St. Stephen in Toledo. As a sign of heaven's favor, at the burial, St. Augustine (seen in the painting as a gray-bearded bishop) and St. Stephen, (the handsome young deacon) appeared and personally placed the count's body in its tomb. The story of the miracle was well known in Toledo, accepted as part of the city's history, which explains why no one in the painting registers surprise or even religious awe.

El Greco has divided his scene in two, with the horizontal line of portrait heads framed by white ruffs and stark black mourning clothes dividing Earth from Heaven. In the lower half of the scene the burial service goes on as usual, saints or no saints. A young boy, El Greco's son, directs the viewer's attention to the miracle, while a priest in a transparent white surplice directs the viewer's gaze up to Heaven where the Virgin Mary and a host of saints are pleading with Christ to bring the count's soul into the light of his presence. The visual link between Heaven and Earth is a tall vertical processional crucifix—an ideal choice since Christian theology teaches that by dying on the cross Christ opened the gates of eternal life to believers.

Young Man Among Roses

By Nicholas Hilliard

The son of a goldsmith who trained to be a jeweler, Nicholas Hilliard (ca. 1547–1619) was accustomed to creating objects that were intricate, finely detailed, and very small. By the time he was twenty-three years old he had developed such a reputation for painting exquisite miniature portraits that Elizabeth I appointed him Court Miniaturist. It is remarkable that given the tiny size of his portraits—his *Young Man Among Roses* measures only 5 inches by 2.75 inches—Hilliard managed to include such delicate details as the pattern of a lace ruff or the cut of a rare jewel.

He avoided chiaroscuro, or shadowing, in his portraits, presenting his subjects as if bathed in natural light. In a treatise he wrote on portrait painting, Hilliard urged the artist to be patient with a sitter and wait until the subject of the painting felt sufficiently at ease that his or her facial expression would show that "the grace in countenance, in which the affections appear."

Young Man Among Roses is unusual for Hilliard as it is a full-length miniature; typically his miniatures showed only the head and shoulders. The subject is young, still boyish in his looks, which his skimpy moustache does nothing to allay.

The identity of the young man has not come down to us, but it has been suggested that he is Robert Devereaux, the Earl of Essex, at age twenty-two and in the first flush of enjoying Queen Elizabeth's favor. He is wearing black and white, Elizabeth's favorite colors, and he is standing among roses known as eglantines, the queen's favorite flower. It's possible this really is Essex, since the way Hilliard has composed this portrait flatters both the young earl and the queen.

ca. 1588

Artemisia Gentileschi

(1593–ca. 1652)

At least twice, Artemisia Gentileschi painted the Jewish heroine, Judith, beheading the enemy of Israel, Holofernes: In one, Judith's maid holds the evil king down while Judith saws through his thick neck as the blood spurts. A variation on this theme shows Judith after the deed is done, the sword on her shoulder, Holofernes' head in her maid's basket. There is also a painting of the Jewish heroine Jael about to drive a metal spike through the temple of another of Israel's enemies, the king Sisera. Some art historians have suggested that these paintings reveal Gentileschi's deep antipathy toward violent men. If that is true, she had good reason—at age eighteen or nineteen, she was raped by her father's friend, Agostino Tassi. Initially Tassi said he would atone by marrying Gentileschi, but when he reneged on his promise Gentileschi's father took Tassi to court. To test whether Gentileschi's testimony against Tassi was true, she was tortured. She stuck to her story and Tassi was convicted and sentenced to a year in prison.

Gentileschi's father, Orazio Gentileschi, painted in the style of Caravaggio, and in many of her paintings Artemisia followed suit. In Rome, Florence, Venice, and Naples she received many commissions from important patrons—including one from Michelangelo's nephew. In 1638, King Charles I of England invited her to his court where she collaborated with her father in painting the ceiling of the Queen's House in Greenwich.

Artemisia Gentileschi was not the only woman artist of this period (as is sometimes claimed): Sofonisba Anguissola worked for King Philip II of Spain, and Lavinia Fontana painted for Pope Clement VIII.

Judith and Holofernes by Artemisia Gentileschi ca. seventeenth century

The Calling of St. Matthew

By Caravaggio

In 1500, the most astonishing artist in Rome was Michelangelo. A century later, in 1600, the artist everyone in Rome was talking about was also named Michelangelo—although we know him by his last name, Caravaggio.

In 1599, thanks to the intervention of his patron, Cardinal Francesco Maria del Monte, Caravaggio received a prize commission—to paint two massive works for the Contarelli Chapel in the Church of San Luigi dei Francesi, the parish of the French community in Rome. Up to this point Caravaggio had painted enchanting genre scenes and still lifes; the two scenes from the life of the apostle, St. Matthew, would be on a far grander scale, and Caravaggio rose to the challenge.

Matthew's gospel (Matt. 9:9) tells how Christ stopped at the place where the tax collector, Matthew, was counting his receipts and said, "Follow me." Instantly, Matthew left his bags of coins and tax ledgers and joined the handful of men who became the Twelve Apostles.

Caravaggio depicts the moment of the call. Christ is off-center and obscured by a shadow in the grungy counting house. Two of Matthew's fellow tax collectors don't even lift their eyes from the pile of coins to see who has stepped into the room. As for Matthew, his expression betrays his astonishment: Eyes wide, finger pointing to his chest, you can almost hear him answer, "Who? Me?"

Look at Christ's outstretched arm, the index finger pointing at Matthew—it is the mirror image of God the Father's gesture at the moment he gave life to Adam in that iconic scene from the Sistine Chapel ceiling. With that gesture, God the Father created the first man. With the same gesture Christ, God the Son, makes Matthew a new man. Caravaggio did nothing accidentally; this painting is a tribute from one Michelangelo to another.

Murals in the Church of Debre Birhan Selassie

ca. 1610

Christianity came to Ethiopia about the year 330 when two young Lebanese Christians, St. Frumentius and St. Aedesius, were shipwrecked on the Ethiopian coast. They were rescued and taken to the king, whom they converted, and once the king became a Christian, the rest of the realm followed. The Muslim invasions of the eighth century largely cut off Ethiopia from the rest of the Christian world, and in that isolation the Church developed its own style of art that drew upon African, Arab, and Byzantine traditions.

The murals that cover every inch of the walls and ceiling of the Church of Debre Birhan Selassie in Gondar are one of the jewels of Ethiopian art. Over the doors that lead to the Holy of the Holies, the church's sanctuary, is a crucifixion scene and a large painting of the Holy Trinity (*Selassie* means Holy Trinity) portrayed as three identical men. On the walls are stories from the Old and New Testaments and the lives of various saints. All of these paintings are wonderful in their way, but the thing that dazzles visitors is the ceiling. The entire ceiling is painted with the heads and wings of hundreds of angels. Typical of Ethiopian religious paintings, the artists at Debre Birhan Selassie used very bright colors, the type generally associated with folk art painting in the United States.

There were once many more such churches in town, but in 1888, followers of the Mahdi, Muhammed Ahmad, from Sudan—the army that killed General Charles Gordon and massacred the populace of Khartoum—ransacked Gondar and burned every church except this one. The people of Gondar say that St. Michael the Archangel descended from heaven and stood before the church brandishing a flaming sword. At the sight of the archangel, the Mahdi's army fled.

Genre Painting

Simply put, genre painting takes as its subjects the humble, ordinary activities of daily life, especially work or recreation: Two farmers gossiping over their tankards of ale, a maid ironing clothes, or a fiddler playing for a family.

Genre scenes can be found painted on the walls of Egyptian tombs, in the margins of medieval Books of the Hours, and on screens and scrolls in Japan and Korea. Pieter Bruegel the Elder was the forerunner of the fashion for genre paintings that in the eighteenth century became extremely popular in the Netherlands, Belgium, England, and France. In France, the great proponents of genre painting were the Le Nain brothers, Louis (ca. 1593–1648), Antoine (ca. 1599–1648), and Mathieu (1607–1677). They painted scenes of peasants, as well as members of the middle class, or bourgeoisie, and the brothers' style was so similar that art critics have a difficult time sorting out attribution.

Genre painting was an alternative for artists as well as patrons to the historical, mythological, and religious subjects that dominated the market at this time. Instead of the miraculous, the heroic, or the earth-shaking, genre artists portrayed the ordinary and the familiar, often while simultaneously making a comment about the human condition ranging from the simple pleasures of family life and friendship to the cruel poverty endured by the peasantry. Louis Le Nain's *Peasant Family in an Interior*, for example, is an optimistic portrayal of a rural family that is reasonably comfortable—they have food, wine, a good fire, and can even afford to keep a cat and a dog.

Peasant Family in an Interior, by Le Nain, 1642

Baroque

ca. 1620

Baroque was the Catholic Church's answer to the Protestant Reformation. Everything the Protestants rejected—the Mass, the sacraments, the veneration of saints, the magnificently decorated churches, the majestic ceremonies—the Catholics celebrated in a spectacular new style of art and architecture. The goal of the baroque was to bring the glory of heaven down to earth. To achieve this, church interiors became theatrical in ways they had never been before, with countless sculptures of saints and angels directing the worshipper's gaze to the high altar. Gone was the calm, contemplative style of Renaissance painting and sculpture, and in its place came vividly colored, intensely dramatic, intensely emotional portrayals of saints in either agony or ecstasy. And it worked—when it came to inspiring religious awe, you couldn't beat baroque.

Protestants recognized the power of baroque and adopted it—but for secular purposes. The baroque was sumptuous; it made its subjects appear heroic; it filled viewers with wonder—which is exactly why Protestant kings and aristocrats embraced it. Their new baroque palaces underscored their authority and lent glory to their dynasty. Catholic kings and aristocrats also recognized the secular uses of the baroque too and followed suit.

The most baroque of all the baroque painters, the master who filled his canvas with vibrant colors, twisted bodies, turbulent skies, high drama, and a large cast of nymphs and angels, pagan gods and Christian saints, was Peter Paul Rubens (1577–1640). His grandest achievement was a series of twenty-one huge oil paintings (they measure on average 15 feet by 25 feet) that trace the life and reign of Marie de' Medici, queen of France. Working with an army of assistants, Rubens completed the commission in two years.

The Reconciliation of Marie de' Medici and Her Son, seen here, is vintage Rubens. Marie's son, Louis XIII, looking like Apollo, lifts her heavenward. One of her breasts is exposed—a reminder to Louis and other viewers that she is a mother. Meanwhile, St. Michael the Archangel, armed with a lightning bolt, destroys the many-headed Hydra, an emblem of confusion, discord, and treachery.

The Reconciliation of Marie de Medici and Her Son, by Peter Paul Rubens, 1621

RAPE OF PROSERPINE

By Gianlorenzo Bernini

When Bernini went to work on a block of stone he had two goals in mind—to have the marble become flesh and to make his figures as natural, active, and full of life as living people. He achieved his goals in *Rape of Proserpine*. Look at Pluto's fingers—they sink into the soft flesh of Proserpine's side and thigh. And look at Proserpine—twisting and writhing, kicking her legs to squirm out of the grasp of the god of the underworld, while striking him in the temple with the flat of her hand. As for Pluto, strong as he is, he still struggles to keep his balance and keep his grip on the flailing young goddess he plans to make his queen. Never before—not in ancient Greece or Rome, not even in the studios of Donatello and Michelangelo—had a sculptor succeeded so completely in breathing life into stone. And Bernini did it consistently—look at his *David*, his *Apollo and Daphne*, his portrait busts of Cardinal Scipione Borghese and Constanza Bonarelli, and most famously, his *Ecstasy of St. Teresa of Avila*.

The inspiration for the sculpture is a story from classical mythology. Proserpine (Persephone in the Greek version) is the beloved daughter of Ceres (Demeter), the goddess of crops, harvests, and all growing things. One day while Proserpine was picking flowers with some nymphs, the earth split open and Pluto (Hades) appeared. He seized Proserpine and carried her off to the realm of the dead. Ceres, heartbroken at the loss of her daughter, neglected the earth. The crops failed, food stores ran out, and humankind began to starve. Jupiter, king of the gods, brokered a deal: For eight months of the year Proserpine would live with her mother on earth, then return to the underworld for four months as Pluto's queen. During those four months, grieving Ceres permits nothing to grow. The myth, then, explains the origins of the seasons.

Storm on the Sea of Galilee

By Rembrandt

It's tragic, but the reproduction on the opposite page is as close as any of us are likely to come to seeing Rembrandt's one and only seascape. At 1:24 in the morning of March 18, 1990, two men dressed as Boston police officers weaseled their way inside the Isabella Stewart Gardner Museum. The cops were not cops—they were art thieves. They bound the museum's two night guards to posts in the basement, then went on a stealing spree through the galleries. By the time they left, their haul included a Vermeer, a Manet, some Degas drawings, and two paintings by Rembrandt, including *Storm on the Sea of Galilee*. Every attempt to recover the lost art has failed, and the last possible sighting occurred in 1997 when unidentified sources drove a reporter for the *Boston Herald* to a warehouse. There, by the beam of a flashlight, he was shown, very briefly, a painting that may have been the missing Rembrandt.

When he painted this work, the master was only twenty-seven years old—a period of his life when he liked action pictures. The storm-tossed boat cuts a sharp diagonal across the canvas; five apostles struggle to save the ship, while seven huddle around Christ, seated in the stern. The scene at the back of the boat is relatively serene, while at the center of the picture is an explosion of white and yellow light, such as a titanic bolt of lightning might produce. The painting also showcases a technique known as chiaroscuro—dramatic, even theatrical contrast between light and shadow—that Rembrandt mastered early on.

The scene of a small ship on the verge of disaster is utterly convincing. In a letter to a friend, Rembrandt declared that in his art his goal was to capture "the greatest and most natural movement."

1633

TRIPLE PORTRAIT OF CHARLES I

By Anthony van Dyck

England's King Charles I was an enthusiastic art collector and a generous patron of great artists of his own day. His favorite portrait artist was the Flemish painter Anthony van Dyck (1599–1641), who developed a new manner of portraiture that blended informality with elegance. It was a style that would dominate portrait painting for the next 150 years.

From 1632, the year van Dyck moved to England, until his death in 1641, he painted at least forty portraits of the king, about thirty of Queen Henrietta Maria, plus countless portraits of the English aristocracy. Van Dyck's paintings of young English lords of this period epitomize the "Cavalier style": High boots; silk and satin doublets; and long, carefully curled hair falling on elaborate lace collars. In fact, a good part of van Dyck's success was his willingness to tinker with nature in order to please his clients. King Charles, for example stood barely 5 feet tall, yet he never fails to look majestic in a van Dyck portrait. The artist extended the same courtesy to the queen. In 1641, when Duchess Sophia of Hanover met Maria Henrietta she confessed that she was surprised by the queen's appearance. Van Dyck's portraits had given her the impression that the queen was a great beauty, but on meeting Henrietta Maria face-to-face, Sophia found "a small woman…with long skinny arms and teeth like defense works projecting from her mouth."

Van Dyck did this unusual triple portrait of Charles I for the sake of a fellow artist. The great Italian sculptor, Gianlorenzo Bernini, had been commissioned to carve a portrait bust of the king. Since Bernini could not come to England and the king certainly could not travel to Rome on such a pretext, van Dyck painted this portrait that showed his patron at three-quarters, full front, and in profile. And he elongated the king's torso a bit to make him look taller.

HELENE FOURMENT IN A FUR WRAP

By Peter Paul Rubens

To the exuberance and sensuality of the baroque style the Flemish artist Peter Paul Rubens (1577–1640) brought his own predilection for fleshy women. In 1630, Rubens, a widower, married Helene Fourment, the daughter of a silk and tapestry merchant; Rubens was fifty-three, Helene was sixteen. In spite of the age difference, it was a love match that produced five children and many lovely and loving portraits of Helene, often in the guise of Venus, the Roman goddess of love.

Rubens' and Helene's marriage spanned the last ten years of his life, which were arguably the artist's happiest. His paintings had made him rich; his service as a diplomat had him respected in the courts of Europe; and two of his most august patrons, Charles I of England and Philip IV of Spain, had knighted him. At the time, no other artist had ever been granted knighthoods by two kings. In 1630, he retired from the diplomatic corps and returned to his family in Antwerp.

Rubens completed this nearly nude portrait of Helene sometime between the years when she was twenty-one and twenty-six. She appears to have just climbed out of bed on a chilly morning: Her white chemise is wrapped around her left arm, and she has thrown a thick fur robe over one shoulder. We do not know if Helene in her twenties already had a double chin and bags around her knees, but that is how Rubens portrays her, and there is nothing critical about it.

It is the position of her arms that give the painting a little extra significance: Rubens copied Helene's pose from a sculpture that was much admired at the time—the *Venus de Medici*, a first-century Greek statue of the goddess.

PENITENT MAGDALENE

By Georges de la Tour

We know very little about the French master Georges de la Tour (1593–1652). For centuries, in fact, he was forgotten by the art world, only experiencing a revival early in the twentieth century. He belongs to a school of art known as tenebrist, a word that comes from a Latin term for "shrouded in darkness." Caravaggio, of course, was among the first and most prominent artists of the seventeenth century to use the play of light and shadow for dramatic effect in his paintings. De la Tour developed his own tenebrist technique, painting scenes illuminated by a single candle.

In the *Penitent Magdalene*, de la Tour portrays St. Mary Magdalene at a midway point between her old life of sexual promiscuity and her new life as a disciple of Jesus Christ who will spend the rest of her days lamenting her sins and doing penance to expiate them. She sits at her dressing table where she used to doll herself up for her next sexual conquest. She wears a red dress and white blouse. Red is the color of sexual passion, while white is the color of purity. That her blouse is open and her breasts almost exposed suggests that Mary is early in her conversion, that the allures of the flesh may still have some hold on her.

In her lap she holds a human skull, a traditional symbol of someone who is trying to be "dead to the world" and all its false pleasures and temptations. But she is seated before a beautiful, expensive mirror, no doubt purchased during her decadent period. A mirror is a traditional symbol of vanity, but in this painting it does double duty, reflecting the light from the candle to cast more light on Mary. The candle itself serves a dual purpose, lighting up the picture while also symbolizing Christ, Mary's new master and the light of the world.

ca. 1635

Arcadian Shepherds (Et in Arcadia Ego)

By Nicolas Poussin

Although his life spanned the heyday of baroque, Nicolas Poussin (1594–1665) steered away from the flash and excitement of the dominant style of his time and created thoughtful, tranquil paintings of scenes from the classical world. His figures are pleasing to the eye and his command of color exceptional—never before or since have there been such attractive, stylish shepherds.

The Latin phrase that is one of the two titles of the picture, *Et in Arcadia Ego*, means, "And I too am in Arcadia." There is a real Arcadia—it is a province in Greece. In antiquity, and again during the Renaissance, and afterward, Arcadia was regarded as an idyllic place, a pastoral paradise, where shepherd boys and shepherd girls lived simple, happy lives. Three of these shepherds, and a woman who is much too well dressed to be a shepherdess, have stumbled upon a tomb bearing "Et in Arcadia ego" as its epitaph. In other words, no one escapes death, not even in Arcadia.

The painting belongs to a type called *memento mori*, another Latin phrase, which means, "Remember, you must die." The *memento mori* most commonly appears in a religious context, reminding the faithful that life is fleeting, that death can come upon anyone at any moment, and so it is wise to repent now while there is still time. Since Poussin sets his scene in pre-Christian Greece, this *memento mori* is a reminder that eventually youth, beauty, pleasure, and strength all wither and fade.

1637

LAS MENINAS

By Diego Velasquez

Snapshots were more than 200 years in the future, yet that is what Diego Velasquez (ca. 1599–1660) gives us in this enchanting, enigmatic painting—a moment frozen in time at the court of King Philip IV of Spain.

In the center of the painting is the Infanta (princess) Margarita, three or four years old, attended by two maids of honor (*meninas*), one of whom is offering her a drink from a red cup on a gold tray. At the far right of the canvas are two dwarves, who are also part of the princess' retinue, and a dozing mastiff. The veiled woman is a chaperone; the gentleman she is speaking with is a bodyguard. At the rear of the painting is another gentleman of the court who has stopped suddenly on a flight of stairs. The man holding the palette who has stepped back from the huge easel is Velasquez. Look at the mirror above the princess' head and you'll see what has caught the attention of everyone in the room—reflected in the looking glass are King Philip and his queen, Marianna of Austria.

Some art critics believe that Velasquez is shown in the act of painting a portrait of the king and queen. Given the arrested action, the looks of mild surprise on the faces of the people in the room, it is more likely that Velasquez was painting Margarita's portrait when the artist, the princess, and her attendants received an unexpected visit from the king and queen.

Velasquez's use of natural light, which puts Margarita and, to a lesser degree, her maids in the spotlight, is lovely, but it is no more than one would expect from a master. More interesting is the depth of perspective: The man on the stairs is either about the walk out of, or into, the painting. And the viewer sees the scene from the perspective of the king and queen. If that mirror on the back wall were a bit larger, we would be reflected it in, too.

Girl with a Pearl Earring

By Jan Vermeer

It makes us shudder to think that when one of the greatest painters of all time got behind in his bills, he handed over one of his paintings to clear the debt. That thought is even more painful when we consider that in the span of his short life Jan Vermeer (1632–1675) produced only thirty-four paintings.

Vermeer painted slowly, touching up, polishing up, fine-tuning every picture. His subjects are subtle, quiet, and often take as their subject the types of things that happen in any household on any given day of the week. A woman stands at a window reading a letter. A lady dozes off in the afternoon. A cavalier's joke makes his girlfriend laugh. These are all commonplace subjects, but Vermeer rendered them so beautifully, so perfectly, that art lovers have been in awe of his paintings for almost 400 years.

One of his favorite devices was to place his people near an open window so the interiors of these lovely Dutch houses are illuminated with natural light. And that splash of sunlight picks out wonderful details—the pattern of a Turkish carpet that covers a table, the details of a map hanging on the wall, the thoughtful expression on the face of women pouring milk, or examining pearls, or playing a harpsichord.

The *Girl with a Pearl Earring* was supposed to be a study, the type of painting an artist dashed off as an exercise. But Vermeer's study is a bona fide masterpiece, and at the heart of it is that earring. He made it with just two strokes of his brush, and that small flash of white in the pearl picks up the white of the woman's collar, the clarity of the whites of her eyes, the flecks of white in the turban. We don't know who the girl is, and it doesn't matter because we can't take our eyes off the pearl.

ca. 1665

CANALETTO

(1697–1768)

In the first half of the eighteenth century, a painting by Canaletto was the must-have souvenir from a Grand Tour of Europe. The British could not get enough of his views of Venice, rich with the pageantry of Venetian holy days and suffused with the misty light of this city by the sea. By 1730, Canaletto was so popular with British travelers and art collectors that he acquired a British agent, Joseph Smith, to arrange the details of commissions and sales with customers in Britain.

As a native son of Venice, Canaletto (his real name was Giovanni Antonio Canal) knew where to find the most enchanting views in his hometown. So it is ironic that his very first Venetian streetscape was not a view across the Grand Canal of the soaring dome of Santa Maria della Salute, but a portrait of a grubby stonemason's yard. Nonetheless, the painting established Canaletto's reputation for two reasons: First, he painted it on-site (the established method at the time was for the artist to sketch a scene and then return to his studio to paint it); and second, his mastery of color and light captured perfectly the character of Venice.

British tourists were impressed by *The Stonemason's Yard*, but they wanted something that suggested the glory of Venice. Canaletto responded with magnificent views of the city's churches, piazzas, and palazzos. Also extremely popular were his depictions of Venice's opulent religious festivals, such as *Return of the Bucintoro on Ascension Day*. And he didn't hesitate to alter topographical details in order to produce a more pleasing painting. As a result, his paintings commanded the highest prices of any artist of his day, and collectors such as Catherine the Great of Russia competed for his best work.

Return of the Bucintoro on Ascension Day by Canaletto, ca. 1732

PORCELAIN INCENSE BURNER

By the Kakiemon family

Sakaeda Kakiemon (1596–1666) was a Japanese potter whose home and workshop were in Nangawara near Arita in the province of Kyushu. About the year 1644, he developed an innovative method of decorating porcelain known as multicolor over-glaze enamel. On the milky white base of the porcelain Kakiemon painted birds, squirrels, quail, bamboo, pine, or chrysanthemums (the national flower of Japan) in lovely shades of red, turquoise, green, yellow, and blue. These decorative elements were charming, but Kakiemon used them sparingly, the better to set them off against the white background of the piece. He also preferred pieces that were square, hexagonal, or octagonal rather than circular—the most traditional shape for porcelain objects.

To create his pieces, Kakiemon first applied the white glaze to a piece, then fired it in the kiln. Once the piece had cooled, he painted his decorative motifs with colored glazes on top of the white glaze, then fired the porcelain again at a lower temperature.

The technique was very popular in Japan, but in 1659, representatives of the Netherlands' East India Company saw Kakiemon's porcelain and were enchanted. They placed a large order that the company's ships carried back to Europe and sold at a high mark-up to the nobility. For many generations thereafter the Kakiemon family's porcelain found eager buyers and collectors in Europe, especially in England, and eventually in America.

This seventeenth-century incense burner was likely the creation of Sakaeda Kakiemon's son, Sakaeda Kakiemon II; it is unusual in that it is round. Too small for use in a temple, it was likely produced for private individuals to burn incense on their home altars.

The descendants of Sakaeda Kakiemon still create Kakiemon porcelain using the overglaze enamel method invented by their ancestor. In 1971, the Japanese government declared Kakiemon porcelain an "intangible cultural treasure."

ca. 1700

JOSHUA REYNOLDS

(1723–1792)

The son of an English parson, Joshua Reynolds was the artist who revived the interest in Renaissance art in England by marrying it to a trend of his own day—a fresh fascination with the natural world.

At age twenty-seven, he went to Rome to study painting. There, and in the other great art capitals of Italy, he was captivated by the work of Raphael, Titian, and Michelangelo—especially Michelangelo. Toward the end of his life, when he was president of the Royal Academy of Art, he told an audience of art students and art lovers, "I should desire that the last words which I should pronounce in this Academy, and from this place, might be the name of Michel Angelo." (Reynolds spelled the name as two words.) After returning to England he hoped to make a living painting epic scenes from classical mythology or ancient history, but there was little demand for such work. What the art-buying public wanted were portraits of themselves. Reynolds bowed to the pressure of the art market, and soon nobles, gentry, and military commanders—all the most distinguished people in Britain—were clamoring for Reynolds to paint their portrait.

Typically, he set his subjects outdoors, although the landscape often looked more Italian than English. Often, as a tribute to his love for the Renaissance, he would include a broken column, or a Roman arch, or a piece of classical sculpture in the scene. If his subject was agreeable, he would portray her in a Greco-Roman fashion. Mrs. John Hale, for example, appears to be dancing in an outdoor pagan festival, while Lady Sarah Bunbury permitted herself to appear dressed as a Roman priestess and sacrificing to the Graces.

Men did not find this style appealing, so Reynolds tended to paint them in a heroic pose against the backdrop of a tempestuous sky or a storm-tossed sea.

Elizabeth Gunning, Duchess of Hamilton and Duchess of Argyll
by Joshua Reynolds, ca. 1760

Dharmapala

Among Tibetan Buddhists—and this gilt bronze sculpture was cast in Tibet—a Dharmapala is a supernatural Defender of the Law (in this case, the law is the six supreme principles of Buddhism). This particular Dharmapala is called Yamantaka, a wrathful, fearsome manifestation of wisdom. Although he has a terrifying appearance, Yamantaka is actually listed among the compassionate deities who come to the assistance of humankind.

His name can be translated as "the Terminator of Death." According to Tibetan Buddhist mythology, Yama, the demon king of death, was slaughtering the people of Tibet. To combat him and save the faithful, Yamantaka took on a frightening appearance with the head of bull, a mouth full of fangs, as well as eight additional faces, thirty-four legs, and thirty-four arms and hands, each of which wielded a fearful weapon. He became a mirror image of Yama, and when Yama saw this manifestation of himself, he was literally scared to death.

By meditating on an image of Yamantaka, a Tibetan Buddhist confronts his or her own fear of death. To overcome that fear is to move a step closer to enlightenment.

This bronze sculpture was gilded with a thin layer of high-quality gold. The face, feet, hands, and other details of Yamantaka were enameled to give it a more lifelike (and therefore more hideous) appearance. Standing almost 18 inches high, it was probably used as a focus of meditation in a private home or in the cell of a monk.

Dharmapala, defeater of the Lord of Death; Tibetan School, ca. eighteenth century

Marriage a-la-Mode

By William Hogarth

An engraver of illustrations for books who also dabbled in portraiture, William Hogarth (1697–1764) was one of the first artists to demand that the law protect his intellectual property. He had an inspiration for reaching a mass market with his art: A new genre that he called "the modern moral subject." He produced a series of engravings that told the whole sordid story of an individual's wasted life, or in this case, of a doomed marriage.

Hogarth skewered characters everyone in his day would recognize: The wealthy but miserly merchant who wants his daughter to marry into the nobility; the gouty cash-poor earl (called Earl Squander in the *Marriage a-la-Mode* series) who is willing to let his son marry outside the nobility in exchange for a fat dowry. Each succeeding engraving in the series shows the unhappy main characters sinking deeper and deeper into degradation until they are murdered, or hanged, or commit suicide. "The wages of sin is death," is almost invariably the moral of a Hogarth series.

While he painted his series, he also produced them as engravings priced for middle-income budgets. There is a strong comic element to Hogarth's work—he is merciless in mocking the rich, the well-born, the supposedly respectable people of English society, but he doesn't spare the money-grubbing merchant class, or the debauched lower classes, either. It is part of Hogarth's genius that in every series of engravings, everyone of every social strata could find someone to laugh at and feel superior to.

ca. 1743

Rococo

Love, youth, beauty, pleasure, and the untroubled life of the aristocracy were the subjects favored by rococo artists. The style developed in France, where artists reacted against the formality that King Louis XIV (1643–1715) had preferred during his seventy-two years on the throne. In furnishings and interior décor, rococo abandoned the straight lines and classical motifs drawn from ancient Greece and Rome; the new style called for sinuous curves and delicate scrollwork, embellished with shells, flowers, and other natural objects.

If visions of heaven inspired baroque, French pastry appears to have been the inspiration for rococo, with its puffy clouds, chubby cherubs, and palette of bright pastels. Portrayals of long-suffering martyrs or dignified gods were out of fashion—if Diana were the subject of a rococo painting, she was seen luxuriating in her bath, or dallying with some handsome swain.

For members of the aristocracy, the world was their playground, and they adored the way rococo painters made them look deliriously happy as they pursued their round of frivolous pleasures. Naturally, love affairs were a favorite occupation, and two French artists, Francois Boucher (1703–1770) and Jean-Honoré Fragonard (1732–1806) turned out a steady stream of paintings of cavorting lovers that were racy without being crudely explicit. Even Boucher's *Music Lesson*, seen here, is a bit suggestive. The couple is alone, unchaperoned, in a lush fantasy garden. And although the young lady keeps her eyes on her music, the young gallant strumming the guitar clearly has other things on his mind.

ca. 1749

The Music Lesson by Boucher, 1749

THE EPISCOPAL PALACE AT WURZBURG

By Giovanni Batista Tiepolo

In a German bishop's palace, Giovanni Batista Tiepolo (1696–1770) brought a touch of the light and warmth of Venice to the icy north. It is a huge fresco that covers an area of approximately 62 feet by 100 feet. The ceiling is Tiepolo's greatest work, yet it was a backwater job. The principality of Wurzburg in the German province of Franconia was a bit player in European politics. In terms of artistic tastes it was behind the times, still regarding the Versailles of Louis XIV as the epitome of high style. The man who commissioned the fresco, Prince-Bishop Carl Philipp von Greiffenclau, had some inkling of these disadvantages and looked to Tiepolo to boost his standing among the other princes—of the Catholic Church as well as of the state.

The theme of the paintings is the four continents. At the center of the fresco is the radiant god of the sun, Apollo, the Greek deity associated with light, beauty, and reason, all of which Europeans were spreading across the globe. Set amid all this supernatural splendor, and easy to spot as the visitor climbs the stairs, is a very large portrait of the prince-bishop, framed in gold, supported by Fame and Truth, while another winged female mythological figure calls attention to von Greiffenclau with a blast from a long, golden trumpet.

This is a propaganda piece, and so the symbolism is not subtle. The personification of Europe is surrounded by figures that represent all the Arts. Near her is a cannon, the emblem of Europe's military superiority. America is seated on a crocodile; near her is a pile of severed heads, and in the background, a cannibal roasts human flesh. Asia, crowned with a turban, sits on the back of an elephant as two men bow low before her and a poor captive struggles to keep up. Africa rides a caravan camel, observed by an old man with a long white beard—the personification of the Nile.

Having secured his reputation by painting one of the largest and most celebrated frescos in the world, Tiepolo promptly returned to Venice.

STILL LIFE WITH FRUIT AND A GLASS

By Jean Chardin

Dutch artists were painting still lifes, assemblages of everyday objects, in the seventeenth century. But the master of the genre was a Frenchman who painted a century later—Jean-Baptiste-Siméon Chardin (1699–1779). His control of color, light, and texture in his still lifes has never been equaled.

Chardin was an anomaly in the eighteenth-century French art scene. His still lifes, however accomplished, along with his scenes of middle-class life, were out of fashion with the upper classes, with one exception: King Louis XV, who did not like the pouffy, superficial, and salacious rococo painters. He purchased Chardin's paintings, gave him a generous annual salary, and arranged for the artist to have a studio and living quarters at the Louvre (which was not yet an art museum; it was still a royal residence).

Chardin had begun as a tradesman who painted signs for other tradesmen's shops. On the side he painted still lifes, and in 1728, he displayed some of his work at an outdoor art fair in Paris. Nicolas de Largillière, a successful portrait artist, spotted Chardin's paintings and launched his career.

His *Still Life with Fruit and a Glass* (also known as *Basket of Plums with Nuts, Currants, and Cherries*) showcases Chardin's facility with different textures: the rough wooden tabletop and the basket; the various skins of the cherries, plums, and almonds; and the smooth water glass. He has arranged these elements into a harmonious composition that is interesting and pleasing. And then there is the light: It almost caresses the fruit, but the focal point is that glass of water. The light bounces off the rim of the glass, and passes through the clear, clean water, illustrating why Chardin's mastery of lighting effects won him the admiration of everyone from the king of France to Henri Matisse. "We have learned from Chardin," the novelist Marcel Proust wrote, "that a pear is as living as a woman, that an ordinary piece of pottery is as beautiful as a precious stone."

THE SWING

By Jean-Honoré Fragonard

The Swing is the emblematic painting of the rococo period. Set in an isolated grove of gnarled trees, a place straight out of a fairy tale, a seemingly innocent pleasure takes a turn toward the naughty. Incredibly, the scene was not dreamed up by the artist, Jean-Honoré Fragonard, but by a patron who commissioned the piece and was very specific about what he wanted.

The Baron de Saint-Julien desired an unconventional portrait of himself with his mistress—and this is the scene he described to Fragonard. Actually, Fragonard was the baron's second choice, but the first artist he had approached had been scandalized by the composition and refused the commission. Fragonard was more open-minded, but even he insisted on one change: Initially, the baron wanted the man pushing the swing to be a bishop; Fragonard convinced the baron to let him paint a cuckolded husband instead.

The two men are in the shadows of the painting—in fact, the baron, reclining upon the ground, is meant to be hiding. The ray of sunlight that has broken into this dim corner of the forest has fallen fully upon the young lady in the swing. As she soars upward, her billowing pink gown flies open, giving her lover a clear view up her skirt. She has kicked off her shoe as a promise of all the other garments she will remove for him.

In case the theme of sexual passion were not obvious, the sculpture of the little cherubs, known as putti, the attendants of Venus, the goddess of love, supply a little extra emphasis. And the complete painting has a sculpture of winged Cupid with his finger raised to his lips makes plain that he's in on the secret romance, too.

Experiment on a Bird in the Air Pump

By Joseph Wright

He's using a theatrical lighting effect worthy of Caravaggio, yet English artist Joseph Wright (1734–1797) is not illustrating a miracle, but a step forward in the history of modern science. Nonetheless, the various poses, gestures, and facial expressions of the onlookers are lifted from religious painting; Wright has done this on purpose, to imply that science has its own sacred character.

The title is a misnomer because the scene is a demonstration rather than an experiment—by 1768, the year of the painting, the principles of the air pump (what we would call a vacuum pump) had been established for about a century. Yet for most people of this period, the idea that the air was composed of various gases, and that air could be drawn out of a glass vessel, was still a marvel. The white-haired gentleman in the red dressing gown is a natural philosopher, as they called themselves at the time; he will conduct the demonstration. Once the air has been pumped out of the glass globe, the white cockatoo will die—a fact that has upset the children.

The natural philosopher looks directly out of the picture at the viewer, as he would at an audience. In the mid-eighteenth century, natural philosophers with a flair for the dramatic traveled the country, putting on flashy scientific experiments and demonstrations of scientific principles for large audiences or private gatherings.

One of the conundrums of the painting is the source of the bright light at its center. No lamp or candle can be seen. This has prompted one art critic to declare that the painting is illuminated by "the light of revelation."

DEATH OF GENERAL WOLFE

By Benjamin West

Young Benjamin West's desire to study drawing was the subject of much discussion among his Quaker congregation in Swarthmore, Pennsylvania. Art was unknown in austere Quaker meetinghouses, where even a simple wooden cross was unwelcome. Furthermore, from the perspective of many Quakers, painting was a frivolous occupation that catered to the whims and vanity of wealthy patrons. On the other hand, the Quakers admired a man who possessed a God-given talent and worked hard to make a success of his gift. In the end, that was the argument that won, and Benjamin West's neighbors encouraged him to pursue his studies as an artist.

West (1738–1820) studied in Philadelphia and New York, but he took time off to fight against the Indians in Pennsylvania. After the war, he traveled to Italy and then to England. It was in London that West made all the right connections. Sir Joshua Reynolds, the foremost painter in England, and Dr. Samuel Johnson, a renowned author and wit, befriended West. But it was when King George III saw and approved of West's work that the young American's career was made. The king commissioned several paintings from him and was so pleased with the result that he made West his personal historical painter, granting him an income of £1,000 per year (worth approximately $124,000 today).

Death of General Wolfe is the type of grand historical scene, full of drama and pathos, that was popular in the late eighteenth century. Major-General James Wolfe, commander of the British forces outside Quebec in 1759, is dying. He has won the French and Indian War and conquered French Canada for England, but it has cost him his life. British officers, soldiers, American militiamen, and a solitary Indian warrior each respond in his own way to the tragedy and keeps the viewer's attention focused sharply on the dying hero. The general's pose, by the way, echoes earlier paintings of the dead Christ taken down from the cross.

Watson and the Shark

By John Singleton Copley

On a hot day in Cuba in 1749, Brook Watson, a fourteen-year-old crewman from an English trading ship, stripped off his clothes and dove into Havana harbor for a refreshing swim. Suddenly, Watson began to scream. A shark attacked him, tearing the flesh from his right leg. As Watson's shipmates came to his rescue, the shark attacked a second time, this time biting off the boy's right foot. Before the shark could make a third assault, the sailors had hauled their friend into their boat.

That is the moment John Singleton Copley (1738–1815) has chosen for his subject—the sailors have reached Watson, the boy is in shock from his terrible wounds (which Copley downplays considerably), and the shark is poised for the third, presumably fatal, attack on his prey.

The painting is full of movement: The shark swings around in an arc, ready to sink its teeth into the boy; the rowers haul on their oars to reach Watson in time; two crewman put themselves at risk as they reach down to grab their friend; and in the prow of the boat a sailor, in a heroic pose, thrusts down with his pike at the shark. The turbulence of the scene in the foreground contrasts sharply with the serenity of the harborscape in the background, just as Watson's naked body emphasizes his vulnerability.

In 1778, Copley exhibited *Watson and the Shark* at the Royal Academy in London. The painting caused a sensation and made Copley's career, elevating him from the status of a provincial artist from Boston to the toast of English society.

Brook Watson, by the way, survived the attack and the amputation of his right leg a little below the knee. In fact, Copley may have had the account of the incident from Watson himself. In his diary for 1774 is an entry, "To Morrow I . . . Dine with a Mr. Watson."

MR. AND MRS. WILLIAM HALLETT

By Thomas Gainsborough

William and Elizabeth Hallett are overdressed for a walk in the woods, but in 1785 there was a rage for portraits of well-born, or well-heeled, individuals opulently dressed in a natural setting. Thomas Gainsborough (1727–1788) was one of the most popular and most accomplished artists of this new fashion. His portraits conveyed perfectly the message that his subjects were sufficiently wealthy to enjoy a life of leisure but knew how to carry their privileges with an air of nonchalance.

The couple is very young at the time of this painting—both were twenty-one. In fact, at the time the portrait was completed, they had not yet been married; the ceremony took place a few weeks after Gainsborough fulfilled his commission.

In France, portraits of careless, lighthearted aristocrats were still in vogue, but in England the established mode was to give an air of dignity, or at least respectability, to the sitters. Impeccably dressed, exquisitely coiffed, and carrying themselves beautifully, William and Elizabeth are the models of English refinement. William is wearing a suit made of black silk velvet, which gives him an air of authority and sobriety, but he wears it unbuttoned, an informal gesture that is appropriate for a morning walk. As for Elizabeth, she is wearing ivory silk. This may be her wedding dress, in which case this could be interpreted as the couple's wedding portrait.

Gainsborough employed light brushstrokes to capture the texture of Elizabeth's muslin shawl and the three large but delicate ostrich feathers that adorn her hat.

There is no record that the Halletts owned a white Pommerian shepherd dog. It may have been borrowed to give the scene a bit of animation.

JOHN JAMES AUDUBON

(1785–1851)

If you like to watch and identify the birds that flit in and out of your backyard, you probably own a bird identification guide with illustrations by David Sibley or Roger Tory Peterson. Well, Sibley and Peterson measure their work against the work of John James Audubon, whose magnum opus, *Birds of America* (published in a series between 1827 and 1838), which features 435 superb watercolors of birds in their habitats, and set the standard for American wildlife artists.

Audubon was born in Haiti, the illegitimate son of Lieutenant Jean Audubon and his mistress, Jeanne Rabin. Audubon's mother died while he was an infant; his father married soon thereafter, and Audubon was raised by his stepmother in France. In Paris, he took lessons from the most popular artist of the day, Jacques-Louis David.

In 1803, when Audubon was eighteen, his father sent him to America; war was raging across Europe at the time, and Audubon senior did not want his son risking his life for Napoleon. The young man lived at an estate called Mill Grove outside Philadelphia—it was here that Audubon first began to study and draw birds.

About the year 1820, Audubon, accompanied by an assistant, set off on a voyage on the Mississippi River to paint American birds. He had almost no money to fund such an expedition, and he often relied on the kindness of strangers for food and shelter. By the time he finished, however, he had a splendid portfolio. When American publishers declined to publish his paintings, Audubon sailed for England, where he found a much more receptive audience. English and Scottish publishers turned out splendid, large-format, full-color prints of his watercolors. Audubon's depiction of birds was scrupulously accurate without being sterile or clinical. He was also a pioneer conservationist who called for the preservation of bird habitats.

Greater Flamingo by John James Audubon, from *Birds of America*, (1827–38)

Apotheosis of Homer Vase

By Josiah Wedgwood and John Flaxman

Anything that harkened back to the classical world was very much in vogue in the last half of the eighteenth century, and everyone from architects to fashion designers to painters catered to the trend. Josiah Wedgwood (1730–1795) and John Flaxman (1755–1826) drew their inspiration from the ancient Etruscans and the modern Chinese. Wedgwood, whose family had been making pottery for four generations, embraced the new style but wanted to create something "unpot-like," as he put it. In other words, he set out to create works of art that could be mass-produced. He took as his model the black pottery created 2,000 years earlier by the Etruscans. By mixing clay with Carr, an iron oxide, and manganese, he developed a new type of stoneware that, when fired, produced finely textured pots in a distinctive blue-black color. Wedgwood marketed his new pottery as "Basaltes," derived from the term "basalt," a type of black volcanic rock.

To the basic black body, Wedgwood applied reliefs inspired by classical scenes, sculptures, and cameos. The style was adopted from potters in Yixing, China, who applied ceramic sprigs of leaves on teapots created for the European market. Wedgwood's favorite designer of reliefs was John Flaxman. Their partnership produced wonderful works of art, including the *Apotheosis of Homer Vase*. Flaxman based the reliefs that decorated the vase on figures he had seen on ancient pottery in the private collection of Sir William Hamilton, Britain's envoy to the king of Naples.

The scene shows the Greek poet being honored by the gods in the afterlife. The finial on the vase's cover is a tiny sculpture of Pegasus, the mythical winged horse. Wedgwood's factory produced a limited edition of fifty *Apotheosis* vases, which were sold by subscription for 50 guineas (a guinea in 1786 was a gold coin worth 20 shillings). Wedgwood was so proud of the vase he donated one to the British Museum.

MARIE ANTOINETTE AND HER CHILDREN

By Elisabeth-Louise Vigee Le Brun

By 1787, Marie Antoinette was in the midst of a serious public relations crisis. It was widely circulated among the French people at every level of society that the queen was a promiscuous trollop; that her children had not been fathered by the king, Louis XVI, but by Marie Antoinette's lovers; that her extravagant tastes were driving the country into bankruptcy; and that she cared nothing for France or its people.

To counter these accusations the queen called upon her close friend and chosen court painter, Elisabeth-Louise Vigee Le Brun, to paint a portrait of herself and her children. Vigee Le Brun rose to the challenge, carefully staging the scene to convey with absolute conviction that Marie Antoinette was the loving, virtuous mother of the king's children.

The queen is dressed in regal red velvet, trimmed with black fur and adorned with white plumes—red, black, and white were the ancient colors of France's royal family.

The princess, Marie Therese Charlotte, clings to her mother and looks at her lovingly. The older prince, Louis-Joseph, points to the empty cradle of his late sister, Princess Sophie, who died in infancy in 1786—thereby suggesting that the queen, like so many mothers of her time, knows the sorrow of losing a beloved child. Seated on Marie Antoinette's lap is the Prince Louis-Charles. He and his big brother both wear the blue silk sash of the Order of the Holy Spirit, which by tradition the kings of France awarded to their sons at birth.

The message of the painting is unmistakable: Marie Antoinette is devoted to France, a loving mother to her children, a faithful wife to the king, and a woman who sympathizes with the troubles of the French people.

Tragically, disaster followed everyone in this painting. Louis-Joseph died in 1789 of tuberculosis of the spine. Marie Antoinette was guillotined. Louis-Charles died of malnutrition and abuse in the Temple prison in 1795. Marie Therese Charlotte survived but spent most of her life in exile from France. She died in 1851.

PORTRAIT OF ELIJAH BOARDMAN

By Ralph Earl

In a full-length, life-size portrait (the canvas measures 83 inches by 51 inches), American artist Ralph Earl (1751–1801) gives a well-to-do dry goods merchant the kind of treatment once reserved for the nobility. Elijah Boardman (1760–1823) was a shopkeeper in New Milford, Connecticut, who became wealthy by selling fine fabrics, as the viewer can see through the open door. Earl shows Boardman as a man of business, standing at his high desk where he did his accounts. But Boardman is also turned out like a member of the gentry: a gold-trimmed vest, gold chain dangling from his waist, gold buttons on the sleeves of his fine coat, and silver buckles on his shoes.

But there is more to Boardman than good business sense and excellent taste in clothes: Look at the books on the desk's shelves. These are not ledgers, but leather-bound copies of Shakespeare, John Milton's *Paradise Lost*, Samuel Johnson's *Dictionary*, as well as editions of *London Magazine*. With these titles, Boardman tells us that he is a learned man with a taste for high-quality literature who keeps up with the times.

Ralph Earl was born in Massachusetts. Like most artists of colonial America he was self-taught, and he was an itinerant. In other words, he did not set up a studio in Boston or Philadelphia and wait for clients to come to him; instead, Earl packed up his paints and brushes and rode from town to town offering to paint portraits for anyone who could pay. In this way he painted at least 183 portraits, almost all of them in America. (During the American Revolution, Earl, a Loyalist, fled to England and did not return to his homeland until 1786, when he began painting portraits again.)

Elijah Boardman, however, sided with the rebels during the Revolution. In later years, he served in the Connecticut House of Representatives before going to the U.S. Senate.

Tea-making in Korea

By Anonymous

There is a long history of genre painting in Korea, particularly of Buddhist or scholarly scenes—monks going about the routine of the monasteries, for example, or Confucian masters in their studies. In the mid-eighteenth century, Korean artists developed their own style of genre painting in which they portrayed everyday scenes from the lives of ordinary people—men sitting on the ground in a circle, watching a wrestling match; or women kneeling beside a stream, scrubbing clothes.

The eighteenth century was a time of change in Korean society. There was an economic boom, and the living standards of the common people rose. As farmers, tradesmen, and shopkeepers prospered, they bought better quality goods, including clothing, for themselves and their families—identifying a person's rank in Korean society by the way he dressed was no longer reliable.

Korea's contact with Europe in terms of trade also increased at this time, and this painting portrays an example of cultural exchange. The anonymous artist shows us the interior of a tea-making factory. There is a Korean foreman overseeing production, while a gentleman from Europe observes. He could be a casual visitor to the factory, but it is more likely that he is the merchant who placed the order for Korean tea.

This work reveals a bit of influence from traditional Korean court paintings. Court artists depicted ranks of aristocrats and courtiers lined up in formal poses as they participate in or witness a court ceremony. While the artist's ranks of tea-makers alludes to formal court art, in this case he gives the viewer, not an assembly of Korean aristocrats, but ordinary Korean workingmen.

DIANA THE HUNTRESS

By Jean-Antoine Houdon

Jean-Antoine Houdon (1741–1828) is best known for his portrait sculptures and busts of the heroes of the Enlightenment—Voltaire, Thomas Jefferson, George Washington, and Benjamin Franklin. These sculptures are wonderfully realistic, but perhaps Houdon's most lifelike work is his bronze sculpture, *Diana the Huntress.*

He portrayed the Roman goddess running after her prey, a bow in her left hand and an arrow in her right (though not in facing image.) In Roman mythology Diana was the goddess of the hunt, but she was also the goddess of the moon (hence the crescent she wears in her hair). Her nudity is lovely but dangerous: Diana was a virgin goddess who disdained gods and men. When a handsome young hunter named Acteon happened to see her bathing in a woodland pool, she transformed him into a stag and sent her hunting dogs to tear Acteon apart. All these elements are combined in Houdon's masterpiece: Diana is beautiful, strong, self-confident, and unashamed. And she is perfectly balanced—Houdon has set the entire weight of the sculpture on one foot, or more accurately, the toes of one foot.

The statue's long arms and legs, and the even, elongated torso, may have been inspired by sixteenth-century portraits of Diane de Poitiers, the mistress of France's King Henri II. In fact, Houdon's Diana looks very much like the Diana in a bronze sculpture Jean Goujon created for Henri II in 1549.

Houdon made many copies of his Diana, including a version in fragile terracotta that is displayed at the Frick Collection in New York City.

À Marat

By Jacques-Louis David

This is a secular holy picture. Jacques-Louis David, for all intents and purposes the artist laureate of the French Revolution, elevated a tawdry murder (in a bathtub, no less) to the level of martyrdom, and transfigured Marat into the savior of the Revolution.

The French Revolution abolished the monarchy and the aristocracy; it then tried to dechristianize French society. Priests and bishops were torn to pieces by blood-thirsty mobs; nuns were hauled off to the guillotine; churches were ransacked; and, at one point, a prostitute was dolled up as "the Goddess of Reason" and enthroned on the altar in Paris's Cathedral of Notre Dame. But the Revolution could not just banish Christ and the saints—it had to find replacements, and the cult of Marat was one of the first and one of the most successful.

Jean-Paul Marat was a fanatical advocate of the Reign of Terror who took great satisfaction in sending countless "enemies of the people" to the guillotine. Opponents of the Terror feared that the infant French Republic would drown in so much blood; one of these was twenty-five-year-old Charlotte Corday of Caen in Normandy. In July 1793, she took a coach to Paris, and talked her way into Marat's house. She found her victim soaking in a bathtub; pulling a long kitchen knife from beneath her skirts, Corday stabbed Marat below the collarbone, severing his carotid artery. Corday was arrested and within days was herself a victim of the guillotine.

Meanwhile, David began work on the painting that would make Marat a secular saint. Drawing upon the iconography of martyrdoms and lamentations over the dead Christ, David placed the ivory-handled knife, the implement of the martyr's death, beside the bathtub. He tidied up the gash, making a neat incision from which seeped a thin trickle of blood—the usual way artists depicted the wound in Christ's side.

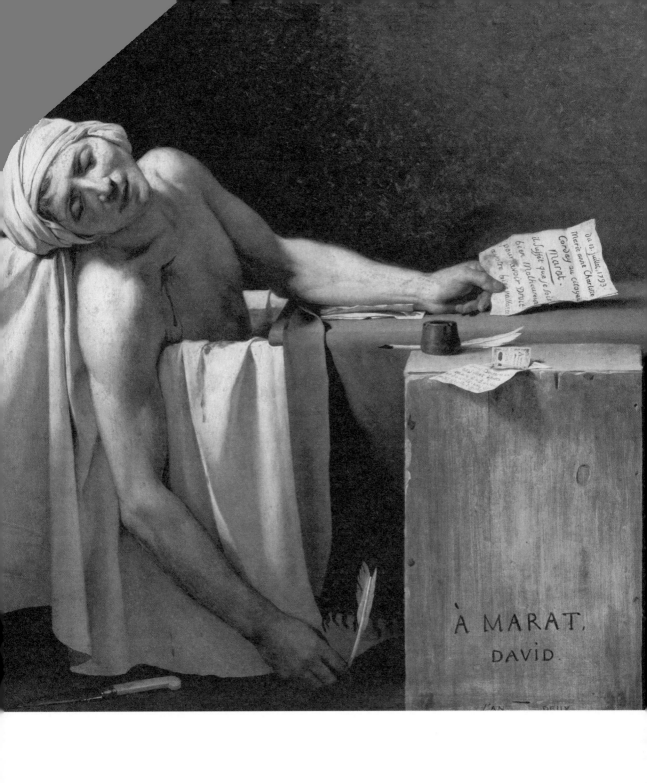

Du 13. Juillet. 1793.
Marie anne Charlotte
Corday au cítoyen
Marat.
il suffit que je sois
bien
Malheureuse
pour avoir Droit
a votre bienveillance

À MARAT.
DAVID.

L'AN DEUX

THE STAIRCASE GROUP

By Charles Willson Peale

Charles Willson Peale (1741–1827) was a Maryland saddlemaker whose gift for drawing, especially portraits, was exceptional, so much so that his friends and neighbors took up a collection to send him to England to study with the transplanted American artist, Benjamin West. When Peale returned to America he painted dozens of portraits of prominent Americans in the Middle Atlantic region, as well as renowned heroes of the American Revolution. Peale himself enlisted in the Pennsylvania militia, and fought with General Washington at the Battle of Trenton.

Peale had sixteen children, among whom were sons he named Rembrandt, Raphaelle, Rubens, and Titian. *The Staircase Group*, also known as *Portrait of Raphaelle Peale and Titian Ramsey Peale*, is a very large canvas measuring 89.5 inches by 39.375 inches; it depicts two of Peale's boys, Raphaelle and Titian, pausing as they climb an enclosed spiral staircase. This is a classic example of trompe l'oeil, a type of painting intended to be an optical illusion. Peale's figures are life-size, and the young men are so carefully portrayed, and the perspective so exact (including the step that seems to jut right out of the painting), that if it were hung so the bottom of the canvas were flush with the floor, the viewer would believe he or she had interrupted a common domestic scene.

And that is exactly what Peale did—he installed the painting inside a door in his own studio. In later years Rembrandt Peale recalled a day when George Washington, a close friend of the Peale family, stopped by the studio to visit the artist. As he passed *The Staircase Group* he tipped his hat, bowed, and greeted Raphaelle and Titian by name.

CUPID AND PSYCHE

By Antonio Canova

The cool dignity of Neoclassism was a reaction to the exuberance and triumphalism of the baroque and the frivolity of the rococo styles. This nod to the art of ancient Greece (where democracy was born) and ancient Rome (which had been a republic before the emperors came along) meshed seamlessly with a new interest in the rights of man and the success of the revolutions in America and France, where the common people had severed their ties to monarchs and established modern republics.

But the late eighteenth century was not entirely cool, aloof, and cerebral. The emotional life, the irresistible force of the passions, was the other side of the Neo-classical coin, and the beginning of the artistic movement known as Romanticism.

We see these two schools of thought in Antonio Canova's (1757–1822) *Cupid and Psyche* (also known as *Love and Psyche,* or *Amor and Psyche*). In the shape of their faces, the arrangement of their hair, and the musculature of their bodies, Cupid and Psyche could have stepped off the pediment of any temple in Greece. But that's where the comparison ends, because the embrace, the emotionalism, the passion conveyed in this sculpture owes nothing to the ancient classical tradition, and everything to the up-and-coming Romantics.

The scene depicts Psyche being awakened from a magical sleep by Cupid's kiss. In Greek, psyche means "soul," and Cupid, of course, is the god of love. The sculpture, then, is an allegory of the human soul awakened by love.

George Washington (Lansdowne Portrait)

By Gilbert Stuart

This life-size, full-length portrait of George Washington acquired its name, "The Lansdowne Portrait," because it had been presented to the Marquis of Lansdowne, an English aristocrat who had sided with the American rebels during the Revolution. The picture was presented to the marquis by William and Anne Bingham of Pennsylvania, the wealthiest couple in America in the late eighteenth/early nineteenth century.

At first glance, this appears to be a conventional, dignified portrait of an American statesman, but Gilbert Stuart furnished the painting with symbols that referred to Washington and to America.

Washington's extended right hand is interpreted as a gesture of farewell—in 1796, he was leaving office as President of the United States. (Washington was sixty-four years old at the time; he would die three years later.)

On the floor under the table are three books: *General Orders*, *American Revolution*, and *Constitution and Bylaws*—references to Washington's role as commander-in-chief of the Continental Army during the Revolution and president of the convention where the U.S. Constitution was debated and adopted.

The two eagles on the golden table leg are taken from the Great Seal of the United States. The sheathed sword in Washington's left hand is the emblem of a gentleman (although by 1796 it was no longer fashionable for men to wear swords as part of formal attire). The sheathed sword represents two facets of Washington's character—a valiant man in time of war, a just man in time of peace.

At the top of the chair behind Washington is a medallion painted with stars and stripes and draped with a garland of laurel, a symbol of America's victory over the British Empire.

The rainbow visible in the top right corner of the portrait recalls the rainbow God set in the sky after the Great Flood as a sign of his new covenant with humankind. It suggests that the new American nation enjoys the approval of heaven.

Naked Maja

By Francisco Goya

Spain in 1800 was in a state of social and political upheaval. King Charles III had tried to modernize his country by encouraging industry and trade and by stripping the Inquisition of its power. After the king's death in 1788, his reactionary son, Charles IV, rolled back his father's reforms. Nonetheless, among the Spanish, that little taste of freedom went a long way.

Francisco Goya (1746–1828) was a fervent liberal who loathed Charles IV and the Inquisition (although after 1799, when he became the king's court painter, Goya kept his opinions to himself). With one client, however, he could be candid. Manuel de Godoy, prince of La Paz, commissioned several paintings from Goya, including a female nude to join his collection of other nude paintings.

By the standards of 1800, the *Naked Maja* was pornographic. Female nudity was tolerated in art if it was integral to the story—a tryst between Mars and Venus, or Diana bathing in a woodland pool—or if it represented the innocence of Eve or the heroism of the Amazons. But here was a life-size painting of an unknown woman, naked, sprawled out on a couch, posing and turning toward the viewer in a manner that looks suggestive if not downright inviting. Even more shocking, Goya painted the woman's pubic hair.

Conservatives in Spanish society were outraged, and the Inquisition summoned Goya to explain himself. A century earlier he might have been sentenced to prison, but by the early nineteenth century the Inquisition's influence had dwindled. The tribunal stripped Goya of his position and income as court painter.

Thomas Cole

(1801–1848)

In America, the style of painting known as the Hudson River School has never lost its popularity with art lovers. The artists' vision of the mountains and rivers of the Catskills and the Adirondacks in New York romanticized the wilderness, editing out the dangers, to portray an American Eden, only lately discovered, barely explored, and completely unspoiled.

The first artist of the Hudson River School was Thomas Cole, an immigrant from England who had a gift for drawing. In his late teens, Cole was designing wallpaper patterns that were reproduced endlessly at his father's wallpaper factory. By his early twenties he was learning to use oil paints and creating his first landscape paintings. In September 1825, he took his first trip into the Catskills.

A few weeks later, Cole returned to his father's apartment in New York City and painted three landscapes: *The Falls of the Kaaterskill, Lake with Dead Trees*, and *A View of Fort Putnam*. He convinced an art dealer to display them in his shop window. They were bought up—for $25 apiece—by the artists John Trumbull and Asher B. Durrand, and by a New York theater impresario, William Dunlap. Trumbull made himself Cole's mentor, introduced him to other artists, and encouraged him to keep painting.

Cole's landscapes are characterized by dramatic lighting, spectacular mountain crags, and gnarled trees. But Cole himself wanted to vary his subject matter with allegorical works. *The Voyage of Life* is a series of four sentimental scenes representing the four ages of man—Childhood, Youth, Manhood, and Old Age, with a guardian angel watching over each stage of the journey. More dramatic is his five-part series, *The Course of Empire*; the fourth painting, *Destruction*, has a cinematic quality worthy of a Cecil B. DeMille movie.

From the Top of Kaaterskill Falls by Thomas Cole, 1826

Wanderer in the Mists

By Caspar David Friedrich

By 1818, the middle and upper classes of Europe and the United States were firmly in the grip of the Romantic movement. Emotional restraint was out of fashion. So, too, were the linear, symmetrical, well-clipped gardens and parks designed in the eighteenth century. People yearned for powerful, life-changing emotional experiences, and sought them in wilderness areas where they could encounter the power of nature, raw and untouched by man.

Wanderer in the Mists (also known as *Wanderer Above the Sea of Fog*), by the German artist Caspar David Friedrich (1774–1840) captures the spirit of Romanticism perfectly. A solitary wanderer, hiking-stick in hand, perches himself on a windswept rock and surveys the mist-shrouded peaks of a mountain range. Is he contemplating his own insignificance in the midst of such untamed natural splendor? Or does he take pride in his strength and courage for reaching this lonely spot? The Romantics would have approved of either emotional response.

Many art critics regard this as the quintessential Romantic painting and Friedrich as the quintessential Romantic artist. He was a tortured soul who once slit his throat in an attempt to kill himself. When he married in 1818 (the year he painted the *Wanderer*), he tried to control his emotional outbursts so as not to frighten his bride. Nonetheless, Friedrich believed that his inspiration depended on wild mood swings. Today we would say he was "conflicted." Friedrich conveys this facet of his personality in this painting, in which turbulent scenery represents his own turbulent emotions.

HAY-WAIN

By John Constable

Light, color, draftsmanship, and composition are perfectly combined in the *Hay-wain*, one of the greatest British paintings of all time. So it is odd that when John Constable (1776–1837) exhibited the *Hay-wain* at the Royal Academy in 1821, no one bought it because almost no one liked it. Confused and disappointed, Constable took his painting home. Three years later he tried again, this time exhibiting at the Paris Salon, and this time it found a buyer—an art dealer named John Arrowsmith. The painting also won attention and acclaim among French art lovers, including a gold medal from France's King Charles X.

The hay-wain of the title is the horse-drawn cart in the stream. A wain is a heavy freight cart used by farmers.

Constable knew this scene intimately. This is the River Stour near Flatford in Suffolk. Constable's father owned and operated a mill nearby, and the cottage on the left belonged to a neighbor, Willy Lott. The cottage still stands, although it has been tidied up for tourists. The landscape has changed, however; the trees are gone, and the river runs higher.

Constable painted this large canvas (it measures approximately 52 inches by 73 inches) using a technique known as impasto: He applied thick layers of oil paint to create texture, then added dabs of white paint to create the impression of sunlight reflecting off the surface of the river and the water dripping from the wain's wheels.

This is a rural paradise where the sun shines, the fields are lush, and the river flows gently by.

1821

MASSACRE AT CHIOS

By Eugene Delacroix

In 1821, nearly 400 years after their country had been conquered by the Ottoman Turks, Greek rebels began a bloody, eight-year-long struggle to win independence for Greece.

About a year after the outbreak of the revolution, 2,000 Greek rebels from the Aegean island of Samos landed on the island of Chios and attacked the Turkish garrison stationed there as well as its Turkish residents. Very few of the Greeks of Chios joined the rebels; nonetheless, the Ottoman government in Constantinople sent an army to punish the people of Chios. The Turkish forces were merciless: They massacred 42,000 Greeks, and rounded up another 50,000, whom they sold in the slave markets of Constantinople, Asia Minor, Egypt, and the Barbary Coast. Some 23,000 Greeks fled their homes. In the end, there were barely 2,000 Greeks left alive on Chios.

In western Europe and the United States, people were outraged by reports of the atrocities at Chios. In response to these reports a young French artist, Eugene Delacroix (1798–1863), painted *Massacre at Chios*, a work that was almost as shocking to the art world as the actual massacre.

Conventions of the time required that paintings of even tragic scenes should strike some redemptive note but Delacroix rejected this notion. In this painting there are no valiant Greek patriots, going down fighting; there is only terrible suffering, despair, and death. The naked infant clinging to the breast of his dead mother became the one detail of the painting that everyone remembered and that fueled international support for the Greek rebels. Many art critics, however, considered the *Massacre at Chios* not only inflammatory, but unfit to be seen. Delacroix's colleague, artist Antoine-Jean Gros, declared the painting was a "massacre of art." In spite of these condemnations, Delacroix remained defiant. The next year he produced another pro-Greek painting, *Greece Expiring on the Ruins of Missalonghi*, where a Turkish army slaughtered more than 10,000 Greek civilians.

ALBERT BIERSTADT

(1830–1902)

Albert Bierstadt was only three years old when his family left their home in Germany and emigrated to the United States. They settled in New Bedford, Massachusetts. In his teens, he showed a talent for drawing, so in 1853 his parents sent him back to Germany to study art at the Dusseldorf School. Three years later he returned, and began painting landscapes of dramatic natural scenes in New England and New York.

Bierstadt's life-changing moment came in 1859 when he joined a team of surveyors who were traveling to the Wind River region of Wyoming. The vast, sweeping, unspoiled landscape—especially the Rocky Mountains—enthralled Bierstadt. During the two years he traveled through the west with the surveyors, he made an untold number of sketches. And when he got back east, these sketches became the springboard for a great many paintings. For the rest of his life he returned time and again to the west, traveling all the way to California, to find new, thrilling vistas for his paintings.

He painted his landscapes on enormous canvases. They suited the scale of the scenery he was portraying, and they gave Bierstadt an advantage when he displayed his work—in an art gallery, his massive paintings made the competition's paintings look puny.

Dramatic lighting effects were his specialty. Since he chose outdoor scenes as his subjects, he portrayed natural light, but he manipulated the natural light so that the rays of the sun shone exactly where Bierstadt wanted them—on a waterfall, or down a river valley, or reflecting off a snow-capped mountain peak. Indians, wagon trains of settlers, and wildlife appear in the pictures, but they are "extras." The landscape and the light are the stars of a Bierstadt painting.

Yosemite Falls by Albert Bierstadt, ca. 1865

GREAT WAVE OFF KANAGAWA

By Katsushika Hokusai

The giant wave captures the viewer's attention so completely that it comes as a surprise to learn that this woodblock print is supposed to offer a view of Mount Fuji. *Great Wave Off Kanagawa* is the first print in a series that Japanese artist Katsushika Hokusai (1760–1849) published as *36 Views of Mount Fuji*.

Traditionally this type of picture, known as a *meisho-e,* or scene of a famous place, would give prominence to the landmark. Hokusai has set that tradition on its head, presenting a fearsome seascape in which Mount Fuji appears tiny and serene in the distance. To give a little more drama to the scene, he has included three Japanese barges caught up in the violence of the wave. You can see the sailors in blue, laying flat on their bellies, clinging to their ships for dear life. And to further enhance the fearfulness of the scene, Hokusai has made the white foam at the crest of the waves take on the appearance of claws.

Prints such as these could be mass-produced cheaply and found a large market among the middle class who could not afford an original painting. But Hokusai also found an audience in Europe for his Mount Fuji prints. It is believed that Claude Debussy's *La Mer* (*The Sea*), and Rainer Maria Rilke's poem "Der Berg" ("The Mountain") were both inspired by Hokusai's *Great Wave*.

1832

Peaceable Kingdom

By Edward Hicks

Edward Hicks (1780–1849) painted sixty-one different versions of the painting known as the *Peaceable Kingdom*. He was an American folk artist, a pretty broad term that can encompass everyone from quilters to makers of weathervanes. In a nutshell, a folk artist is an individual whose style is not influenced by artistic trends and who has no formal or academic training in art.

Hicks had a good sense of design, and he liked strong colors. He had, in other words, a knack for understanding how to catch a viewer's attention—a skill that also made him an accomplished and sought-after sign painter. In fact, he never really thought of himself as a fine artist—he regarded his work as a craft.

As Hicks was a Quaker minister, it was not surprising that the inspiration for the *Peaceable Kingdom* paintings came from the book of Isaiah 11:6–9, which reads in part, "The leopard shall lie down with the kid; and the calf and the young lion and the fatling together; and a little child shall lead them."

The world the Old Testament prophet describes is a place of perfect harmony, free from all dangers, but Hicks has rendered it more as a cute, cuddly place. The beasts have the appearance of plush toy animals, and the adorable little children look like dolls. In the background is a historic scene—William Penn's treaty with the Indians of Pennsylvania. The British Crown had given Penn possession of Pennsylvania and the authority to found a colony there. As a devout Quaker, Penn was unwilling to drive the Indian inhabitants of Pennsylvania from their ancestral homes. In 1682, at a place called Shackamaxon, Penn and the leaders of the Delaware or Leni Lenape tribe, met and worked out a mutually satisfactory arrangement. He paid the Leni Lenape £1,200, a considerable sum for the time, for land in eastern Pennsylvania. The colonists and the Indians then signed a peace treaty. Penn's treaty became a model of fair dealing and initiated between the colonists and the Leni Lenape "a chain of friendship" as the Indians called it.

The Burning of the Houses of Lords and Commons

By J. M. W. Turner

After dark on October 16, 1834, a fire broke out in one of the cellars of the Houses of Parliament. Soon the entire medieval palace that had been the seat of English government was swallowed up in flames. Immense crowds hurried to the banks and bridges of the River Thames to witness the disaster. Among them was a portly fifty-nine-year-old gentleman, J. M. W. Turner (1775–1851), an artist fascinated by light, color, moments of high drama, and the uncontrollable forces of nature. This catastrophe delivered everything Turner desired in a painting. Hiring a boat, he had himself rowed across the river for a better view; once the boatman got as close as he dared to the conflagration, Turner made lightning-fast sketches of the scene.

Three months later Turner began to paint. In the upper left hand corner of the canvas, the buildings of Parliament explode in red and yellow flames that streak upward, fading into a giant grayish white cloud of smoke that almost obscures the deep blue and turquoise of the night sky. Balancing the opposite end of the painting is the massive white stone bridge, packed with people watching the spectacle. In the foreground are even more spectators crammed together on the riverbank.

It is a magnificent painting, but look at it beside the work of other popular artists of the 1830s such as Franz Xavier Winterhalter, Charles Eastland, and Edwin Landseer and you can understand why Queen Victoria was convinced that Turner was mad. Compared to the highly polished, elegant, representational paintings that dominated the art world at this time, Turner's expressionistic style appears wild and out of control. And wild and out of control is what this scene requires—with its enormous, billowing flames and mesmerized crowd of onlookers, Turner immortalizes a national disaster of the first magnitude.

WINSLOW HOMER

(1836–1910)

In 1861, *Harper's Weekly* magazine sent Winslow Homer, one of its best freelance artists, to Washington, D.C., to provide illustrations of the inauguration of the new president, Abraham Lincoln. When the Civil War began about six weeks later, *Harper's* gave Homer a full-time assignment following the Union troops and providing illustrations of battle scenes and camp life, as well as portraits of the commanders, officers, and ordinary soldiers. At the end of the war in 1865, Homer produced a superb painting, *A Veteran in a New Field*, which showed a Union soldier back home; his uniform jacket lies on the ground behind him, and he is wielding a scythe, mowing his family's field.

In 1865, Homer went to Paris for a year. The Impressionist movement was in full swing, but Homer did not adopt the new style. Back in the United States he painted realistic scenes of country life. At some point he began experimenting with watercolors, the medium that would elevate him to the rank of America's greatest watercolor artist. His watercolors possess a fresh, spontaneous quality, but also a real command of color and composition. Typically, art lovers associate Homer and his watercolors with Maine, but he did some of his finest work in the Florida Keys, Cuba, and the Bahamas.

He loved painting in the tropics where the colors were so vivid—emerald, coral, indigo. He liked the unself-consciousness of the black inhabitants of the islands, who did not have to be guarded about what they did, or what they said, or at whom they looked, as was the case in America. The *Turtle Pound,* painted in the Bahamas, is vintage Winslow Homer—colorful, vigorous, intimate. The watercolor portrays two handsome Bahamian men, one of whom is hauling up a large captive sea turtle they will have for dinner. The contrasting colors are wonderful: the bronze skin of the men against the bleached boards of the pound and their black hair against stark white clouds.

White Cloud, Head Chief of the Iowas

By George Catlin

In his own language, White Cloud's name was Mew-hu-she-kaw. He is portrayed here in the full splendor of a chief, but by the time George Catlin (1796–1872) painted him, White Cloud's tribe, the Iowa, had dwindled to fewer than 500 men, women, and children. Furthermore, the United States government had forced the tribe to leave their homelands in eastern Iowa, give up their nomadic existence as hunters, and settle down as farmers on a small reservation in Nebraska.

This portrait was not made in Iowa or Nebraska, but in London. Catlin had taken some of his best paintings of American Indians, as well as tribal artifacts from his private collection, and traveled to London where he mounted a special Native American exhibit. White Cloud, who had known Catlin since he was a boy, offered to join the program and bring some of his warriors to England; Catlin agreed, and the chief and a small band of Iowas made the long journey from Nebraska to London. There, wearing their traditional garb, they performed tribal dances in what Catlin called the Indian Gallery. This was a money-making enterprise for White Cloud and his warriors—their families back home, in fact the entire tribe, had become desperately poor.

Catlin portrayed White Cloud in the finery of a great chief—the skin of a white wolf, a bear claw necklace, and a deer's tail headdress dyed red.

George Catlin had begun life as a lawyer in Pennsylvania, but he gave up this career to travel among the Indian nations west of the Mississippi and paint them before they and their way of life vanished forever. Between 1830 and 1839, he painted 500 portraits and scenes of Indian life, and he also collected an enormous number of Indian artifacts. However, the cost of maintaining his collection was too much for one man.

Catlin lobbied the U.S. government to purchase his Indian Gallery as a legacy for future generations. When they did not, Catlin went bankrupt in 1852. A wealthy Philadelphia businessman paid his debts and, shortly after Catlin's death, donated the Gallery to the Smithsonian.

COMTESSE D'HAUSSONVILLE

By Jean-Auguste-Dominique Ingres

Jean-Auguste-Dominique Ingres (1780–1867) has caught the twenty-seven-year-old countess just as she returns home from the opera. Her gold evening wrap is tossed on an armchair; her opera glasses stand on the mantelpiece. Lying beside them are the notes and cards that accumulated while she was out; she has flipped through them and tossed them in an untidy pile. Now she has turned toward the viewer as if he or she has said something that requires a thoughtful response.

Ingres took three years to complete this portrait of Louise, Comtesse d'Haussonville (1818–1882). It was the position of the raised left arm, the crook of the finger, and the reflection in the mirror that gave Ingres the most trouble—he wanted this part of the composition to be perfect. And it is. The pose is utterly natural, perfectly graceful, with a touch of girlishness.

Rather than a straightforward, up-and-down pose, Ingres has positioned the countess in a way that creates visual interest and dramatic tension. There are two diagonal lines here—one the long diagonal of her body leaning against the fireplace; the other the short diagonal of her slightly bowed head and neck. The two diagonal lines intersect at the countess's shoulder.

The colors are also wonderful. The countess's glorious light blue evening gown is set against the dark blue cloth that covers the mantle. The yellow of her discarded cloak is picked up in her gold ring and bracelet, the gold ornaments in the room, and the gold frame of the mirror. The splash of red ribbon in the countess's hair draws the viewer's eyes upward to her lovely face and large gray eyes.

BARBIZON SCHOOL
(1848–1870)

In 1848, as the dust from various revolutions was settling all across Europe, artists Jean-Francois Millet (1814–1875) and Theodore Rousseau (1812–1867) pooled their meager resources and moved 30 miles from Paris to the village of Barbizon on the edge of the Forest of Fountainbleau, where the cost of living was much more affordable than in the capital. Here, with Jean-Baptiste-Camille Corot (1796–1875) and Charles-Francois Daubigny (1817–1878), Millet and Rousseau began a new type of nature painting in which the painters carried their equipment outside and painted *en pleine air* (in the open air). Because of the name of the village, their style became known as "the Barbizon School."

The Barbizon artists often took landscapes as their subject, but they were also interested in painting realistic scenes of rural life. These were not the buffoons of Breugel or the chiseled Greek shepherds of Poussin—these were real peasants, and the Barbizon painters' goal was to portray them as they were without prettifying them, or politicizing them, or making them "stand" for something.

Nonetheless, in 1857 when Millet exhibited *The Gleaners* (seen here) at the Paris Salon, he was attacked as a political and social radical who tried to undermine French society by exalting the working class. Gleaners, by the way, go through a field to collect stray stalks and grains of wheat that the harvesters missed. It was tedious, arduous labor, and members of the monied classes took it as an insult that Millet had chosen gleaners as a subject. Even the size of the canvas offended them—it measures 33 inches by 44 inches. One art critic, Paul de Saint Victor, sniffed, "[Millet's] three gleaners have gigantic pretensions, they pose as the Three Fates of Poverty . . . their ugliness and their grossness unrelieved."

The hostility toward *The Gleaners* was so intense that Millet, reluctantly, agreed to sell it to a British collector for a paltry 3,000 francs—1,000 less than his original asking price.

The Gleaners by Jean-Francois Millet, 1857

Sudden Shower at the Atake Bridge

By Ando Hiroshige

From the time he was twelve years old, Ando Hiroshige (1797–1858) had worked as a fireman, his father's profession. Then one day, by chance, he saw the prints of Hokusai; from that day on, he yearned to become an artist.

Hiroshige was a natural. Like Hokusai, he created *ukiyo-e*, "pictures of the floating world," the name for the exquisite but inexpensive landscape woodblock prints artists produced for the popular market. He published his prints in several great series, including *Fifty-three Stations of the Tokaido* (the highway that connected Edo—modern-day Tokyo—with Kyoto), *Celebrated Places in Japan*, and *Sixty-nine Stations on the Kiso Highway*. His prints have a lyrical, some art critics have even said poetical, feel. His landscapes are so enchanting that the viewer would like to go to Japan at once and experience firsthand the intense colors; the strangely gnarled trees; the exquisite houses, temples, and bridges; and the shadowy mountains in the distance. In most cases, however, Hiroshige improved upon nature; very few of the "views" in his prints record these scenes as they actually appear.

One of his most interesting prints is *Sudden Shower at the Atake Bridge*, also known as *Evening Shower at the Atake Bridge*. It is an austere work, in which he used a limited palette of colors, only a few human figures, and, in the background, a man propelling a boat. The one part of the scene to get detailed attention is the Atake Bridge.

This print is of interest for another reason—it caught the eye of Vincent Van Gogh, who did his own version of it. Van Gogh's is a much "busier" painting: The river is green and choppy; the boat much sharper; the surface of the bridge is yellow; and the viewer can make out the scenery on the far shore. Van Gogh also painted a frame in vivid green and red around his painting. Talented as Van Gogh was, many prefer Hiroshige's original.

CHILDE HASSAM

(1859–1935)

Childe Hassam's mother and father traced their ancestry back to English Puritans who settled in Massachusetts in the seventeenth century. A distinguished ancestry did nothing for the family's fortunes, however, and after a disastrous fire destroyed his father's business, Hassam was compelled to give up his plans for college and get a job. For three weeks he worked in the accounting department of Little, Brown, the Boston book publishers. At the end of the three weeks, he was fired; his supervisor suggested he go become a painter. And that is what Hassam did. By 1882 he had his own studio in Boston; the city's directory listed his occupation as "artist."

Since he had no formal training in art, he studied by attending art exhibits, where he noticed that the trend was for realistic paintings of rural life. He followed the fashion. But after a trip to Europe in 1883, Hassam came under the influence of the Impressionists. He returned and began painting in a way that Americans had not seen before—a style that borrowed techniques from the naturalistic and the Impressionistic painters and that took as their subject daily life in American cities.

At the time of its debut, *Boston Common at Twilight* was considered very modern. At the far left of the canvas are trolley cars crowding the street, a symbol of commerce, rush, and activity. The rest of the scene, however, is serene, as a mother and her two little girls stop to feed the birds in Boston Common, the park that by the time Hassam painted this work (1885–1886) had become an oasis of calm in the bustling city.

This is one of Hassam's "tonal" paintings, dominated by shades of rust and rose. The light cast by the setting sun has even lent a pinkish cast to the snow.

Boston Common at Twilight, 1885

ACADEMIC ART

As the name suggests, Academic Art was taught at the art schools of Europe. The goal of the curriculum was to give students a firm grounding in the traditional themes of Western art and to ensure that they possessed not just raw talent, but a high degree of technical ability. Art schools in the United States, Latin America, and Australia followed the example of the European academies and set the same standards for their students.

In the nineteenth century, the most prestigious art organization in the world was the French Academy, which operated the École des Beaux-Arts in Paris. The French Academy also awarded the most coveted art prize, the Prix de Rome.

The Impressionists, and then the radical innovators generally lumped together under the heading of "modern artists," rejected the Academic style. The influence of modern art is still so pervasive that not only have most Academic artists been forgotten, but their work is still routinely dismissed as utterly deficient in artistic merit. This point of view is insufferably snotty, ignoring as it does the genius of such overlooked artists as Jean-Leon Gerome, Lawrence Alma Tadema, Frederick Arthur Bridgman, David Roberts, Gustave Doré, and William Adolphe Bouguereau, whose painting, *Charity*, is seen here.

While these artists showed great mastery, they did not break new ground, and that contributed to their downfall. By the last half of the nineteenth century, the rules at many of the national academies of art had become so rigid that any type of innovation in style, technique, or composition was banned from the official academy art exhibitions. In 1863, the situation in France reached a crisis when established artists such as Édouard Manet and James McNeill Whistler were barred from the Paris Salon. Consequently, France's emperor, Napoleon III, opened the Salon des Refuses, the Salon of Rejected Art, where Manet, Whistler, and other artists like them could exhibit their work.

Charity by William Adolphe Bouguereau, 1859

GRANDMA MOSES
(ANNA MARY ROBERTSON MOSES)
(1860–1961)

By the time she was in her seventies, Grandma Moses' arthritis was so bad she could no longer embroider. When she found she could hold a brush, she began to paint.

Anna Mary Robertson was born in Greenwich, New York, the year before Abraham Lincoln became president. She had four sisters and five brothers, and at age twelve she went to work on a neighbor's farm as a hired girl. Fifteen years later she was still there; that year, she married the farm's hired man, Thomas Moses.

The newlyweds bought their own farm in Virginia, and in addition to running the house and raising the children, Anna Mary made her own butter and potato chips, which she sold locally. When she began to paint she turned to her memories of what she called "old timey" life in rural America. She painted scenes of farm work, the excitement of the first snowfall or the first flowers of spring, the pleasures of a big family Thanksgiving.

She had no training in art at all, yet once she started exhibiting her paintings and offering them for sale, she found an enormous audience (and eventually a mentor in Otto Kallier, owner and director of the Galerie St. Etienne in New York).

Grandma Moses' style has been described as naïve, nostalgic, and primitive (in a good way). Even European art critics fell under the spell of her paintings, hailing them as "full of naïve and childlike joy," and exclaiming that they were "adorable."

Moses painted on Masonite, laid atop an old kitchen table, and she painted her pictures from the top down. Once she had an idea, she became lost in her work. "I forget everything," she said, "everything except how things used to be and how to paint it so people will know how we used to live."

At the time of her death, Grandma Moses had completed more than 1,000 paintings, 25 of them during the last year of her life.

Come On Old Topsy by Grandma Moses, 1948

FREDERICK REMINGTON
(1861–1909)

Frederick Remington is renowned as an artist whose works in paint or in bronze captured life in the American Wild West just as it was about to vanish forever. Beginning in the 1880s, he drew illustrations of western and military themes for some of the most popular magazines of his time, including *Harper's Weekly*, *Century*, *Collier's*, and *Boys' Life*. To make his work convincing he traveled out West many times, making sketches, taking photographs, and collecting cowboy, Indian, and pioneer artifacts that he could use as props once he got back to his studio.

Remington did not romanticize the West. He understood that life on the Great Plains was hard, and often cruel. He knew that the Indians' traditional way of life was almost over, and so too was the life of the freewheeling cowboys. This recognition that two cultures were pitted against one another on the frontier, and that his favorite subjects were on the verge of extinction, brought a level of raw tension to Remington's work that does not exist in the work of other American artists, such as George Catlin and Albert Bierstadt, who took the West and its people as their subjects. *Shotgun Hospitality*, for example, shows a cowboy, his shotgun across his lap, as he shares his campfire on a frigid night with three Indians.

In his writings about the West, Remington tended to be utterly conventional: Indians could be noble but were still savages; white soldiers were heroic guardians of the advance of civilization into the wilderness. Very likely, he was writing in the way his audience (and his publishers) expected, because there is no such condescension in his art.

Pony War Dance by Frederick Remington, 1897

Symphony in White No. 2

By James McNeill Whistler

Many Americans have been described as self-made men or women; James McNeill Whistler (1834–1903) was self-invented. He was born in the industrial city of Lowell, Massachusetts; his father was an engineer who specialized in designing railroads. Such a background had no cachet, so Whistler relocated to Europe, where he passed himself off as a cavalier of the Old South, a member of America's plantation aristocracy.

Although his pedigree was a sham, his talent was genuine and extraordinary. In Paris, the greatest artists of the day—Gustave Courbet, Édouard Manet, Edgar Degas—took up Whistler as their protégé. Camille Pissarro proclaimed, "This American is a great artist and the only one of whom America can be justly proud." It was a backhanded compliment to American talent, but Pissarro meant well.

Whistler was a proponent of "art for art's sake." He refused to paint pictures that conveyed a message, taught a moral lesson, or told a story. To emphasize his point he gave his paintings unconventional names: For example, *Arrangement in Grey and Black, No. 1* is better known as *Whistler's Mother*. But Whistler's title tells the viewer what the artist attempted to do in the picture—study shades of grey and black in an eye-catching composition.

Symphony in White, No. 2 (also known as *The Little White Girl*) is Whistler's study of shades of white and cream. The woman holds a fan, the type mass-produced in Japan for the Western market. On the mantelpiece are examples of Japanese porcelain and a spray of pink azaleas such as appears in Asian paintings. These small touches reflect Whistler's interest in Japanese aesthetics.

Algernon Charles Swinburne, moved by the wistful, dreamy expression of the woman, wrote a poem inspired by the painting:

> *Glad, but not flushed with gladness,*
> *Since joys go by;*
> *Sad, but not bent with sadness,*
> *Since sorrows die.*

MAX SCHMITT IN A SINGLE SCULL

By Thomas Eakins

Between 1870 and 1874, Thomas Eakins (1844–1916) went through a "rowing period," when he painted many scenes of racing sculls. Max Schmitt (1843–1900) was a close friend of Eakins and a champion oarsman. Schmitt is pictured on the Schuylkill River in Philadelphia near the Girard Avenue Bridge (seen in the background). As Schmitt had just won a single-scull race, this painting pays tribute to his victory. In fact, the painting is a snapshot in oil of the race. Eakins has set the scene late in an autumn afternoon (Schmitt won the race at 5 p.m. on October 5, 1870). The spot where the scull is positioned is exactly where Schmitt crossed the finish line. The rower in the background, coming in a distant second, is Eakins himself, who enjoyed rowing but was not in the same class as his friend.

Eakins was the artist who would shift the focus of American painting from landscapes to the human figure. In terms of style, H. Barbara Weinberg of the Metropolitan Museum of Art in New York City has described Eakins as "America's greatest, most uncompromising realist." His subjects tended to be friends or members of his family. He favored outdoor scenes, especially athletes in action. His paintings set indoors tend be moody, full of shadows, and populated with quiet women and children.

His interest in realistic depictions of people led him to study human anatomy, and made him perfectly at ease with nudity at a time when nudity, even in art, made most people uncomfortable. In 1886, while lecturing on anatomy before a class of female students, Eakins removed the loincloth of the male model, to better trace the path of a particular muscle. Outraged students and their parents forced Eakins to resign his post at the Pennsylvania Academy.

Piet Mondrian

(1872–1944)

Piet Mondrian was an idea painter, whose art was guided by principles as firmly set in stone as the rules of Academic Art. He saw no purpose for art other than to express beauty, and to achieve that goal, he stripped his paintings down to the two most basic elements—line and color (hence, the blocks of color boxed in by stark black lines).

Early in his career as an artist, Mondrian was breaking out of the mold. His landscapes, dominated by shades of orange and purple, were garish, especially when compared with conventional paintings by his fellow Dutch Impressionists.

It is likely that his inspiration for the boxy style with which he is so closely associated came to him while he was staying on the island of Walcheren. The perfectly flat landscape, relieved only by church steeples, resembles the vertical and horizontal lines of Mondrian's paintings. (From 1908 to 1916, Mondrian visited Walcheren every year.)

The emergence of the style known as Cubism meshed seamlessly with Mondrian's own ideas about the geometric fundamentals of painting. Eventually, he became so disinterested in the conventions of naturalistic painting, he even stopped giving his works titles. He called his paintings "Compositions," and often assigned them a number.

His "grid paintings" became his trademark—stark white canvases, strong black lines, and occasional blocks of pure primary colors—red, yellow, blue—the colors from which all other shades are derived. Contrary to what Mondrian desired, viewers tend to free-associate when viewing his work, seeing a street plan, or a city map, or even a circuit board in Mondrian's paintings.

Composition No. 1, with Red and Black by Piet Mondrian, 1929

AUBREY BEARDSLEY

(1872–1898)

Precocious and often perverse, Aubrey Beardsley was the poster boy for the decadence of late nineteenth-century Europe. By age fifteen he had illustrated the novels *Madame Bovary* and *Manon Lescaut*. At age eighteen he met Oscar Wilde, who invited him to illustrate his play *Salome*.

His style of illustration was based on figures from ancient Greek vase paintings and the abstract patterns of Islamic art. His art is undeniably, unabashedly erotic, often with a sharp sinister cast.

Almost all his works are black-and-white ink drawings (only two oil paintings by Beardsley are known). Swirling lines, grotesque characters, and terrifying women were among his most common motifs. He restrained himself a bit when he illustrated Sir Thomas Malory's *Le Morte d'Arthur*, but Beardsley was incapable of exercising complete control over his wicked imagination. One illustration, "La Beale Isoud at Joyous Gard," portrays an elegant woman in a lovely enclosed garden. But the border around the illustration is a parody of a medieval Book of the Hours: From stylized branches hang oversized pears, each sporting a pair of female breasts with nipples.

Beardsley's illustrations have led to speculation about his sexuality. He was a member of Oscar Wilde's circle of homosexuals, but there was a rumor that he had gotten his elder sister pregnant (she miscarried). Another theory claims that given Beardsley's weak physical condition—he had been dying of tuberculosis most of his life—he was foppish and affected, but ultimately asexual.

In 1897, Beardsley converted to Catholicism (some sources claim his conversion came as early as 1895). In March 1898, he was dying. On his deathbed, fearful of the price he might have to pay for his art in the afterlife, he wrote a note to his publisher. "Jesus is our Lord & Judge. I implore you to destroy all copies of *Lysistrata*....By all that is holy—all obscene drawings." Beardsley's publisher ignored the artist's final request.

Third Tableau Illustration for Das Rheingold by Aubrey Beardsley, 1896

Volga Barge Haulers

By Il'ya Yefimovich Repin

In terms of subject matter, Il'ya Yefimovich Repin (1844–1930) cannot be pigeon-holed. He is often described as a painter whose work advanced the revolution in Russia, but he also painted religious genre paintings, historical paintings, portraits of Leo Tolstoy and Modest Mussorgsky, as well as portraits of the Russian ruling class, including a very fine full-length, full-color sketch of Nicholas II, the last tsar.

Volga Barge Haulers is regarded as his most damning painting of the social order in Russia during the late nineteenth century. Here are eleven desperately poor men, some of them on the verge of physical collapse, performing a job that could be done more efficiently (not to mention humanely) by a team of oxen—that is, haul a barge ashore.

The Russian term for barge haulers is *burlak*, which is also a term used to describe the poorest of the poor. Repin's painting is the type of work of art that troubles the viewer's conscience: The burlaks are dressed in rags, they are dirty and unkempt, the leather straps cut into their chests as they drag the boat, and although they are resigned to this work, some still rebel against the injustice of being used like beasts—especially the man in the reddish rags who looks directly at the viewer.

The light falls directly on the one young man in this team, the only one whose head is lifted up, who tries to adjust his hauling strap. He appears to be the hope of the future, of a Russia when there will be no more burlaks, no more cruel exploitation.

c1873

Proserpine

By Dante Gabriel Rossetti

According to classical mythology, Proserpine, the beloved daughter of Ceres, the goddess of the harvest and all growing things, was abducted by the god of the underworld, Pluto. During her captivity, heartbroken Proserpine ate nothing except four pomegranate seeds. In brokering a deal between Ceres and Pluto, Jupiter, king of the gods, decreed that Proserpine must be released eight months out of the year, but the remaining four months she must return to the underworld.

The model for this painting was Jane Burden Morris, wife of the artist William Morris. Jane was carrying on an adulterous affair with Dante Gabriel Rossetti (1828–1882), and Proserpine's doleful expression may refer to Jane's predicament—trapped in a marriage from which she cannot escape. The pomegranate, then, is the emblem of her captivity.

Rossetti was one of the founding members of the Pre-Raphaelite Brotherhood, an association of artists who took their inspiration from the art and literature of the Middle Ages, and sought to create visual images that recovered the pure, natural style that they believed reached its culmination in the Renaissance master, Raphael.

New pigments came on the market in the mid-nineteenth century that gave artists a new spectrum of fresh, brilliant colors unlike anything that had been available before. The Pre-Raphaelites delighted in these new paints, and to make them even more vibrant, they first painted the entire canvas with bright white paint. This white undercoat made the subsequent layers of color fairly leap off the painted surface, as we see here, particularly in Proserpine's flaming red hair and shimmering dark green gown.

J. C. LEYENDECKER

(1874–1951)

In his teens, Joseph Christian Leyendecker worked by day as an office boy at J. Manz & Co., a Chicago printing house, then took art lessons at night at the Chicago Art Institute. At some point his superiors saw his schoolwork, because at age nineteen they gave Leyendecker the assignment of creating sixty illustrations for a new edition of the Bible the company was planning to publish.

Leyendecker got his first taste of celebrity in 1896 when he won a cover competition sponsored by *Century* magazine (Maxfield Parrish came in second place). The prize brought Leyendecker a steady stream of requests for cover art from such prestigious national magazines as *Collier's* and *The Saturday Evening Post*. His association with the *Post* lasted forty years, during which time he painted 320 covers for the magazine.

Outside of publishing, one of Leyendecker's most successful relationships was with Arrow Shirts. He was the company's favorite illustrator of handsome, full-color ads for their dress collars and dress shirts. The model for the Arrow Shirt Man was the strikingly handsome Charles Beach. Women across the country wrote love letters to the Arrow Shirt Man, but Beach was already in a relationship—with Leyendecker.

Leyendecker's favorite subjects were youthful, active, well-dressed men and women who projected a lifestyle that consumers would envy and want to emulate. It was a method that worked—it sold shirts, socks, magazines, and during World War I and World War II, it sold war bonds.

Leyendecker died of a heart attack in 1951. When his sister and Beach began to clean out the mansion where they had all lived together in New Rochelle, New York, they found hundreds of canvases, the original paintings from which the magazine covers and advertisements had been shot. Most of the canvases were sold at a yard sale, in which original Leyendeckers went for $75 apiece.

Kuppenheimer: Wolfhound by J. C. Leyendecker, ca. 1925

Prima Ballerina

By Edgar Degas

This is a rare scene for Edgar Degas (1834–1917). Generally, he preferred to portray dancers before the performance or the dance lesson begins. He liked the informality of such moments. But in the *Prima Ballerina* (also known as *The Star*), he takes us onstage where a dancer is in the middle of her solo and is performing exquisitely. Actually, given the angle of the scene, we are viewing the dance from above the stage—one of the catwalks where the stage crew managed the lighting, scenery, and curtains. It is a behind-the-scenes view that the audience will never experience, and in that respect this painting is vintage Degas; he used to say that he wanted to "paint life through a keyhole." This predilection for indoor scenes, by the way, set him apart from his fellow Impressionists, who reveled in landscapes.

This is not an oil painting but a pastel, an exquisite drawing made with drawing crayons. We think of crayons as waxy things children use. Pastel crayons are much more sophisticated: They are made of powdered pigments combined with a non-waxy binding agent, usually gum tragacanth in Degas' day; they are closer to chalk than to wax crayons. Like children's crayons, pastels are about the size of a finger, and they snap easily, but the breadth of colors available in pastel crayons and the effects a master such as Degas could achieve with them compensated for their breakability problem.

Ballerinas were one of Degas' obsessions (along with horse races, nudes, and laundrywomen). He painted these subjects again and again, striving each time for perfection. In the *Prima Ballerina*, he may have achieved it.

ca. 1876

POINTILLISM

French painter Georges Seurat (1859–1891) invented Pointillism, an unusual technique in which he arranged tiny dotlike brushstrokes of primary colors on his canvases. By arranging these dots with contrasting colors beside or around them, the artist created an impression of secondary or intermediate colors. Study a pointillist painting up close and you will see the individual dots; then, back away a few steps and the dots of color blend together, as if the viewer's eye were mixing the paints on a palette. And when light strikes the painting, the colors become brilliant and fairly shimmer. It is a lovely technique, but so time-consuming that very few Impressionist or Post-Impressionist painters adopted it (Paul Signac and Henri-Edmond Cross being among the exceptions).

As often happened in the history of art, this innovative method was derided by the critics, who coined the term "pointillism" as an insult.

Typically, painters mix their pigments, then apply them in longish brushstrokes—not in tiny dabs. Pointillism, then, has more in common with commercial color printing that uses miniscule dots of cyan, magenta, yellow, and black to create various shades and hues.

Seurat, like such classic Impressionist masters as Claude Monet, was interested in the play of light in a painting, but while most Impressionist painters also introduced a sense of movement in their paintings, Seurat's figures are motionless, as if he had pushed the freeze-frame button on a DVD player. We see this clearly in his most famous painting, *Sunday Afternoon on the Island of La Grande Jatte*. It is a huge picture—81 inches by 120 inches—that took Seurat two years to complete. By the way, it is also the only masterpiece to inspire a Broadway musical—Stephen Sondheim's *Sunday in the Park with George*.

Sunday Afternoon on the Island of La Grande Jatte by Georges Seurat, 1884–1886

Haida Mask

Among the Haida people from the Pacific Northwest of North America existed secret religious societies that performed dances in which they wore wooden masks or carried wooden puppets that represented *gagiid*, or the spirits of the forest. A *gagiid* mask can be either male or female, it usually has a wrinkled face and a gaping mouth, and the mask tends to be painted bluish-green. Sometimes earrings were added to the mask.

Masks were also worn at potlatches, ceremonial banquets where a family observed a wedding or a funeral with feasting, dancing, and speeches. The culmination of a potlatch came when the host distributed gifts of food and blankets to his guests.

Once Christian missionaries made inroads among the Haida, the secret societies died out and Haida mask-making with them.

The Haida have a very long tradition of woodcarving. Beginning about 2,000 years ago, the Haida made canoes and rattles, carved and painted boxes and chests, and fashioned the equipment and furnishings necessary for a potlatch, and they traded these items with neighboring tribes for food, furs, and other necessities. When sailors, explorers, traders, and settlers arrived in the Pacific Northwest in the 1840s, they were astonished by the high level of craftsmanship of Haida woodcarving. Recognizing that they had a new market, Haida artists began creating pieces for Americans, Canadians, and Europeans. One of the most popular items were Haida masks, which, to meet the demand, the woodcarvers turned out by the thousands. Today, most Haida masks found in private and museum collections were made in the nineteenth century, not for religious rituals but for the tourist trade.

ca. 1880

A Thunder or Spirit Being

By Black Hawk

The winter of 1880–1881 was an especially hard one at the Cheyenne River Reservation in South Dakota. Black Hawk (ca. 1832–1890?), a medicine man of the Sans Arc, or Itazipacola, band of the Lakota people, was responsible for several women and many children, but he had no supplies to get them through the winter. He also had no money, and he would not beg, but his friend, William E. Caton, who ran the trading post at the reservation, knew Black Hawk was a talented artist. The trader offered to buy, for 50 cents each, as many drawings of Lakota life as Black Hawk cared to create. Furthermore, Caton would furnish the paper, colored pencils, and ink for the project.

That winter, Black Hawk produced seventy-seven drawings that he sold to Caton. The early drawings were of supernatural creatures such as the Thunder or Spirit Being on the facing page, which Black Hawk saw in his dreams. Soon he veered away from his dreams and began to record scenes of traditional Lakota life—dances, courtship, the hunt, as well as depictions of horses, buffalo, deer, bighorn sheep, and even prairie dogs.

Black Hawk's drawings fall into a category known as Plains Indians Ledger Art. There was a long tradition among the Plains tribes of painting on buffalo hides. In the last half of the nineteenth century—as buffalo became scarce, but contact with white traders became more frequent—Plains artists switched to paper, often from ledger books (hence the name, "Ledger Art"), and adopted the colored pencils and ink that were also available at trading posts.

William Caton recognized Black Hawk's work as an artistic treasure, and took all seventy-seven drawings to Minneapolis where he had each one properly mounted and bound in a book. The book has survived, intact, to this day. What became of Black Hawk, however, is unknown. It is said that he was killed at the Wounded Knee massacre in 1890, but that report has never been confirmed.

FRANZ MARC
(1880–1916)

One of the gloomiest forms of art is German Expressionism, filled as it is with disturbing, even creepy figures, distorted faces, and contorted bodies. Franz Marc is Expressionism's cheerful, colorful alternative.

Like his colleague, Wassily Kandinsky, Marc agonized over the materialism of late-nineteenth-century society. While Kandinsky felt that recognizable figures must be abandoned in painting because the spiritual could only be communicated through color, Marc believed that some figures did suggest purity—those figures were animals, and most often in Marc's case, horses.

Humankind was tainted by all manner of vices, Marc believed, but animals were pure. He painted animals because he was convinced that just seeing such primal, uncontaminated creatures did the soul good. "An animal's unadulterated awareness of life," Marc said, "made me respond with everything that was good in me."

But if Marc felt that natural creatures were the embodiment of goodness, he felt no obligation to paint them as they were. He assigned certain attributes to certain colors that viewers, who know Marc's method, can use as a guide to "read" his paintings. "Blue is the male principle, astringent and spiritual," Marc wrote. "Yellow is the female principle, gentle, gay and spiritual. Red is matter, brutal and heavy and always the color to be opposed and overcome by the other two."

During World War I, Marc fought for Germany. In 1916, an order came down that renowned artists serving in the army should be kept out of the line of fire. At this time Marc was at the Battle of Verdun. Before that order could be executed, shrapnel from an exploding shell struck him in the head, killing him instantly.

Little Yellow Horses by Franz Marc, 1912

LUNCHEON OF THE BOATING PARTY

By Pierre-Auguste Renoir

In an art movement renowned for its bright, sunny canvases of outdoor life, Pierre-Auguste Renoir's (1841-1919) *Luncheon of the Boating Party* stands alone as the most joy-filled Impressionist painting. This large party of friends—lovely, charming young women, and dashing, athletic young men—have just polished off a fine meal, washed down with goodish amount of French wine. It is a sunny afternoon; they have dined on a balcony overlooking the River Seine. The bright blues, yellows, reds, and whites proclaim that it is summertime, and the informal poses—look at the young man in the foreground on the right, straddling his chair—convey the close friendship of this group.

The light is wonderful. Look at the top of the canvas and see how Renoir has captured the effect of sunlight still making its way through the striped awning. That diffused light reflects off the wine bottles, glasses, and the bare arms of the men and women.

Early in his career as an artist, Renoir imitated the earth tones of Gustave Courbet, but soon he gave them up for bright, cheerful colors. It is impossible to look at a Renoir and not be enchanted by the loveliness of his brilliant but perfectly balanced colors.

Renoir could not bear depressing pictures. "There are quite enough unpleasant things in life without the need for us to manufacture more," he once said. "For me a picture should be a pleasant thing, joyful and pretty—yes, pretty!"

In *Luncheon of the Boating Party,* Renoir has raised "pretty" to the level of masterpiece.

A Bar at the Folies-Bergère

By Édouard Manet

ca. 1881

Édouard Manet was the great innovator of the Impressionist movement. During the 1860s, he conducted a kind of salon for artists at his Paris studio; Edgar Degas, Claude Monet, Alfred Sisley, and Pierre-Auguste Renoir were regulars, and Paul Cezanne and Camille Pissarro stopped by from time to time. Manet's method of painting was *alla prima*, or all at once. Artists from previous decades and centuries had painted in layers, gradually refining their colors, and then adding a glaze to give the painting a smooth surface. Manet wanted to be able to paint from life, whether a landscape or a model posing in his studio, and he wanted to complete the painting in one sitting. One of his shortcuts was the elimination of gradations of color. He selected or mixed the color he wanted, then painted it on the canvas in a largish spot. Manet's fellow Impressionists, Monet especially, modified this technique, reducing Manet's large patches of color to little flecks or dabs.

A Bar at the Folies-Bergère is Manet's final masterpiece. He was dying when he painted it; too weak to go to the Folies-Bergère to paint the concert-hall-and-café from life, he had a bar set up in his studio. He did not completely surrender his standards, however—the young woman behind the bar was a real barmaid, not an artist's model.

The composition is a bit off. Behind the barmaid is a large mirror. In it, on the left, you can see the audience enjoying the evening's entertainment. On the right side of the canvas is a reflection of a gentleman, perhaps placing an order, perhaps chatting up the barmaid. Either way, she seems unimpressed.

This is a portrait of a glittering, colorful, exciting world that Manet loved and was about to leave. He died the following year.

FERNAND LÉGER

(1881–1955)

Cubism was the ideal art movement for Fernand Léger, a man who trained as an architect, but he adapted the style to suit his own predilections. The muddy tans and grays employed by Cubism's purists bored Léger; so did all those rectilinear shapes. He introduced to Cubism a full palette of bright colors, as well as cylinders or similar circular or rounded shapes.

During World War I, Léger served in the French army, where he nearly died in a mustard gas attack. While convalescing he painted *The Card Players*, a scene of robot-like soldiers playing cards inside what appears to be a giant machine.

After the war, Léger painted scenes of working people, but in the Cubist style. He wanted ordinary people, not just art critics and intellectuals, to be able to respond to his paintings.

He was fascinated by the modern, the mechanical, and the newest technologies. After World War I, when the film industry was getting off the ground, Léger worked for a time in the cinema. He designed the laboratory set for Marcel L'Herbier's film, *L'Inhumaine* (*The Inhuman One*), and he collaborated with Man Ray, Dudley Murphy, and George Antheil to produce a movie of his own, *Ballet Mecanique* (*Mechanical Ballet*).

The Constructors, painted in 1950, is emblematic of Léger's interests in architecture, bright colors, ordinary workingmen, and a mechanized society. Although Léger for many years had been interested in creating "art for the people" and portraying the working class, it was not until 1945 that he finally joined the Communist Party.

The Constructors by Fernand Leger, 1950

MADAME X

By John Singer Sargent

At age twenty-seven, John Singer Sargent (1856–1925) was an ambitious American artist in Paris, eager to make a splash in the art capital of the world. He approached a beautiful fellow American, Virginie Avegno Gautreau, a New Orleans heiress who had married a French banker, with an offer to paint her portrait. Madame Gautreau agreed at once, but the portrait progressed slowly: The lady did not like to stand still for any length of time; Sargent couldn't find a pose that suited him. At one point he complained that Madame Gautreau's beauty was "unpaintable." But once he decided to take advantage of the lady's striking profile, he made progress.

With the consent of the Gautreaus, Sargent exhibited the portrait at the Paris Salon of 1884. For discretion's sake he entitled the painting *Madame X*, but it was an empty gesture—everyone in town knew this wealthy, glamorous leader of Parisian society. Besides, the identity of the lady was not the issue.

Critics and art lovers alike savaged the portrait. They ridiculed the turn of Madame Gautreau's right arm, her pallid complexion, her daring décolletage. Worse, Sargent had initially painted one strap hanging off the lady's shoulder, a detail that added a touch of erotic frisson to the portrait, but that also caused an uproar among the Salon's attendees.

Horrified to find themselves at the center of a scandal, the Gautreaus pleaded with Sargent to withdraw the painting. He hoped to mollify his critics by painting the strap back on *Madame X*'s shoulder, but the exhibition committee would not permit him to make any adjustments to his work while the Paris Salon was in progress.

Angry and humiliated, Sargent left Paris for America. Nonetheless, he always considered this portrait to be one of his best.

Shaw Memorial

By Augustus Saint-Gaudens

On May 28, 1863, Bostonians thronged the narrow streets of the old town to cheer as the men of the 54th Massachusetts Volunteer Infantry Regiment marched off to fight for the restoration of the Union and the emancipation of the slaves. The 54th was an all-black regiment, 1,000-men strong, and among its ranks were two sons of Frederick Douglass and a grandson of Sojourner Truth. Leading the regiment was their twenty-five-year-old colonel, Robert Gould Shaw, himself a Boston man. As he rode past his family's home, Shaw saluted his parents and his bride (they had married only a month earlier). About eight weeks later, Shaw and approximately one-third of the men of the 54th Massachusetts would be dead, killed storming Fort Wagner outside Charleston, South Carolina.

Twenty years after Shaw and his men fell in battle, the city of Boston commissioned Augustus Saint-Gaudens (1848–1907) to create a memorial sculpture. In his teens, Saint-Gaudens had begun carving fine cameos; by 1883 he was the most celebrated sculptor in America, the man who had created the pensive *Standing Lincoln* bronze for Chicago's Lincoln Park and the mournful Clover Adams Memorial in Washington, D.C.'s, Rock Creek Cemetery.

Initially Saint-Gaudens had planned an equestrian sculpture of Shaw alone, but Shaw's mother didn't care for it—too pompous, she said. His next inspiration was a bronze relief of Shaw and the men of the 54th. Cast in very high relief (the figure of Shaw on horseback is almost fully rounded), the sculpture has incredible vitality. Led by drummer boys, the soldiers almost rush forward to death and glory. Although the face and pose of each man in the sculpture is individualized, the overall effect is of perfect solidarity. It is one of the most successful, most magnificent public sculptures in America.

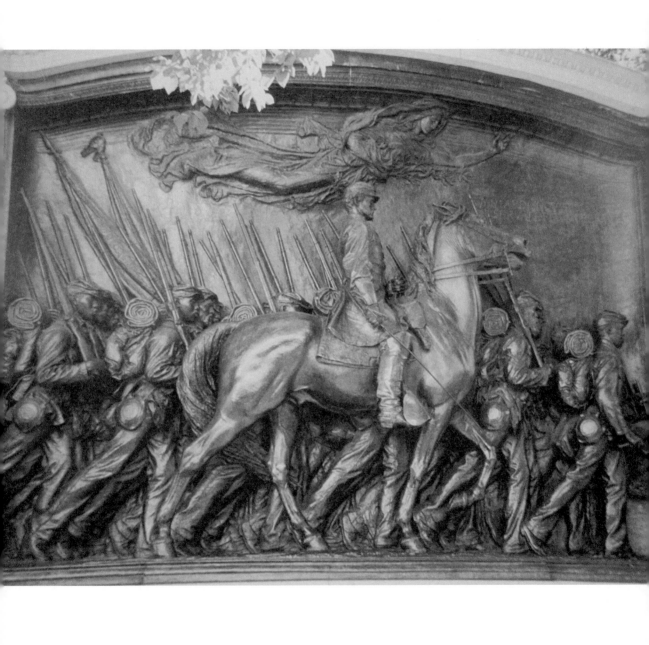

AMADEO MODIGLIANI

(1884–1920)

Although he was Italian and Jewish, African masks were the greatest influence in Amadeo Modigliani's art. Throughout his brief life he would create works that imitated the simple lines and uncomplicated shapes of African art. His sculptures tend to be flat and elongated, and the same masklike faces appear again and again in Modigliani's paintings.

A very handsome young man, many women found Modigliani impossible to resist—and he felt the same way about women. His one-night stands and love affairs, fueled by large quantities of booze and drugs, undermined his precarious health. Since childhood he had suffered from chronic bouts of pneumonia and tuberculosis, and his self-destructive behavior did no good to his damaged lungs. He had to give up stonecarving and woodcarving because it became too strenuous for him; he switched entirely to painting because it did not require intense physical effort.

Most of Modigliani's paintings are of women, and many of these are nudes. He developed a recognizable style—skin painted ochre, long thin nose, almond-shaped eyes, and elongated, gracefully curving neck, with the rest of the body drawn with long, sinuous lines. There is a delicacy, even a gentility, to Modigliani's art that stands in sharp contrast to his wretched private life.

In 1917 in Paris, he had his one and only exhibition of his work, thirty-two paintings and drawings. The show opened and closed on the same day, however, after the chief of police stopped by the gallery and encountered paintings of nudes in which no attempt had been made to conceal or obscure the models' pubic hair.

He fell in love with Jeanne Hébuterne, and together they had two children. But Modigliani could not support his family; he relied on a steady stream of cash gifts from a Polish poet and art dealer, Leopold Zborowski. Given Modigliani's habits, it was never enough. Besides, no amount of money could reverse his health crisis. The final three years of Modigliani's life were nightmarish. He died of tubercular meningitis in a charity hospital. A few days later, Hébuterne (who was nine months' pregnant at the time), threw herself from a fifth-floor window of her parents' house, killing herself and her unborn child.

Young Brunette by Amadeo Modigliani, 1917

THE KISS

By Auguste Rodin

It comes as a surprise that Auguste Rodin (1840–1917) intended this ardent sculpture to be part of his monumental *The Gates of Hell*. Originally, the couple were to represent a pair of thirteenth-century star-crossed lovers, Francesca da Rimini and Paolo Malatesta, who fell in love while reading the story of Lancelot and Guinevere and were killed by the enraged Giovanni Malatesta—Francesca's husband and Paolo's brother. That was Rodin's original intention, but ultimately a loving couple, even an adulterous one, seemed all wrong for *The Gates of Hell*. Rodin kept the sculpture as a stand-alone piece entitled *The Kiss*.

Rodin's lover and, to some extent, collaborator was Camille Claudel (1864–1943), a brilliant sculptor in her own right. It has been said that the couple often worked together on the same piece, although the finished product bore only Rodin's signature. Some biographers believe that Claudel suggested ideas; other biographers contend that Rodin stole his lover's ideas. For fifteen years it was an intense, loving relationship. Rodin broke it off in 1898, which gave Claudel the opportunity to create her own body of work. The rejection, however, preyed on her mind and she went mad.

The woman in *The Kiss* is not in a submissive pose; she is as passionate as the man. Rodin made a bronze version of *The Kiss* that he submitted to the 1893 World's Columbian Exposition in Chicago. The Exposition's jury accepted the piece, but considered it too racy for display in the open where everyone would see it. They installed *The Kiss* in a private gallery where it could be seen only upon request.

Outside Chicago, *The Kiss* proved to be very popular. Rodin created four marble copies, and many copies in bronze.

MARCEL DUCHAMP

(1887–1968)

In 1913, the Armory Show in New York City introduced Americans to the avant-garde art that was sweeping across Europe. Accustomed as Americans were to realistic painting and sculpture, their sudden exposure to nonrepresentational work came as a shock. President Theodore Roosevelt stormed out of the Armory, declaring, "That's not art!" Nonetheless, more than 100,000 people came to the Amory Show. One of the paintings exhibited there was Marcel Duchamp's *Nude Descending a Staircase, No. 2*. Rather than trying to capture a single moment in time in his painting, Duchamp captured *several* moments, as the nude keeps moving down the diagonal of the canvas like a series of stop-action photographs—except there is nothing realistic about this nude.

Duchamp's paintings are no longer shocking, as art lovers have become accustomed to abstract art. His "readymade" art is a different matter and still provokes heated debate. There is the intellectual school of thought that sees Duchamp asking intriguing questions about what is art and what is not art. Others feel that Duchamp was poking fun at the art world's tendency to take itself much too seriously. Even so, if his readymade is supposed to be equivalent to fine art, then the joke has gone too far.

Duchamp's readymades were common objects from everyday life. His first readymade was a bicycle wheel mounted on top of a stool. At least in this instance he actually *made* something, but he also took some common thing, such as a snow shovel, gave it a title (*In Advance of the Broken Arm*, in this case), signed it, and set it up in an art gallery. According to Duchamp, now the utilitarian object was art.

His most notorious piece was the porcelain urinal he entered (under the title *Fountain*) in a show sponsored by the Society of Independent Artists. His colleagues rejected the piece, which was probably exactly what Duchamp wanted, since their reaction revealed just how avant-garde they were willing to be.

Hat Rack and Urinal by Marcel Duchamp, 1915

STARRY NIGHT

By Vincent van Gogh

In May 1889, Vincent van Gogh committed himself to the sanitarium of St. Remy, a former monastery about 20 miles from Arles in the south of France. He had two rooms at the hospital, one of which served as his studio so he could still paint as he tried to recover his peace of mind. He wrote to his brother Theo, "This morning I saw the country from my window a long time before sunrise, with nothing but the morning star, which looked very big." It's possible that the sky van Gogh saw in those hours before dawn became the inspiration for *Starry Night*, the best known and most beloved of the masterworks he painted while at St. Remy.

The scene is dazzling: churning clouds, whirling stars, and a brilliant, golden crescent moon surrounded by a large yellow halo. The drama and movement of the night sky stands in sharp contrast with the serene view of the sleeping village and the gentle pattern of undulating lines in the countryside.

The one point in the landscape almost as full of energy as the sky is the large cypress tree in the foreground, its branches leaping like a flame.

Some critics have observed that, in the nineteenth century, cypress trees were often planted in cemeteries, and so became an emblem of death. There is some question if that is what van Gogh had in mind, because another letter leads us to believe that by painting the cypress he wasn't introducing a solemn note to the scene: "Why, I ask myself, shouldn't the shining dots of the sky be as accessible as the black dots on the map of France? Just as we take the train to get to Tarascon or Rouen, we take death to reach a star."

Vision of the Holy Grail

By Edward Burne-Jones

Many artists of the last years of the nineteenth century were eager to overturn traditional ideas about beauty and break into new forms of self-expression. Edward Burne-Jones was not among them. His art reflected Victorian England's fascination with its past and its self-confidence in the present and the future. He was a Pre-Raphaelite, one of the greatest of that movement, and like his colleagues, studied the masterworks of the Late Gothic and early Renaissance periods. Burne-Jones believed that the sacred, the supernatural world of Christianity, was real; that love was worthwhile even if it brought pain to the lovers; and that suffering could be redemptive. These were values that had their roots in the Middle Ages, and beyond, and that still resonated in the Western world in 1890s. However, these ideals were about to be swept away and derided, which makes Burne-Jones' work even more poignant.

This tapestry, *Vision of the Holy Grail*, is one of a series of six that tell the legend of the Holy Grail, the cup Christ used at the Last Supper and in which Joseph of Arimathea caught drops of the Lord's blood as he hung on the cross. At some point after the twelfth century, the Grail legend merged with the King Arthur legend, and that is the inspiration for Burne-Jones's tapestries. Of the 150 Knights of the Round Table who set out to find the lost Grail, only three were deemed worthy by heaven to see it: Sir Galahad, kneeling at the door; Sir Bors, kneeling some distance behind; and Sir Percival, standing behind Bors.

The design of the tapestries is inspired by medieval tapestries, but not slavishly so. The *mille fleur*, or thousand flowers, motif in the foreground is taken from medieval tapestries. The cutaway of the house so we can see inside, where three angels watch over the Grail, is a convention of medieval art. But the three-dimensionality of the figures, their faces, their gestures, their clothing, are all Pre-Raphaelite.

At the Moulin Rouge: The Dance

By Henri de Toulouse-Lautrec

Henri de Toulouse-Lautrec was a transitional artist whose work looked back to the Impressionists' keen interest in contemporary life, while adopting the new Expressionist ideas about odd shapes and colors. The creepy bluish-green lighting of the dance hall, and the man in the foreground who is walking right out of the canvas are examples of the Expressionists' fascination with the unconventional.

The painting is a slice of Parisian life, specifically the life of Henri de Toulouse-Lautrec (1864–1901). He was a French aristocrat whose stunted growth in childhood gave him a dwarfish appearance as an adult. He never felt at ease among his own class, so he moved down to the opposite end of the social spectrum—the prostitutes, dancers, actresses, and habitués of cafes and nightclubs in Paris's seedier districts. The Moulin Rouge, named for the red windmill perched on its roof, was one of the nightclubs Toulouse-Lautrec frequented.

He liked cabarets, theaters, and brothels because in these places people pretended to be someone or something other than their true selves. When he was at such places, he sketched what he saw; sometime later, some of the people he sketched would appear in one or another of his paintings. The long-legged gentleman dancing, for example, was known as Valentine the Boneless—a nickname that paid tribute to his nimble foot work on the dance floor.

Toulouse-Lautrec was such a fixture at the nightclubs and cabarets that he was hired by the owners to paint advertisements for upcoming performances. Original lithographs of Toulouse-Lautrec's posters are as collectible (and much more affordable) than his oil paintings.

Max Ernst

(1891–1976)

Surrealism encouraged oddball methods among artists, and Max Ernst was among the oddest. He hoped that by tapping into his unconscious he could produce visionary works of art. He tried automatic drawing, in which he just let his hand grasping a pencil wander at will across a sheet of paper, but the results were more of a scribble than a vision.

Still hoping that intuition would guide him, he developed two techniques he called "frottage" and "grattage." Frottage involved laying a sheet of paper on top of a textured surface such as a wooden board or a tangle of twigs and dead leaves, then drawing the bumps they created on the paper. For grattage, Ernst scraped layers of dry paint off a canvas, hoping that it would produce an interesting outcome.

For a time he believed he had a spirit guide, a green bird named Loplop, who materialized from the artist's unconscious, bringing him the inspiration he longed for. Often these visits from Loplop generated nightmarish visions such as *The Robing of the Bride*, in which a nude female with the head of an owl is draped in red.

He found a friend (and for a brief time, a wife) in Peggy Guggenheim, the American heiress and patron of many artists of the twentieth century. Their marriage lasted only four or five years, but Guggenheim continued to encourage Ernst, buying many of his paintings for her private collection, housed today in her palazzo on Venice's Grand Canal.

Night Fish by Max Ernst, 1972

ERTÉ

(1892–1990)

In St. Petersburg, where he was born, this artist's name was Roman Petrov de Tyrtov. Outside of Russia he called himself Romain de Tirtoff, or R. T.—pronounced *Er Té* in French. He came from a distinguished family—his father was an admiral in the Tsar's fleet. While still in his teens, Erté defied family tradition, announcing he would not attend naval college but study design instead.

Erté's work epitomized the glamour and sophistication of Art Deco. Fashion magazines, stage companies, and movie studios clamored for him. He was able to transfer his idea about art into lavish stage sets and costumes; his clients included the Ziegfeld Follies, the Follies Bergere, and the Hollywood mogul Louis B. Mayer, who put him to work designing sets and costumes for the 1925 silent-film version of *Ben-Hur*. His drawings for costumes, sets, and scenes as he imagined they would (or should) appear in various films have become a favorite with collectors. These sleek, bold images are reproduced as prints, posters, greeting cards, and of course on coffee mugs and T-shirts.

In 1976, he produced an *Alphabet Suite* and *Numeral Suite* in which letters and numbers are produced by (mostly nude) figures of men and women twisted into unabashedly erotic positions.

His taste ran to the exotic and outrageous. In many of his illustrations, women wear long sleeves that drape down to the ground—it is one of Erté's trademark design motifs.

Erté's designs did not imitate much found in nature, and he intended it that way. "Look at me," he once said, "I'm in another world—a dream world that invites oblivion."

Adoration by Erté, 1986

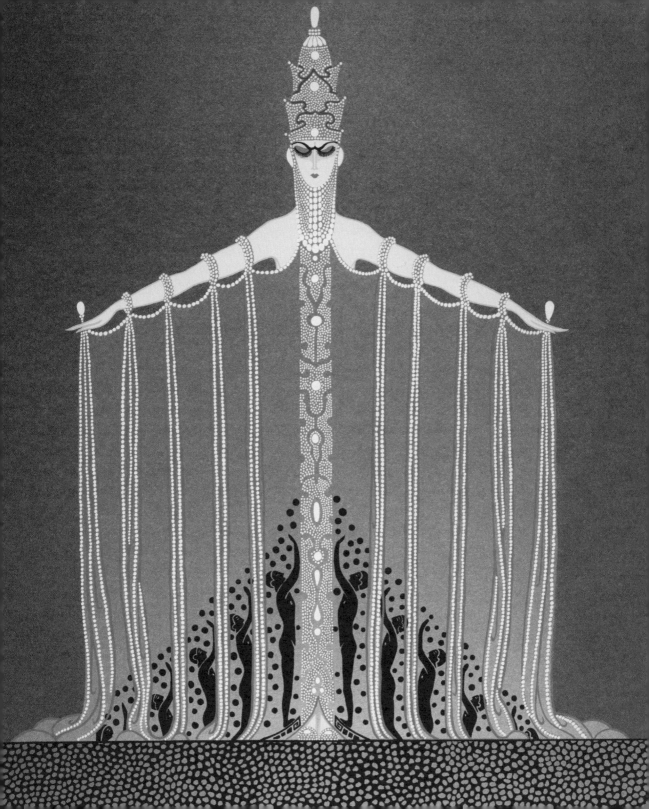

Peacock Window

By John La Farge

In his stained glass windows, John La Farge (1835-1910) combined his near-comprehensive command of religious imagery with his admiration for Renaissance art. He also showcased his understanding of the new effects of light and color, made possible by the development of opalescent glass, which is pressed rather than blown and has a cloudy, sometimes veined appearance like marble. For the *Peacock Window*, however, La Farge employed a much more difficult technique—*cloisonné*, or fused, glass.

In Early Christian iconography, the peacock is the symbol of immortality, which explains why La Farge's bird is more magnificent than any real-life peacock. Shades of gold are the dominant colors of the bird's plumage, accented with blues and greens for the eyes of the tail feathers. The peacock is perched on the limb of a peony tree, its blossoms in full flower. Below flows a quiet stream. Beyond the bird is a twilight sky rendered in dark purples and blues.

Some of the glass is held in place with thick strips of lead—the traditional medium in a stained glass window. But La Farge has used thin threads of copper for the composition of the peacock. In the same way, the glass of the flowers, the stream, and the sky is thick, while the glass used for the bird is thin and transparent. This delicacy, combined with the colors of the peacock, gives it a jewel-like quality.

The *Peacock Window* is one of La Farge's final works and represents his attempt, toward the end of his life, to develop new types of stained glass. As splendid as this window is, La Farge was not happy with it—he believed that even after repeated firings in his kiln, the *cloisonné* glass had not fused perfectly.

THE BATH

By Mary Cassatt

Mary Cassatt (1844–1926) enjoys the distinction of being the only American and the only woman welcomed into the circle of the original French Impressionists, a group that included Édouard Manet, Edgar Degas, Claude Monet, and Camille Pissarro. She developed an especially close friendship with Pissarro, who taught her how to draw and paint in the Impressionist manner. She once said of her friend, "He could have taught stones how to draw correctly."

Mothers and children were Cassatt's favorite subject, and one that she never idealized. Close observation of mothers caring for their children had taught her that, in addition to an unbreakable, loving bond, motherhood involved a high degree of responsibility, as well as moments of sheer drudgery. *The Bath* conveys all those facets of motherhood. With one hand the mother holds her child firmly in her lap; with the other she washes the child's foot. Washing in a basin is inefficient, and messy. The odds are very good that the bath will end with puddles on the floor. But the task is necessary, and the mother performs it with love.

This painting's from-the-top-down perspective is something Cassatt borrowed from Japanese woodblock prints, which were popular in late nineteenth-century France. Many of these Japanese prints portrayed women going about their daily routine, which would have reinforced Cassatt's own interest in mother-and-child scenes.

In terms of composition, Cassatt contrasts round shapes—the basin, the pitcher, and the chubby arms, legs, torso, and head of the child—with the vertical stripes of the mother's dress. A sweet touch is the reflection of the mother and child in the basin of water.

THE SCREAM

By Edvard Munch

Like the *Mona Lisa*, Edvard Munch's (1863–1944) *The Scream* is one of those paintings everyone knows. It is so familiar that it has been endlessly parodied in everything from cartoons to the iconic shot of the child actor Macauley Culkin in the hit movie *Home Alone*.

Munch tells us how the idea for the painting came to him. He was walking with friends outside Norway's capital, Christiania (now Oslo). "I was walking along a road with two friends," he recalled. "On one side lay the town, below me the fjord. I felt tired and sick. The sun was setting and the clouds turned red as blood. I sensed a scream passing through nature. I felt as though I could actually hear the scream."

Whether Munch was in the throes of a panic attack, a case of agoraphobia, or a hallucination brought on by excessive drinking, the painting that resulted from his experience still shrieks at us. The colors are shrill and garish, painted in heaving bands like sound waves.

The Scream is not unique in Munch's body of work. Many of his paintings are steeped in anxiety if not outright trauma, including such unsettling works as *Madonna* (who looks more like a vampire than the Virgin Mary) and *Dead Mother*, which portrays a shocked little girl standing at her mother's deathbed.

Munch's paintings emerge from the Symbolist movement in art, which looked to ancient mythology and the images from dreams to represent truths about the soul and the psyche. Munch felt *The Scream* captured his own turbulent mental condition: On the back of his painting, he wrote, "Could only have been painted by a madman."

1893

ART NOUVEAU

By the late nineteenth century, factories in Europe and the United States could mass-produce just about anything. Factory-made items were functional, of course, and most were inexpensive, but they were not attractive. The Art Nouveau (or New Art) style rose in reaction to the bland functionality of industrial-made goods.

The fine arts—painting and sculpture—were not influenced in any significant way by Art Nouveau. But the decorative arts, graphic arts, and architecture took up the new style enthusiastically.

It began in Belgium where two architects, Henry Van de Velde (1863–1957) and Victor Horta (1861–1940), designed building interiors characterized by ornate, asymmetrical patterns. Everything from staircase railings to window frames was reimagined into wild arabesques or undulating curves. For this reason Art Nouveau was known originally as *le style Belge* (the Belgian style).

The craze for the curvaceous lines of Art Nouveau swept the Western world, with everything from furniture to advertising posters to subway stations and even public toilets designed in the new style. The guiding principle of Art Nouveau was that art should be everywhere. In keeping with that dictum, Louis Comfort Tiffany produced table lamps that were works of art, as well as visually stunning stained glass windows unlike anything ever before seen inside a church. René Jules Lalique created exquisite glass perfume bottles, vases (such as the Tulipes vase on the facing page), chandeliers, and even sublime hood ornaments for automobiles.

There was Art Nouveau pottery, tableware, furniture, posters, illustrated books, jewelry, clocks, and porcelain figurines. With such a wide range of items in the new style, almost everyone could afford something Art Nouveau. It was high-quality decorative art for the masses.

Tulipes by René Jules Lalique

WHERE DO WE COME FROM? WHAT ARE WE? WHERE ARE WE GOING?

By Paul Gauguin

Paul Gauguin (1848–1903), a successful French stockbroker with a wife and five children, did not start painting until he was an adult. He had a natural talent, however, that was recognized and encouraged by Camille Pissarro, Vincent van Gogh, and Claude Monet. As he became more interested in painting, he longed for subjects that would capture the primitive essence of humankind. "[Europe] is artificial and conventional," he complained. "In order to do something new we must go back to the source, to humanity in its infancy." He believed he would find an unspoiled world in Tahiti, so he left his job, his wife, and his children for the South Pacific.

Tahiti was not the earthly paradise he had expected. Gauguin forgot that Tahiti was a French colony. Consequently, the island was filled with Europeans—colonial administrators, missionaries, and expatriates like himself searching for an easy life. He stayed anyway, and began to paint in a style similar to traditional Polynesian art.

Gauguin said *Where Do We Come From? What Are We? Where Are We Going?* should be read from right to left: The baby on the ground represents the carefree days of childhood; the group in the center represents the busy-ness of adult life; and the elderly woman at the far left represents resignation at the coming of death. The blue idol, Gauguin said, was an emblem of "the Beyond."

True to his Impressionist roots, Gauguin painted this large canvas in thick brushstrokes using vivid colors. Typical of Gauguin's personal style, the landscape in the background resembles nothing in the real world, and he has not bothered with the laws of perspective. He did these things consciously, as part of his effort to recapture the vitality of primitive art. He said, "To me barbarism is a rejuvenation."

Tamara de Lempicka

(1898–1980)

This wealthy Polish socialite invented the sexy side of Cubism. Tamara de Lempicka adopted the sharp lines and angles that fascinated the Cubists, but they were not the focus of her paintings. Instead, they added precision to her portraits of glamorous women and sophisticated men. De Lempicka's paintings reflected her interests—wealth, beauty, elegance, and sexuality.

De Lempicka's friends and acquaintances included European royalty, émigré Russian aristocrats, Hollywood stars, and great artists such as Pablo Picasso, Georgia O'Keeffe, and Willem de Kooning. Many of her paintings were portraits of her friends. In the 1920s, she was in such demand that she could charge 50,000 French francs for a portrait—or about $200,000 in modern American dollars. In 1929, she painted her self-portrait, *Tamara in the Green Bugatti*. Years later her daughter, Kizette, said that this painting captures how her mother saw herself, "Her hands are gloved, she is helmeted, and inaccessible; a cold and disturbing beauty."

While she borrowed ideas from the Cubists and the Art Deco movement, ultimately de Lempicka's style was uniquely her own, and she had complete confidence in what she was doing. She did not care for the Impressionists, whom she thought were inept draughtsmen; she derided Braque for painting with "dirty" colors; and as for her friend Picasso, his paintings "embodied the novelty of destruction."

Years before anyone else in her social circle, de Lempicka realized that another world war was coming. She convinced her second husband, Baron Raoul Kuffner, to sell off his estates in Eastern Europe, deposit the proceeds in a Swiss bank, and move with her to America. They settled in Beverly Hills, where de Lempicka welcomed to her home and studio the closest thing America had to aristocracy—movie stars. Tyrone Power and George Sanders were her close friends.

Her final years were not happy. She did not understand or approve of the social upheavals of the 1960s and 1970s. She retired to Mexico, where she found a home among a community of aging jet-setters and young aristocrats. She died there at age eighty-two in 1980.

Young Girl in Green by Tamara de Lempicka, 1930

POLACCA POLYCHROME CANTEEN

By Iris Nampeyo

Beginning in 1883, Dr. Joshua Miller settled in Arizona where he spent a good deal of time traveling to pueblos to treat the Hopi Indians. One of his patients was a renowned potter, Iris Nampeyo (ca. 1860–1942), whom he treated for trachoma, an eye condition. As a token of gratitude and friendship, Nampeyo made this splendid pottery canteen for the doctor.

In her own language, Nampeyo's name was Num-pa-yu, which means "snake that does not bite." While she was still an infant, her family also gave her an English name, Iris. Nampeyo's grandmother taught her the art of making pottery, and by the time she was in her teens, she was bringing in a steady flow of cash thanks to her sales at the trading post operated by Thomas Keam. Because of his encounters with artists such as Nampeyo, Keam became an ardent collector of Native American artwork and artifacts.

Nampeyo became interested in reviving the traditional shapes and decoration of ancient Hopi pottery, but very few examples survived. An archaeologist working in the area, J. Walter Fewkes, learned of Nampeyo's interest and began bringing her shards of pottery he excavated at Sityaki, a Hopi site occupied from the fourteenth to the seventeenth centuries. The Hopi of Sityaki polychromed their pottery, which inspired Nampeyo's decoration of this canteen.

Iris Nampeyo's descendants continue to make pottery, although they often put a contemporary spin on the Hopis' traditional shapes.

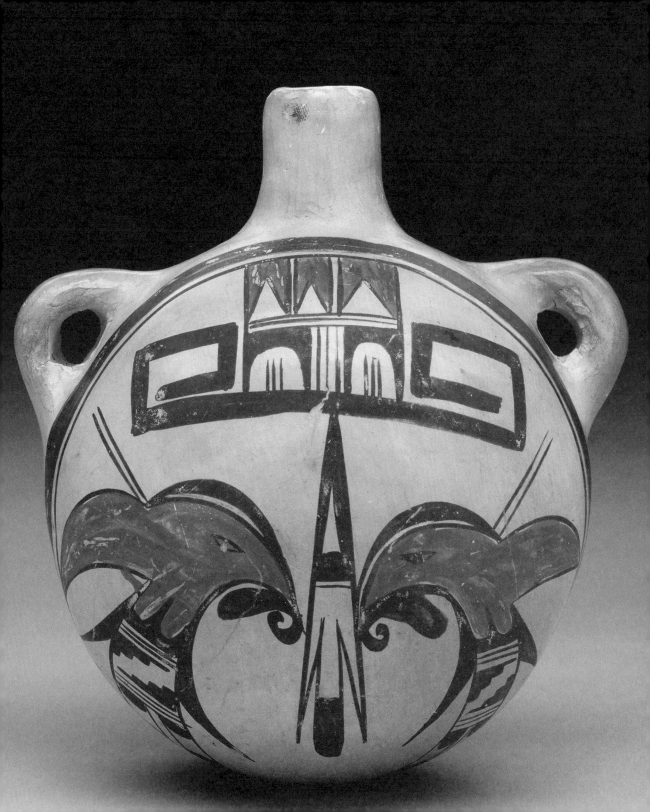

Park Guell Mosaics

By Antoni Gaudí

At the end of the nineteenth century, Count Eusebi Guell planned to convert a bare Barcelona hilltop into a luxury housing development. When the count's plans to make a fortune in real estate flopped, the mountain became a municipal park, with architectural elements designed by Barcelona's most fantastical artist, Antoni Gaudí (1852–1926). Technically, Gaudí could be described as an Art Nouveau artist, but his style is so entirely his own that he has always been difficult to categorize. Initially, Gaudí's intensely original style put off many of his fellow architects; his only patron at this time was Count Guell, which explains how Gaudí became involved in turning an unsuccessful housing project into a park that has become an international destination.

Gaudí designed huge bird's-nest-shaped planters and colonnaded walkways where the stone columns have the appearance of trunks of palm trees, but the park's main draw is the ceramic mosaics. Gaudí designed a long, serpentine bench, its back covered in a riot of colorful mosaics. As the bench curves around, it forms several little conversation areas.

Cubes of colored glass were used to create Byzantine mosaics, but Gaudí used broken pottery, old tiles, and broken stones. The overall effect is of brilliant color, like the classic *azuelejo* ceramics of Spain and Portugal. However, the energy of these mosaics is twentieth-century, and the barely controlled style could only be Gaudí.

A grand staircase, completely covered with mosaics in shades of white, cream, and ivory, leads up to a terrace. Guarding the staircase is a large multicolored mosaic dragon, one of the best-loved art treasures in Barcelona.

Ceramic Tile by Antoni Gaudí

THE WISTERIA LAMP

By Louis Comfort Tiffany

The genius of American designer Louis Comfort Tiffany (1848–1933) was his ability to capture the Art Nouveau style in works that combined superb artistry with the latest technology. At the beginning of the twentieth century, as more and more homes were wired for electrical light, Tiffany believed there was a market for beautiful table lamps. He had already designed stunning stained glass windows; now he would make exquisite lamp shades from the same material.

The Wisteria Lamp is one of Tiffany's masterpieces. Everyone notices, of course, the beauty of those cascading pieces of stained glass, but the genius of Tiffany as a designer was taking what was essential to the construction of the shade—the leading that holds the bits of glass in place—and shaping them so that they contribute to the overall design. Then, he cast the bronze lamp stand as the trunk and roots of a wisteria vine.

We speak of Tiffany as an artist, but he thought of himself as a craftsman. "Craftsmen," he said, "are nearer the people, for they fabricate useful objects belonging to daily life, while the artist who produces objects of the fine arts, so called, is more remote." True to his philosophy, Tiffany designed a wide range of decorative items, most of which were within reach of the typical American middle-class budget. By 1906, his studio offered shoppers more than 125 glass lamp shade designs, ensuring that almost every family could afford to light up their home with something beautiful from Tiffany.

ca. 1902

MONT SAINTE-VICTOIRE

By Paul Cezanne

The airy, ethereal quality of Impressionist paintings that most museum-goers find so appealing troubled Paul Cezanne (1839–1906). He came to believe that Impressionism ought to be a more substantial style, in the tradition of the Old Masters. "I wanted to make of Impressionism something solid and enduring," he explained, "like the art in museums."

Cezanne abandoned the little dabs of color favored by many Impressionists and began building his scenes with blocks of color. To underscore his new interest in the substantial, he chose to paint, not delicate water lilies floating in a still pool, but a mountain. After all, what could be more solid, more permanent than a mountain? The one he chose, Mont Sainte-Victoire, was very familiar to him; it rises near Aix-en-Provence where Cezanne was born. Cezanne painted this mountain more than sixty times.

This version, painted toward the end of his life, demonstrates Cezanne's technique. There is geometry at work here, with blocks or cubes of color arranged atop and beside each other, sometimes set at angles to give the scene a little more three-dimensionality (for example, the cluster of buildings at the lower part of the painting).

The colors, like the scene, build in the same way a child builds with wooden blocks—from dark shades of greens offset with blocks of orange and red, up the sides of the mountain to the sky, where whites, grays, blues, and purples dominate. The wonder of this painting is not only its solidity (which gives us a foretaste of Cubism), but also the harmony of the colors.

Fauvism

While touring Paris's Autumn Salon of 1905, art critic Louis Vauxcelles wandered into a gallery where he found a classical sculpture standing on a pedestal. On the walls were paintings by Henri Matisse (1869–1954), André Derain (1880–1954), and Georges Rouault (1871–1958) whose wild, uncontrolled use of color—red trees, purple faces—shocked the poor man. Noting the contrast between the traditional sculpture and the avant-garde paintings, Vauxcelles said, "Donatello parmi les fauves," or "A Donatello surrounded by savage beasts." That's how the term *Fauvism* was born.

There is a touch of the wild beast to these paintings, insofar as the garish colors attack the senses. Matisse, Derain, and their peers were experimenting with clashing colors and flattened perspective. For the sake of self-expression they were taking a new technique to its logical extreme. Since there was no political or social or psychological theory behind Fauvism, it did not last long. In three years, the Fauvists had taken riotous colors as far as they could go.

The idea of painting with pure colors was first suggested by Gustave Moreau, a controversial artist who taught at Paris's École des Beaux-Arts. Matisse and Rouault were among his students; as Matisse recalled later, "[Moreau] did not set us on the right roads, but off the roads. He disturbed our complacency."

Derain's *Turning Road* would disturb anyone's complacency. Yet if the colors are out of control, the composition is balanced and more or less restrained: The curve of the road, the swaying of the trees, and the rushing movement of the villagers all give the painting coherence.

The Turning Road by Andre Derain, 1906

THE HUNGRY LION THROWS ITSELF ON THE ANTELOPE

By Henri Rousseau

Henri Rousseau (1844–1910) modeled his lion and antelope on an example of the taxidermist's art displayed at the Jardin des Plantes, a combination botanical garden, natural history museum, and zoo in Paris. Rousseau was a frequent visitor to the Jardin, which accounts for the lush (if stylized) jungle and cruel (yet also cuddly) wild beasts in this painting.

When he first displayed this work at the Autumn Salon of 1905, Rousseau provided a caption: "The hungry lion throws itself upon the antelope, devours him; anxiously the panther awaits the moment that he too can claim his share. Birds of prey have torn a strip of flesh from the poor animal that is shedding a tear!" It is interesting to recall that the Autumn Salon art show gave rise to the term "Fauvism," or art of savage beasts, in reference to the work of Matisse and Derain among others. Rousseau, however, was not a Fauvist, yet his painting is truly savage.

Rousseau's style is described as Naïve, or Primitive (in the sense of uncomplicated rather than crude). While today he enjoys a reputation for charming composition and lovely use of color, in his own day he suffered ridicule from the art critics and the gallery-going public, who dismissed his work as childish. The mockery stung, for Rousseau longed for acceptance and recognition. It was some consolation that Pablo Picasso, Paul Signac, and Constantin Brancusi admired his work and offered him their friendship, but Rousseau never won the acclaim he hoped for.

When he died, only seven friends came to his funeral, among them Brancusi and Signac, and the poet Guillaume Apollinaire, who wrote his epitaph, promising to smuggle into Heaven "brushes paints and canvas / That you may spend your sacred leisure in the / light of truth Painting."

LES DEMOISELLES D'AVIGNON

By Pablo Picasso

When Gertrude Stein viewed this painting for the first time, she exclaimed that it was "a veritable cataclysm." She meant that in a good way, and art critics and art lovers ever since have regarded *Les Demoiselles d'Avignon* as a milestone, one of the most influential works in the history of modernist art.

The painting reveals two primary influences: the rising style known as Cubism that Pablo Picasso (1881–1973) and Georges Braque would champion, and African and Oceanic masks. In fact, it was *Les Demoiselles* that brought Picasso and Braque together—once he saw it, Braque realized that he and Picasso shared similar ideas about the possibilities of Cubism. Cubism pared images down to basic geometric shapes—and certainly the five women in the painting appear to be made almost entirely of sharp angles.

Picasso had a few masks from Africa and Oceania in his studio. He admired their vitality but was fascinated by what he considered their brutality. That spirit comes through in the painting, too—where a nineteenth-century Romantic painter might have shown five lovely women lounging on the grass, Picasso gives us five bold women exposing themselves and indifferent to if anyone is looking. In fact, the five demoiselles are prostitutes, and Picasso's original, deliberately provocative title for the painting was *The Philosophical Brothel*. (Avignon Street in Barcelona, Picasso's hometown, was notorious for its brothels.)

Some art critics have seen other influences in the painting, including El Greco's almost surreal painting of the Apocalypse, *Opening of the Fifth Seal*, and Cezanne's *Les Grandes Baigneuses*.

Picasso used heavy globs of paint that he spread across the canvas in thick, fast, slashing brushstrokes. One critic, Pierre Daix, described them as "vehement," which certainly conveys that fierce vitality Picasso admired in the masks.

CUBISM

Following the advice of Paul Cezanne literally, Pablo Picasso and Georges Braque began breaking down the subjects of their paintings "in terms of the cylinder, the sphere, and the cone." In 1908, Braque exhibited some of these paintings; in his review of the exhibition, art critic Louis Vauxcelles complained, "Braque scorns form and reduces everything, sites, figures and houses, to geometric schemas and cubes."

In spite of the grumbling of the critics, Braque and Picasso kept experimenting with this new style. The paintings from their next phase were of skewed planes with sharp edges sliding into or away from each other. They abandoned any attempt to give their paintings depth, or to suggest three-dimensionality. And they even gave up the use of color—all the paintings from this period of Cubism were done in an unappealing grayish tan.

Having mastered the geometric or abstract possibilities of Cubism, Braque and Picasso began playing with the concept, introducing unexpected elements to their paintings such as enigmatic musical notes or incomplete words. Having given up perspective, they gave their paintings texture by applying sand to the wet paint.

By 1912, the Cubists were using color again, and they were making paper collages. Sometimes they used fragments of newspaper; in other instances they used art paper to create a collage that looked like polished marble or the grain of fine wood.

By 1914, Picasso was losing interest in Cubism, but Braque, joined now by Henri Matisse and Fernand Leger, among others, kept testing the possibilities of the style into the 1920s.

Woman Playing a Guitar by Georges Braque, 1913

The Kiss

By Gustav Klimt

Two essential influences in the style of Austrian artist Gustav Klimt (1862–1918) were a Scottish artist, Margaret Macdonald, who incorporated semiprecious stones into her work, and the gold background of the Byzantine mosaics of Ravenna and St. Mark's Basilica in Venice, which Klimt visited in 1903. These sources are the origin of the gold and jewel-like colors of Klimt's paintings.

For *The Kiss*, Klimt drew upon a third source, Friedrich Schiller's 1785 poem, "Ode to Joy," which Beethoven incorporated into his Ninth Symphony. "Be embraced, millions!" Schiller wrote. "This kiss to the entire world!" Intimate, erotic, yet very tender, the link to Schiller's poem and Beethoven's symphony gives *The Kiss* a cosmic dimension.

The woman wears a gown covered with colorful circles within circles; stark dark rectangles cover the man's robe, yet they are both enfolded in a golden cloak that unites them. The man is already lost in the kiss, while the woman has turned her face away, as if she were still considering her options before she surrenders completely to sexual passion. This is a romantic piece but with a degree of tension to it—the couple hasn't slipped into ecstasy yet.

The man's face is obscured, but we see the woman from head to toe. Klimt worshipped women: He glorified female sexuality; he reveled in their power over men. And so he shows this woman completely, kneeling upright on a ground thick with flowers and golden vines, dressed in a glorious gown, wearing flowers in her hair, and undecided what she will do next, because she has not yet returned the kiss.

ASHCAN SCHOOL

From time to time you'll encounter an art book that refers to this style of painting as "New York Realism," but "the Ashcan School" is far more common. The name was coined by a New York art critic who was repulsed by the artists' choice of subject matter: interiors of grimy saloons or crowded street scenes in a neighborhood of dilapidated tenements. The leader of the movement was Robert Henri, an artist who rejected the polished, restrained style of Academic paintings in favor of art that was emotionally unrestrained. His fellow Ashcan artists were John Sloan, Everett Shinn, William Glackens, George Luks, Ernest Lawson, Maurice Prendergast, and Symbolist Arthur B. Davies. One New York journalist called them simply "the Eight," but they were also known in some art circles as "the Apostles of Ugliness."

The Ashcan artists' style itself didn't bother art critics—they weren't much more radical than Thomas Eakins. It was their subject matter that bothered their critics. Portraits of the urban poor and views down an alley made viewers uncomfortable. Even worse perhaps was George Bellow's dramatically lit boxing scene, *Stag at Sharkey's*: This is no portrayal of the manly art of pugilistics; this is a slugfest.

Jacob Riis is often listed as a member of the Ashcan School even though he used photography to capture urban life. But while most people derided Ashcan paintings, Riis's heartrending photographs, especially of orphaned or abandoned street kids, galvanized the social reform movement in early twentieth-century America.

For a time Edward Hopper was affiliated with the Ashcan School. In fact, his most famous painting, *Nighthawks*, could be considered a classic Ashcan scene.

Wet Night on the Bowery by John Sloan, 1911

Danse II

By Henri Matisse

Like other artists of the Fauve school of art, Henri Matisse (1869–1954) reveled in bright colors. His figures look like they have been cut out of sheets of colored tissue paper (something he would, in fact, do later in his career). But if Matisse was a "beast" (*fauve* is French for wild beast), he was a very happy one. Few paintings of the twentieth century are so suffused with joy as the works of Matisse. He once wrote, "What I dream of is an art . . . devoid of troubling or depressing subject matter."

In March 1909, a wealthy Russian businessman, Sergei Shchukin, commissioned Matisse to paint two large canvases for his home, the Trubetskoy Palace in St. Petersburg. Dance was to be the theme of one painting and Music the theme of the other. An early color sketch for Dance (known as *Danse I*) is part of the collection of the Museum of Modern Art in New York City. The pair of Shchukin paintings is still in St. Petersburg, at the Hermitage Museum.

Danse II is exuberant, with five nudes cavorting in the open air—one of whom has literally been danced off her feet. The painting is in Matisse's classic and easily recognizable style: solid blocks of vivid color with little or no shading; flattened perspective (although in this case he has rounded out the dancers a bit); and nudes at play.

At first glance the painting seems so simple (and in many ways it is), but Matisse's basic-but-beautiful drawing of the dancers, along with their joyous body language, result in a work that is wonderfully expressive. And when you consider that the canvas measures approximately 8.5 feet by 13 feet, the visual impact of seeing it live must be forceful.

FUTURISM

Futurism, the art movement, was founded by an Italian poet, Filippo Tommaso Marinetti (1876–1944), who believed he understood the central feature of twentieth-century life. In his "Futurist Manifesto," published in 1909 in the Paris newspaper *Le Figaro*, Marinetti said, "We declare that the splendor of the world has been enriched by a new beauty: the beauty of speed. . . . All subjects previously used [in art] must be swept aside in order to express our whirling life of steel, pride, of fever, and of speed."

In addition to an addiction to the whirling pace of modern life and the excitement of new technologies, the Futurists espoused the total destruction of anything that smacked of tradition and the past—marriage, religion, art museums, and so on. Or, as Marinetti put it, "We rebel against that spineless worshipping of old canvases, old statues and old bric-a-brac, against everything which is filthy and worm-ridden and corroded by time."

It came as a surprise to no one that much of Futurist art not only appeared to be careening along at 100 miles per hour, but was also intensely violent. A classic example is Carlo Carra's *Funeral of the Anarchist Galli,* which portrays a riot that broke out between the mourners and the police.

Carra's *Leaving the Theater* is not aggressive, but it is damning. Theater-going, of course, is the kind of passive, old-fashioned entertainment the Futurists' scorned. The theater patrons, therefore, are wrapped up like shrouded corpses. In the rear, a black carriage drives away—another funereal symbol. And the blizzard itself is nature's way of cooperating with Futurists by burying the old world.

Futurism as a distinct art movement did not last long, largely because it was more a rant than an idea. In the 1920s, many former Futurists shifted from art to politics, joining the fascist movements that sprang up in Europe at the time.

Leaving the Theater by Carlo Carra, 1909

I AND THE VILLAGE

By Marc Chagall

The artist, a Hasidic Jew from the village of Vitebsk in Belarus, was born Moishe Segal. When he emigrated to Paris he attempted to play down his Jewish identity by changing his name to Marc Chagall (1887–1985). His name may have been French, but his subject matter and his symbols were still Jewish. His surreal paintings of life in a *shtetl*, the Yiddish term for a Jewish village in Central or Eastern Europe, are imbued with nostalgia—Chagall's paintings are probably the only ones that are both surreal *and* sentimental.

The two major images in this painting are the head of a goat and the face (painted green) of a villager. They are positioned near to one another; their expressions convey affection and friendship because, in a rural village, people and animals live in close proximity and are dependent upon each other.

The odd angles of the painting come from Cubism; the scene of the village woman milking a goat, painted upon the cheek of the big goat, is a foretaste of Surrealism. A Jewish villager with a scythe over his shoulder walks through a village dominated by an Orthodox church. A small cross dangles from a chain around the neck of the green-faced man, who also grasps a miniature Burning Bush, through which God first spoke to Moses, between his thumb and index finger. These disparate elements suggest that Jews and Christians, like people and goats, lived together at Vitebsk, and perhaps they were interdependent, too. It is harder to make sense of the two upside-down houses, and the upside-down woman in the farmer's path. It is part of the whimsical nature of Chagall's paintings. He once said, "For me a painting is a surface covered with representations of things…in which logic [has] no importance."

SELF-PORTRAIT

By Egon Schiele

The art movement known as Expressionism comes from the artist's goal to express the emotions stirred up by looking at a particular person, object, or scene. Expressionists did not want viewers to be detached judges; they wanted them to be emotionally engaged by works of art. To get this powerful reaction, Expressionists painted in ways that ranged from the vivid to the vile. Eager to shock, the Expressionists distorted their subjects, often to the point of grotesquerie.

Expressionism flourished through most of the twentieth century. The series of calamities that took place during the early years of the movement—World War I, the Russian Revolution, the flu pandemic—confirmed the Expressionists in their belief that the world was a hellish place full of awful people.

Austrian painter Egon Schiele (1890–1918) was the bad boy of the early Expressionist movement. His paintings are just brimming over with anxiety, frustrated sexuality, and what today we might call self-esteem issues. He painted himself many, many times, almost obsessively, and almost always in a style that makes viewers cringe. Schiele usually portrayed himself naked and undernourished, his body twisted in a contorted pose.

As disturbing as Schiele's work is, he enjoyed success as an artist. He was called up to serve in the Austrian army during World War I, but his superiors, unwilling to endanger the life of a promising young artist, kept him away from the front and assigned him to light duty guarding Russian prisoners of war in Prague. After the war, his work sold well in galleries in Zurich, Prague, and Dresden, and he was in demand as a portrait painter.

In 1918, having survived the war, Schiele and his wife Edith were living in Vienna, awaiting the birth of their first child. In October both fell ill with the Spanish flu, the epidemic that was sweeping across the globe. Egon and Edith died within three days of each other.

COMPOSITION VII

By Wassily Kandinsky

Like so many artists of the late nineteenth and early twentieth century, Wassily Kandinsky (1866–1944) was fascinated by the possibilities of color to express ideas and arouse emotions. For centuries, one of the primary criteria for assessing a painting or a piece of sculpture was how well it corresponded to the person, place, or thing it was trying to represent. Kandinsky rejected representational art, throwing his support behind the "modern desire for rhythm in painting, for mathematical, abstract construction, for repeated notes of color."

That phrase, "notes of color," is not an idle metaphor. Kandinsky envied composers who, through their music, could touch the heart, the mind, and the soul of an audience. It became his goal to develop a kind of "pure painting," as he called it, that would be as forceful as a piece of fine music. To reinforce the link between his paintings and music he created a series of paintings he called "compositions." Tragically, the first three paintings in the series were destroyed during World War II, and the only photographs of them are in black-and-white.

Composition VII is considered Kandinsky's finest of his pre–World War I paintings. He made thirty preliminary sketches and studies before he sat down to paint the final version. When he was ready, he completed it in just four days.

The swirling colors and tangle of unrecognizable objects or patterns or forms are off-putting because we can't make sense of what it is supposed to represent. Even some art historians, people who should know better, have tried to "see" in this painting a hurricane, or even Noah's flood. But Kandinsky gave us the key—focus on the colors. Observe how he has placed them on the canvas, what color he has placed beside another, and let yourself react to the arrangement. The point of a Kandinsky painting is not to recognize, or to think, but to feel.

WATER LILIES: GREEN REFLECTIONS

By Claude Monet

Beginning in 1892, Claude Monet (1840–1926) worked to transform a marshy tract of land next to his house in Giverny into a Japanese-style water garden. Once the marsh had become a pool, he introduced water lilies, "for the pleasure of the eye," he explained, "and for motifs to paint." Over the course of many years he painted the floating world of the water lilies often—approximately 250 times. He dreamed of a grand tribute to his favorite corner of his garden in which eight of his huge panel paintings of water lilies would hang in a gallery, completely encircling the viewer. He got his wish at Paris's Musee de l'Orangerie where his water lilies cover the walls of two lovely oval-shaped rooms.

All of the canvases measure approximately 6.5 feet high. They vary in length, however, with the longest measuring more than 55 feet.

To achieve the beautiful play of light and color, Monet painted with a broad brush. He applied layer upon layer of color—up to fifteen layers in some places—and varied his brushstrokes to form different shadows and textures. Look at a Monet painting up close and all you can distinguish are dabs of color. Step back, and suddenly all those dabs come magnificently together.

Monet was the most prolific, the most beloved, and the most influential artist of the Impressionist movement. One of his paintings—*Impression: Sunrise*—even gave the movement its name. His primary interests were color and light rather than lines and shapes. To explore the possibilities of this method he sometimes painted the same subject at various hours of the day, demonstrating how color and light change.

DADAISM

The whole point of Dadaism was to be provocative: to confuse, to shock, to outrage. The artists' goal was to clear the way for new ideas about art and new techniques by undermining established notions about what is art. While the Futurists declared war on traditional art, the Dadaists were more like goofy teenage boys making fun of the grown-ups: hence, Marcel Duchamp's painting of the *Mona Lisa* with a mustache and goatee and Arthur Craven's art lecture/striptease before an audience of well-heeled art lovers.

Dadaism began in 1916 in Zurich when poet Hugo Ball persuaded a bar owner to rename his establishment the Cabaret Voltaire and to let Ball use the place for meetings with and impromptu performances by avant-garde artists. The Cabaret Voltaire became a favorite hangout for painters such as Jean Arp and Max Ernst, Ball's fellow poet Tristan Tzara, plus many singers, musicians, and writers. The place served as an informal art gallery and concert hall—on any given night the regulars could not be certain what would happen: perhaps a puppet show put on by Emmy Hennings, Ball's wife, or a noisy argument over whether Dadaism should mean something (the consensus had always been that Dadaism did not mean anything at all).

The origins of the word *Dada* is up for grabs. Some historians believe Tzara, a Romanian, often responded to an argument he didn't like with the Romanian expression, "da, da," the equivalent of today's "yeah, right." Another possibility is that it comes from a French colloquial phrase, "C'est mon dada," or, "It's my hobby."

German Dadaist Hannah Hoch (1889–1978) put her own spin on readymades, taking ordinary objects and displaying them as works of art: She cut out words, letters, and pieces of photos from newspapers, then glued them together as a collage, or photomontage. *Da-Dandy*, seen here, is her send-up of the Dada movement (among Dadaists, self-mockery was perfectly legitimate).

Da-Dandy by Hannach Hoch, 1919

PORTRAIT OF COLONEL T. E. LAWRENCE

By Augustus John

It stands to reason that Augustus John (1878–1961) would paint Colonel T. E. Lawrence (better known as "Lawrence of Arabia") in the Arab garb he favored when he was supporting the Arab Revolt against the Ottoman Empire. The painting captures the way Lawrence viewed himself and the way the British public liked to imagine him—gallant, flamboyant, and chivalrous, an English Saladin.

In the early decades of the twentieth century, John was the most sought-after portrait artist in Britain. He always got down on canvas a good likeness of his sitter, but he did much more—he could give the viewer a sense of the subject's personality. The Irish poet William Butler Yeats, and Yeats's friend and patron, Lady Gregory, asked John to paint their portraits. So did the novelist Thomas Hardy and playwright George Bernard Shaw. He spent particular attention on faces—in a John portrait they are always very strong, the eyes and mouth being especially expressive.

John had shown talent as a boy and had studied at an art school in London. In 1897, while swimming, John made a bad dive and suffered a serious head injury. Afterwards, family and friends noticed a change in his personality and in his art—he became more daring, more impetuous. It is thought that the head injury altered John's personal life, too. He convinced his wife and his mistress to live together with him under the same roof (along with the seven children John had fathered between the two women). But even this bohemian arrangement did not keep him from other love affairs—later in life he had a daughter with the widowed mother of Ian Fleming, author of the James Bond novels.

GOLDEN BIRD

By Constantin Brancusi

Don't call this sculpture abstract! It was a word Constantin Brancusi (1876–1957) loathed. "The people who call my work 'abstract,'" he said, "are imbeciles; what they call 'abstract' is in fact the purest realism, the reality of which is not represented by external form but by the idea behind it, the essence of the work."

Before he pursued his career as a sculptor, Brancusi trained in his native Romania as a woodcarver and a stonemason. For *Golden Bird* he used all three of the materials he knew so well—wood, stone, and bronze. The sculpture stands 85.75 inches high and is one in a series of approximately thirty *Bird* sculptures he created over many years. (There may have been more—about fifty of his sculptures are believed to have been lost or destroyed.) He was not repeating himself; in each new version Brancusi tried to purify, to refine his concept until it was stripped to its fundamental form. He polished the bronze to a very high shine, hoping to create the illusion, when light reflected off the piece, that it was not metal but pure radiance. The *Bird* series was inspired by a Romanian folk tale of the Maiastra, an enchanted golden bird that could foretell the future and restore sight to the blind.

In 1926, Brancusi sold a *Bird* to the American photographer, Edward Steichen. Customs officials inspected the contents of the package and declared that it was not a work of art but some kind of industrial equipment. As a work of art, the *Bird* would not have been taxed, but as an industrial item it was subject to a very high import duty. Steichen disputed the tax in court; a year later, a judge ruled in Steichen's favor—Brancusi's *Bird* was a work of art.

PROMETHEUS

By Maxfield Parrish

Maxfield Parrish (1870–1966) produced his best work during the early years of the twentieth century, the golden age of illustration in America. He brought a level of artistry to his work that his fellow illustrators recognized (and perhaps envied). Norman Rockwell said of him, "I'm an illustrator. Maxfield Parrish was a painter-illustrator."

Like every other child, Parrish grew up drawing pictures, but unlike most children he had real talent. He began painting full-color illustrations for books, including *Arabian Nights* and Nathaniel Hawthorne's *A Wonder Book* and *Tanglewood Tales*. His illustrations caught the eye of magazine publishers—soon he was painting covers for *Collier's* and *Life*. Wanamaker's department store, Edison-Mazda Lamps, Colgate, and Oneida Cutlery hired Parrish to paint full-color advertisements for their products.

Androgynous nudes in fantasy world settings were his trademark, but the sign of his genius was his way with colors. Parrish mixed new shades that were dazzling—including the famous "Parrish blue." One of his techniques was glazing, in which he painted a layer of bright oil colors, then applied a coat of varnish. He repeated this process until he achieved the desired depth of color and luminosity.

Prometheus was one of the advertisements he painted for Edison-Mazda Lamps. In Greek mythology, Prometheus was the Titan who stole fire from the gods and gave it to mankind. In Parrish's painting, it is an Edison-Mazda electric lamp that Prometheus brings down from heaven.

Almost all of Parrish's paintings were reproduced—so much so that reproductions made him independently wealthy. The sales of prints, posters, and wall calendars of his artwork provided him with a comfortable living until his death at age ninety-five.

Art Deco

Ancient Greek and Roman ideals of beauty inspired the Italian Renaissance. Celebrating the goals of a Marxist society is the aim of Socialist Realism. In fact, philosophy or politics have been behind most artistic movements throughout history. The Art Deco movement is unique because it is the first art movement without pretensions to politics or philosophy—it was intended to be purely decorative.

Technology, geometry, and the art of Ancient Egypt, Africa, and pre-Columbian America were among the most important inspirations for Art Deco. Deco artists preferred sleek, sharp lines, but they also liked bright, vibrant colors. For their sculptures they used up-to-date materials such as stainless steel and aluminum, but for smaller, decorative objects they might combine aluminum with such ancient mediums as lacquer or inlaid wood (a classic example being the elevator doors in New York City's Chrysler Building, a monument of Art Deco).

The "Roaring Twenties" were the glory days of Art Deco, and after the tragedy of World War I, artists celebrated a decade of peace, prosperity, and the liberation of old social norms by designing opulent, exuberant interiors for everything from movie theaters to ocean liners. Artists and illustrators brought the chic, sleek look to their canvases and magazine covers. The stylish models in Tamara de Lempicka's paintings have the precise, polished, detached look of a modern woman, while illustrator Heinz Schulz-Neudamm's movie poster for Fritz Lang's 1927 science fiction film, *Metropolis*, is utterly ultramodern.

From furniture, to fashion, to architecture, Art Deco dominated the 1920s especially. Danish silversmith Georg Jensen introduced the public to Art Deco silverware; Irish artist Harry Clarke crafted magnificent Art Deco stained glass windows; and the French firm of Cartier created marvelous Art Deco watches and jewelry.

Art Deco endured through the Great Depression of the 1930s. Ultimately, it was the shortages of World War II, combined with a sense that the opulence of Art Deco was out of place in wartime, that drove Deco out of style.

Design for a Screen by Elena Zababurina, 1937

Socialist Realism

Socialist Realism was a type of art adopted wholesale in the Soviet Union to glorify the Russian Revolution, the political leaders of the USSR, and the workers. In the 1930s, Soviet newspapers, *Pravda* especially, offered artists and authors helpful advice on how to select suitable subjects for their work. Artists were urged to paint pictures that portrayed the peasants' "socialist joy" over collectivization. Authors were encouraged to write novels whose main characters were "people from the Magnitogorsk Construction Site, the Dnieper [Dam] Project . . . the builders of a new life."

From the point of view of the Soviet government, all material goods belonged to the state; since they defined art as a commodity, artists were obliged to produce work that would contribute to the good of the state, exactly as a worker in a steel mill would. Since the Soviet state was the only buyer for paintings and sculpture, artists were essentially state employees. Therefore, it was in their interest to create the kind of art their one and only client wanted.

Socialist Realism had to be representational; the workers must be able to understand what the picture is about; it should depict typical scenes from day-to-day life; and it should support the aims of the Soviet government. For example, a Socialist Realism still life by Vladimir Krikhatzkij is entitled *Lenin's Room in Simbirsk 1878 to 1887*. It is an approach to art that just begs to be parodied—and it was. But for the artists of the period who were compelled to paint pictures of a benevolent Stalin receiving flowers from a group of adoring children, the situation was not funny. Cubism, Fauvism, Expressionism, any kind of abstract art was banned. Even Impressionism was damned by the state as "decadent bourgeois art."

Alexander Gerasimov's *Lenin on the Tribune*, seen here, is vintage Socialist Realism. Even before the Revolution in 1917, Gerasimov was denouncing avant-garde art. After the Revolution he dutifully turned out paintings that glorified Lenin, Stalin, and other Soviet leaders. His reward was to be appointed head of the Union of Artists of the USSR and the Soviet Academy of Art, in which capacity he persecuted artists who would not paint in the Socialist Realism style.

Lenin at the Tribune by Aleksandr Mikhailovic Gerasimov, 1947

SURREALISM

Here we have the first case of psychoanalysis inspiring a new school of art. Influenced by Sigmund Freud's and Carl Jung's writings on the subconscious mind, Andre Breton—a French poet, magazine publisher, and art collector—advanced the idea of a style of art that defied logic and reason for the sake of art. It delivered a surprising, shocking, even incomprehensible visual wallop.

The goal of the Surrealists was to liberate the imagination. In an effort to free themselves from traditional notions of what was beautiful and what made sense, they experimented on themselves with free association and dream analysis. Their works often have the appearance of a hallucination, or the visions of a madman, but most Surrealists rejected the notion of insanity. Salvador Dali, one of the foremost Surrealists, once said, "There is only one difference between a madman and me. I am not mad." Along with Dali, artists Giorgio de Chirico, Max Ernst, Alberto Giacometti, and Man Ray joined the Surrealist movement.

Perhaps the classic example of the Surrealists' desire to undermine reason and the senses is Rene Magritte's painting, *The Treachery of Images*. It is a simple, straightforward image of a tobacco pipe, such as one might see in a catalog. But written beneath the pipe is the inscription, "Ceci n'est pas une pipe." Or, "This is not a pipe."

The 1930s was the Surrealists' Golden Age, with major exhibitions of their work in London, Paris, and New York. For the Paris show, the Surrealists asked Marcel Duchamp to design the exhibition. He transformed the art gallery's main hall into a cave with 1,200 bags of coal suspended from the ceiling and a single light bulb as the only illumination. At one end of the hall were mannequins dressed in a bizarre and unsettling manner by Surrealist artists. Underfoot were dead leaves. And the air was fragrant with the smell of roasting coffee. The visitors who had come to the opening in evening dress were horrified—a reaction that delighted the Surrealists.

Oedipus Rex by Max Ernst, 1922

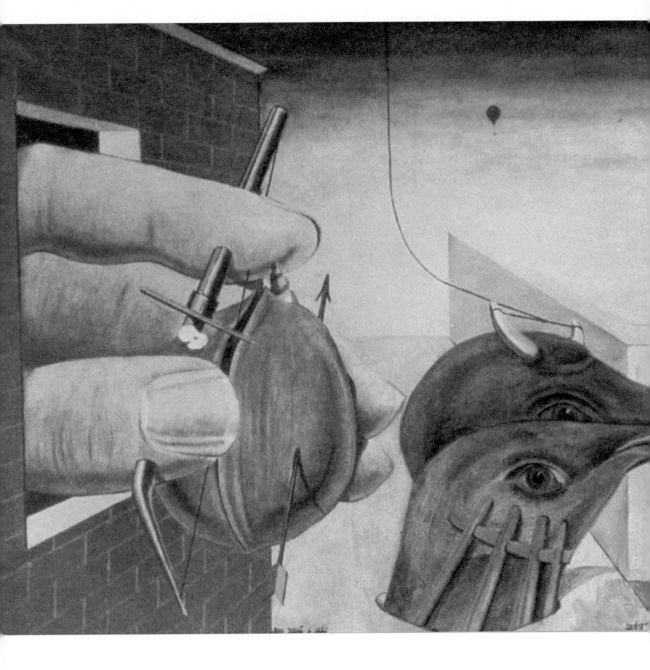

THE PROTEST, FROM THE POLITICAL VISION OF THE MEXICAN PEOPLE

By Diego Rivera

Diego Rivera (1886–1957) was a fascinating man. He revived, virtually single-handedly, the art of fresco. He was a devout Marxist who cheerfully accepted commissions from capitalists (including Henry Ford, the Rockefellers, and the directors of the American Stock Exchange). And he had a stormy love life with his fellow artist, Frida Kahlo.

Rivera believed in creating public art for ordinary people to enjoy every day. He felt that art galleries and museums were fine in their own way, but in essence they were elitist. His murals of Mexican history—from the civilization of the Aztecs through the Spanish Conquest to the Mexican revolutions of the twentieth century—are in the National Palace, right off the Zocalo, Mexico City's main square, where people can wander in off the street to view them.

Rivera's style was influenced by the Socialist Realism movement that was coming into vogue in the Soviet Union. And his *Political Vision of the Mexican People* does glorify the proletariat and make a clear statement that Communism is the way to liberate the masses from poverty, ignorance, and exploitation. This scene, *The Protest*, is peaceful, with working men, joined by at least one soldier on the far right side of the canvas, voting in favor of a resolution held aloft by the man in blue overalls. Other scenes in the same series show workers and peasants arming themselves to bring about the revolution by violent means.

Rivera was a difficult man to get along with; even his fellow Communists found him unpredictable. While in Moscow attending the celebrations of the tenth anniversary of the Russian Revolution, Rivera derided members of the Central Committee for "smirking with satisfaction, drooling with superiority." He even mocked Stalin, describing him as a character with "a peanut shaped head, surmounted by a military haircut, decked out with a magnificent pair of long moustaches." Yet if he found it hard to tolerate the Party elite, he remained committed to the Mexican people, painting mural after mural that called for revolution.

ROBERT RAUSCHENBERG

(1925–2008)

After doing a stint in the Marine Corps, Robert Rauschenberg studied art in Paris on the G.I. Bill. The European art scene left him cold, however, particularly the angst-ridden work of the Expressionists. From Paris he headed to Black Mountain College. This experimental school in a small town in North Carolina had attracted some of the most innovative artists of the twentieth century—Willem de Kooning, Robert Motherwell, as well as dancer Merce Cunningham and musician John Cage. Black Mountain inspired Rauschenberg to be daring and experimental in his work.

In the late 1950s he made what he called "combines," three-dimensional collages that combined unlikely elements. His most famous combine was *Monogram*, which featured a stuffed angora goat, a tire, a police barrier, the heel of a shoe, a tennis ball, and paint. Explaining his combines, Rauschenberg said, "I think a painting is more like the real world if it's made out of the real world."

In the 1960s, Rauschenberg began silk-screening photos of people and things everyone recognized instantly, such as John F. Kennedy, a sculpture of Abraham Lincoln, and baseball games, then painting over them to change the photographs to abstract forms. Rauschenberg's interest in printing led him to experiment with transferring images onto unusual surfaces such as aluminum and Plexiglas. He also created collages.

The combines, of course, are related to Marcel Duchamp's readymades. While Duchamp dared art critics and the public to find meaning in his objects, Rauschenberg went in the opposite direction, insisting that his work had meaning, and as the artist he was the one who assigned it. An extreme example: Once, he was invited to submit a piece for a group exhibition at the Galerie Iris Clert in Paris. His submission was a telegram sent to the gallery that read, "This is a portrait of Iris Clert if I say so."

Double Feature by Robert Rauschenberg, 1959

ALEX KATZ

(b. 1927)

Alex Katz's signature style is known as modern realism. Most of these paintings are portraits, done in smooth, flat perspective, bright colors with limited shading, and sharp lines. The background in these portraits is spare, as in *Dusk*, seen here, and sometimes nonexistent. It is representational art, and the likenesses of the sitters are good, but in these portraits Katz has pared down the face and body—they aren't quite abstract, but they are certainly uncomplicated. A few of his pieces from the late 1950s/early 1960s are freestanding cutout portraits painted on wood or aluminum, which only emphasizes the flat, linear, formal look Katz favors.

Early in the 1950s, when Katz was fresh out of art school, his major influences were the Abstract Expressionists such as Jackson Pollack. But little by little he began introducing more and more recognizable figures into his work. Katz's interest in representational paintings of landscapes as well as portraits put him at odds with most of his contemporaries and placed him outside the avant-garde movement, which by the 1950s was considered mainstream. For many years, Katz found only a limited audience for his work and not much in the way of praise from the critics. In a 2006 interview with *ArtInfo* magazine, Katz said, "I think for years people thought of me as a bad Pop artist or a bad photorealist."

With the return of interest in realism in the 1990s and 2000s, Katz has finally found acclaim and a large international audience for his work.

Dusk by Alex Katz, 1996

THE DEERSLAYER

By N. C. Wyeth

Over the course of forty-two years, N. C. Wyeth (1882–1945) painted more than 4,000 illustrations for books and magazines, most famously twenty-six books for Scribner's Illustrated Classics, with eight to sixteen color plates per volume. These editions are still in print.

Wyeth's fearless, clean-cut heroes became the prototype for heroes that appeared in movies, television, and now computer games. Steven Spielberg and George Lucas both grew up reading the classic adventure stories Wyeth illustrated, and Wyeth's heroes were the models for Indiana Jones.

The two greatest influences on Wyeth's career were the landscape artist George L. Noyes, who gave the young man private lessons, and the renowned illustrator Howard Pyle. Thanks to Noyes, Wyeth created magnificent landscapes, and thanks to Pyle, Wyeth acquired the knack of imagining himself in a scene before he began to illustrate it.

He had an inherent sense for drama, and he knew how to pull his viewers into a painting. Wyeth also had a masterful command of human anatomy—as a result, his figures appear solid, three-dimensional, and utterly convincing. The Impressionists were his strongest influence, and in spite of his tremendous success as an illustrator, he wanted to be recognized as a fine artist. Toward the end of his life, with his family's finances completely secure, he spent more time on what he considered "serious" paintings. He experimented with thin oil paints and egg tempera; he tried styles that resembled the work of Thomas Hart Benton and Grant Wood. He was afraid he would be remembered only as an American illustrator rather than as an American artist.

Not only is Wyeth is remembered as an artist, he is also known for founding a dynasty of artists that includes his son Andrew Wyeth and his grandson Jamie Wyeth.

THE PERSISTENCE OF MEMORY

By Salvador Dali

Dali painted his surreal, hallucinogenic scenes in a realistic way—which just makes the painting ever so much creepier. This is a horrific landscape, but it looks like a real landscape nonetheless. In fact, those gold-colored cliffs in the background are a typical feature of the landscape of Catalonia, Dali's home province in Spain.

The theme of the painting appears to be the breakdown, the decay of time—represented by the melting watches. Time, as measured by a watch, is rational, orderly, and predictable—everything Surrealism rejects. Memories of events that occurred long ago persist, but the memory is often distorted.

The detail of the ants swarming over and devouring one watch, as if it were a bit of food left over from a picnic, is bad enough, but the truly dreadful image is the unidentifiable grayish thing that dominates the center of the picture. Look at it sideways and you'll notice it is the profile of Dali's face with his tongue sticking out, which only makes the thing more grotesque.

To produce such paintings, Dali developed what he called "the paranoiac-critical method," a way of inducing psychotic visions or periods of delirium that he would then paint. It is said that to produce these psychotic episodes Dali would stand on his head for prolonged periods of time. Another technique he used was to hang a fork from around his neck, then deprive himself of sleep. When finally he dozed off, his drooping head would strike the fork, which would wake him up, and he'd paint whatever he had been dreaming.

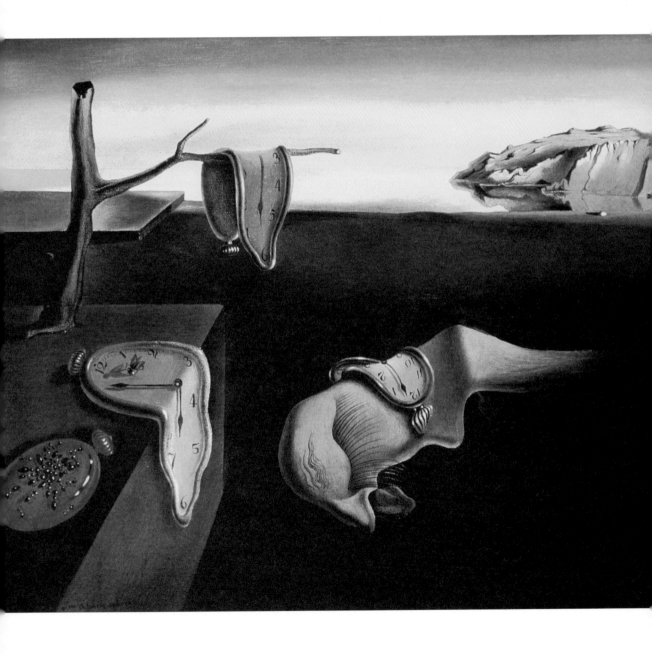

My Uncle

By Isamu Noguchi

Isamu Noguchi (1904–1988) was an extremely prolific, multitalented artist. He was an acclaimed sculptor, a landscape designer who created parks and children's playgrounds, and an innovative creator of public art. He also designed fountains, furniture, and lamps, as well as stage sets for Martha Graham's dance company. Among his most renowned public pieces are a metal relief sculpture, *News*, in New York's Rockefeller Center; *Portal* in Cleveland, Ohio; and his *Bolt of Lightning* memorial to Benjamin Franklin in Philadelphia.

His goal was to bring sculpture into everyone's daily life. For some, this was achieved by purchasing one of his exquisite lamps for their home or office. For others, it was seeing one of his monumental public sculptures in a plaza or some other public area. As a man of Japanese descent born in the United States, he tried to combine the twentieth-century Western aesthetic of abstract art with the Japanese admiration for the beauty and elegance found in simple shapes.

During his long career he would sculpt 120 portrait heads, but only on three occasions did Noguchi work in ceramics. The first instance was in 1931 when he made this terracotta portrait of his uncle, Totaro Takagi. When Noguchi was growing up, Uncle Takagi had been kind and loving; in later years, he invited Noguchi to live with him when the artist came to Tokyo.

Noguchi portrays his uncle as a man getting on in years, serene, pleasant, approachable, with a hint of a smile. The modeling is incredibly lifelike and conveys clearly that this piece is a work of love.

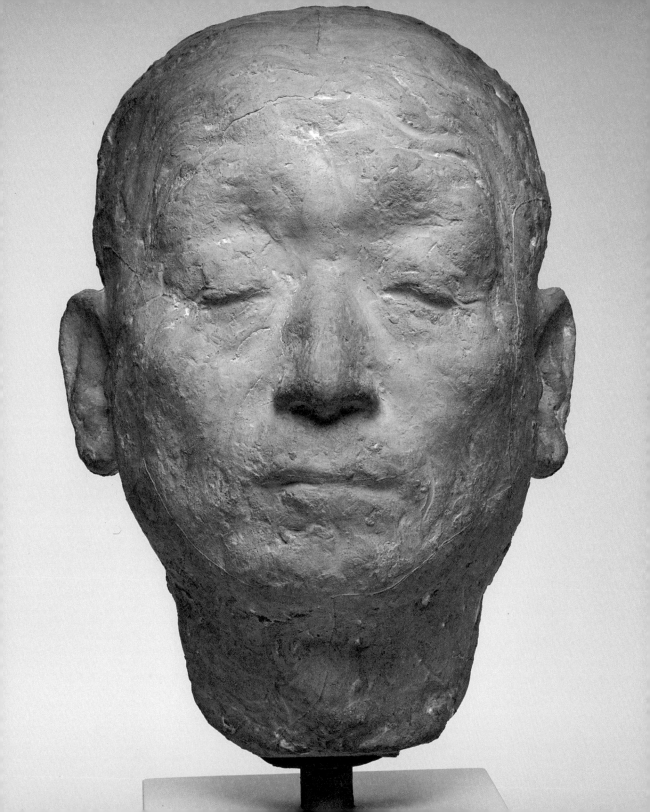

THE PARENTS

By Kathe Kollwitz

The sculptures of the German artist Kathe Kollwitz (1867–1945) emerged out of her personal sorrows. When World War I broke out in 1914, Kollwitz's nineteen-year-old son, Peter, left university to enlist. Two months later he was dead, killed in action. When Kollwitz received the news she told a close friend, "There is in our lives a wound that will never heal. Nor should it."

During the war she conceived the idea of sculpting a memorial to her son, but every design she attempted displeased her. Finally, in 1931, she began work on two sculptures, a mother and a father, each on their knees and bowed down with grief. Kollwitz and her husband, Karl, were the models for sculptures, and she planned to install them on either side of Peter's grave. The piece is called *The Parents*, or sometimes just *Memorial*, and it was officially dedicated in 1932 at the Roggevelde German War Cemetery outside the village of Vladslo in northern Belgium. As Kollwitz planned, the statues guard Peter's grave. Typical of Kollwitz's style, the bodies of *The Parents* are shapeless—the statues' posture is expressive, as are the hands and faces.

The year after the installation of *The Parents*, the Nazis declared Kollwitz's art "decadent," forbade her to exhibit her work, and forced her to resign from the faculty of the Academy of Art. The Gestapo hounded the Kollwitzes, threatening to send them to a concentration camp (Kathe and Karl resolved to kill themselves if it came to that). In 1940, Karl died. In 1942, Kollwitz's grandson, named Peter after his uncle, was killed at the Russian Front. In 1943, Allied bombs destroyed Kollwitz's house, studio, and much of her artwork. She fled to Dresden where an admirer, Prince Ernst Heinrich of Hesse, offered her a home. Kollwitz died there just weeks before the war in Europe ended.

Ram's Head White Hollyhock and Little Hills

By Georgia O'Keeffe

It was Georgia O'Keeffe's (1887–1986) particular gift to be able to paint objects with great precision, yet in a manner that made them appear abstract. She was born on a Wisconsin dairy farm, fell in love with and married photographer Alfred Stieglitz in New York City, and found a lifetime of inspiration in the American Southwest, especially New Mexico, where she made her home.

She has become most famous in recent years for her giant paintings of flowers. Some viewers have insisted that O'Keeffe's flowers represent male and female genitalia—an interpretation that O'Keeffe always denied vigorously (although those denials may have been a ruse on her part to keep people interested in her flower paintings).

She drew from abstract and surreal art when it suited her. Her paintings of pueblos are in the abstract tradition, while *Ram's Head White Hollyhock and Little Hills* owes its composition to the Surrealists.

Living as she did in the wild places of New Mexico, it was not unusual to see on the plains or in the desert the skulls of sheep or cattle bleached white by the sun. In the 1930s, when she first started living in New Mexico, she went backpacking and certainly would have encountered animal bones.

If at the core of abstract art was the desire to reduce objects to their basic geometrical form, what is more stripped down than a skull? Here are the jagged ovals of the eye sockets, the weird rectangle of the nasal cavity, and the graceful curve, with a twist, of the horns. O'Keeffe has suspended the skull over the landscape, like a totem or protective spirit, and suspended beside it a single white hollyhock (for reasons that defy explanation). It is all at once beautiful and mysterious and creepy and utterly unforgettable.

FIDELMA

By Paul Cadmus

Paul Cadmus (1904–1999) was a painter who rejected Abstract Expressionism—the style that dominated the art world in the first half of the twentieth century—and insisted upon painting in a realistic manner. He called himself a "literary painter" because there is a narrative quality to his work. During the 1930s, when his work was just beginning to get attention, some of the narratives Cadmus told in his paintings got him into trouble.

In 1934, his *The Fleet's In* was exhibited at the Corcoran Gallery in Washington, D.C. The painting depicts rowdy U.S. sailors, in uniform, passed-out drunk, consorting with prostitutes, trying to pick up women, and in one case, picking up a man. The Secretary of the Navy demanded that the painting be removed from the museum.

Coney Island is a painting Pieter Bruegel would have loved—a beach overcrowded with boors. The realtors of Brooklyn didn't think there was anything funny about Cadmus's painting. They took it as an insult, one that would depress the neighborhood's housing market, and they threatened to sue the Whitney Museum, where *Coney Island* was on display.

As for his colleagues in the art world, they ignored Cadmus. "I have never been part of any avant-garde [movement]," he said, and so his peers consigned him to artistic limbo. Nonetheless, Cadmus continued to paint in his own way, including many portraits of family and friends, including this one of his sister, Fidelma.

He was a slow painter, rarely finishing more than two paintings a year, but he produced many more sketches, usually male nudes, for which his companion, Jon Anderson, frequently served as the model. Toward the end of his long life a visitor, wishing to pay a compliment, said he believed Cadmus had done more drawings of naked men than any other artist. "Well," Cadmus replied, "there was Michelangelo."

ca. 1936

Two Fridas

By Frida Kahlo

Almost all of Frida Kahlo's (1907–1954) paintings are self-portraits. Her work, then, chronicles her life in very intimate ways.

Her style was drawn from two sources, Surrealism and the naïve-yet-graphic little paintings known as *retablos*. A *retablo* is a painting of a miracle that devout Mexican Catholics paint themselves and hang at the altar or shrine of the saint who answered their prayers. It is religious folk art.

Kahlo married fellow Mexican artist Diego Rivera for the first time in 1929. In 1939, the year she painted this double self-portrait, she divorced Rivera. The painting represents her emotional turmoil at this difficult time. The Frida on the right wears a traditional *tehuana* dress such as a woman from the villages of Mexico would put on every morning. The Frida on the left is dressed in an elaborate white gown such as the lady of a grand hacienda would wear. The hearts of both Fridas are exposed. The Frida on the right holds a small cameo of Diego Rivera as a child; from the cameo springs an artery that coils around the two Fridas, uniting them, but it ends with the Frida on the left severing the artery with a pair of surgical scissors, spilling blood onto her lap.

The faces of the Fridas are impassive—she always painted herself in this cool, detached manner. But the sky behind them is turbulent, suggesting again Kahlo's mixed emotions over her divorce.

The year after she completed this self-portrait, Kahlo and Rivera remarried. Their second marriage was as stormy as their first, and often they did not live in the same house. But their admiration for each other's work was unshakable—each routinely referred to the other as the greatest living Mexican artist.

Parson Weems' Fable

By Grant Wood

As is the case with his iconic painting, *American Gothic*, there is an ambiguous quality to this painting. Grant Wood (1891–1942) painted it at a time when academic historians were debunking the myths and legends that had grown up around George Washington. This painting depicts the most famous legend of all. Little George has been given a hatchet as a gift and has used it to chop down one of his father's prize cherry trees. When confronted, George replied, "I did it, Pa, I cannot tell a lie."

Well, maybe Washington couldn't tell a lie, but Weems could. He made up the story, inserting it in the fifth edition of his book, *Life of George Washington, the Great*. In the parson's defense, his little fabrication did teach generations of American schoolchildren the virtue of honesty.

So, here is Weems, drawing back a curtain to reveal an unreal version of his fable. The house looks like a stage set. The trees are almost surreal in their perfection. And little George has the face and powdered wig of the mature George Washington as painted by Gilbert Stuart (and still seen today on the one-dollar bill). As is the case with fables, the scene is pretty, but not true—in the sense of true-to-life as well as in the sense of historically accurate.

On the other hand, the picture is appealing, just as the cherry tree story is appealing. It teaches a sound moral, and it encourages admiration for a great American. It is a part of American folklore, and that is a legacy that ought not to be discarded. In other words, Wood knows the cherry tree episode is a myth but determined that it is a myth worth repeating.

SUMMERTIME

By Edward Hopper

Viewing an Edward Hopper (1882–1967) painting feels like intruding—the people on the canvas are so still, so alone. Even in his iconic painting, *Night Hawks*, no one at that all-night diner is engaged in conversation. Silence and isolation are the primary themes of Hopper's work.

His paintings are characterized by stark light and deep, interesting shadows. Buildings that appear in his work are large blocks; lines are very sharp; people are stylized, even stiff. His scenes are set in small seaside towns in New England, or in big cities; both settings are linked by the same message—the lack of community in modern life. *Summertime*, seen here, shows a pretty young woman in a cool summer dress all alone on a stoop staring out on an empty street. There are no neighbors to chat with. Another painting, *Morning in the City*, portrays a pretty woman, naked, staring out of her bedroom window; the white towel in her hands tells us that she is fresh from her bath. She's alone, too—no husband or lover spent the night with her.

Hopper's work isn't political—he has no save-the-world message to convey. Nor is it ironic—he never makes fun of his subjects. His paintings are moody, contemplative, and very often melancholy. At the core of Hopper's paintings are human emotions, which explains his broad appeal—viewers look at a Hopper painting and recognize the scene as something commonplace in daily life and sense the emotion behind it.

And there is one other facet of modern city life Hopper understood—the opportunities to watch what complete strangers were doing without being seen by them. *Night Hawks*, after all, is viewed from the sidewalk looking in. And there are other night scenes by Hopper from the same perspective, including scenes of apartment interiors that one glimpses from the window of a speeding elevated train.

Woman I

By Willem de Kooning

Among the most distressing paintings of the Expressionist period are Willem de Kooning's (1904–1997) *Woman* series (he did six paintings). *Woman I*, of course, is the first. Some art critics have tried to tone down this aggressive, fearsome work by saying that de Kooning's painting is a portrait of female energy and power.

The sources for this image include the Venus of Willendorf (the huge sagging breasts); Kali, the Hindu goddess of death and destruction (those nasty fangs); and, perhaps, Artemisia Gentileschi's paintings of Judith beheading Holofernes (*Woman I*'s muscular arms look like they could behead a man).

Some art critics believe de Kooning intended this work to convey a degree of voluptuousness. True, the breasts are exposed, and the legs are apart, but the effect is not erotic—it's frightening: The wide, angry eyes and the snarling mouth are menacing. And the style with which de Kooning has painted this figure is anything but seductive—his jagged lines and slashing brushstrokes are violent and aggressive.

In the 1940s, de Kooning had started painting pictures of women, but they were generally abstract—more symbols of the feminine than human figures. The early paintings from the series that began with *Woman I* were featured in a New York gallery in 1953 where they attracted a great deal of attention. The show spotlighted Abstract Expressionist artists, yet here was de Kooning, an Expressionist, painting not abstract shapes but a human figure. The critics and the gallery-goers found the ferocity of the women and the vulgarity of the style hypnotic. These angry women made de Kooning's career.

RECLINING FIGURE

By Henry Moore

Henry Moore's (1898–1986) bronze or marble sculptures of reclining figures are one of the icons of twentieth-century art. His inspirations for the form, which he turned to time and again during his long, prolific career, were a Toltec/Mayan sculpture of a reclining man known as a Chac Mool and the four reclining sculptures carved by Michelangelo to adorn the Medici Tombs in the Church of San Lorenzo in Florence.

Moore's reclining statues are almost always female, and frequently nude. Since no one would describe these statues as representational, Moore suggests the femininity of his figures by the statue's undulating curves and hollowed-out spots, which are meant to represent the womb. Moore was commissioned for this particular *Reclining Figure* by the directors of the Festival of Britain, a public celebration organized in 1951 to lift the national morale during the economic hardships that plagued the United Kingdom after World War II. Moore produced this sculpture in bronze in a special limited edition of five.

Moore was an Englishman, born in Yorkshire. As a child he made figurines out of clay and wood. In 1924, he visited Italy and France. It was on this trip that he saw a plaster cast of the Chac Mool at the Louvre and the reclining Michelangelos in the Medici Chapel. Over the decades his reclining sculptures changed. The early versions tended to be heavy, substantial, and more recognizably human. In later years he was less interested in mass and began to experiment with abstract shapes, curving lines, and hollows or openings in the sculpture. His work was extremely popular, and by 1977 he was an extremely wealthy man—so much so that every year he was paying the British government about £1 million in taxes. To help alleviate this burden, he established the Henry Moore Foundation, a registered charity, to preserve his work and encourage public appreciation of art.

Untitled

By Mark Rothko

Mark Rothko (1903–1970) gave form—you might even say rules—to Expressionism. His composition, or format, is roughly rectangular shapes aligned on a vertical canvas. The field around the blocks is painted a single color. He began this type of painting about 1949 and continued in this style to the end of his life. Occasionally he varied the format by arranging his blocks of color on a horizontal canvas. Many of his later paintings are dark, but they are still instantly recognizable as the work of Rothko.

Rothko's blocks of color are never random. This *Untitled* painting (they are all named "Untitled") with its large block of grayish blue above a block of orange set in a tangerine field is as warm and cheerful as a summer afternoon. Other "Untitleds" are angry, unsettling, or serene, depending upon the emotional response Rothko wished to evoke. This is nothing new—going all the way back to cave paintings, artists have been using color to get a reaction from viewers.

Some art critics say that Rothko's blocks of color speak to each other on the canvas, that the unfinished edges suggest the colors are vibrating with energy. The paintings can be read that way. Rothko insisted that he was aiming for an emotional reaction. "I am not interested in the relationship between form and color," he said. "The only thing I care about is the expression of man's basic emotions: tragedy, ecstasy, destiny." He also believed there was a profound spiritual dimension to his paintings, that his large canvases could fill a viewer with awe (for the maximum experience, he encouraged viewers to stand exactly 18 inches from the canvas—close enough to engage with it while also being overwhelmed by it).

Pop Art

Pop Art is a kind of joke, a way to skewer the intensity and self-importance of the Abstract Expressionists. If the Abstract Expressionists weighed down their works with imagery that suggested gloomy references to World War II and solemn moral judgments about the human condition, Pop Artists would celebrate the ordinary, the ephemeral, and the ubiquitous. If the Abstract Expressionists fretted over capitalism, the Pop Artists made postwar euphoria and 1950s consumerism their gods, reveling in the new "throwaway" culture.

Advertisements, comic books, catalogs, logos, Hollywood glamour photos—anything that was aimed at a mass audience inspired the Pop Artists. Perhaps the classic, even the definitive work of Pop Art is the very first Pop Art painting/collage, *Just What Makes Today's Homes So Different, So Appealing?* created by Richard Hamilton, John McHale, and John Voelcker in 1956. The scene is the interior of a 1950s "dream home" with Danish Modern furniture, a large picture window, and the latest entertainment gadgets such as a television and a reel-to-reel tape recorder. And front and center on the coffee table is that emblem of convenience in the kitchen, a canned ham. Of course, living in the dream home is the dream couple—a peroxide blonde bombshell preening on the sofa, and a he-man bodybuilder. Even the title for the work sounds as if it has been lifted straight from an advertising campaign. It is an unabashed celebration—as well as a send-up—of the stuff with which we stuff our homes.

1956

Just What makes Today's Homes So Different, So Appealing?
by Richard Hamilton, et all, 1956

TROPICAL GARDEN II

By Louise Nelson

The wits of the art world refer jokingly to Louise Nelson's (1899–1988) work as "art in a box." She was an Abstract Expressionist who built—assembled is a better word—sculptures using discarded boxes, lumber, and other objects that had been thrown away. One of her assemblage sculptures stood three stories high.

Found objects appealed to Nelson for many reasons. She liked their ready-made form; she was not wild about carving or sculpting; assembly enabled her to create her work of art quickly; and the more pieces she added, the more enclosed her sculpture became. She did not intend these box sculptures, such as *Tropical Garden II*, to be seen in the round. Like the relief sculptures carved during the Middle Ages, Nelson envisioned her box assemblages against a wall. Painting the sculptures solid black also simplified the process of creation. Originally she had experimented with other colors, but black delivered the most satisfactory results, particularly in terms of light and shadow. Nelson was especially interested in shadow, which she once described as "the fourth dimension."

In addition to regarding her work as assemblages as well as sculptures, Nelson also thought of them as architecture. Her boxes are not completely shut; they are intricate forms with openings in them that let in light and air.

Nelson once said, "When you put together things that other people have thrown out, you're really bringing them to life—a spiritual life that surpasses the life for which they were originally created."

MINIMALISM

Like Pop Art, Minimalism was a reaction against Abstract Expressionism. The leading proponent of Minimalism was Frank Stella (1936–). In some respects, he was looking back to the Cubism of the early part of the twentieth century when artists such as Braque and Picasso had pared down the figures in their paintings to their fundamental geometric shapes. Stella and the artists who joined him—Richard Serra (1939–) and Agnes Martin (1912–2004), for example—also were interested in a work of art's most basic building blocks. They jettisoned everything from recognizable figures to shades of color to symbolism to art that would evoke particular emotions. Some people said (and still say) they ripped the heart out of art, producing stark, lifeless, dehumanized objects. Minimalist sculptor Donald Judd (1928–1994), for example, would not produce a sculpture that represented anything found in the real world.

Most people do not care for Minimalist art. A notorious case arose in Lower Manhattan in 1981. As part of a U.S. government-sponsored "Arts-in-Architecture" program, Richard Serra was commissioned to provide a sculpture for Federal Plaza in downtown New York City. He delivered a work he called *Tilted Arc*, a plate of rusting steel 120 feet long and 12 feet high, and pitched at a slight angle. From the beginning, the people who worked at Federal Plaza loathed *Tilted Arc*. They considered it a depressing eyesore. Eventually they petitioned to have the steel wall removed. The controversy raged on between art critics and the people who had to live with Serra's work. In the end, the employees at Federal Plaza won, and in 1989 *Tilted Arc* was dismantled and carted off to be sold as scrap metal.

View of "Fulcrum" by Richard Serra, 1987

THREE FLAGS

By Jasper Johns

Three Flags is an example of reverse perspective. In traditional paintings, the perspective recedes backwards, leading the viewer into the scene. Jasper Johns (1930–) has painted three canvases of flags, the smallest on top, so that the painting(s) are projecting outward at the viewer.

Three Flags emerges from the Pop Art movement in which an artist takes familiar icons that everyone recognizes and presents them in the traditional media of painting or sculpture so that they achieve the status of fine art. The fact that a flag is flat and that it is composed of solid blocks of color makes it especially appealing to advocates of the kind of modern art that rejects conventional techniques such as perspective, attempts to make figures on a painted canvas look three-dimensional, and shades of color.

Of course, it is not a flag such as flies from flagpoles. This is a painting on a canvas, and as a result it has texture and irregularities in its stars and stripes that would not be tolerated in a real American flag. Johns has also taken it out of any context so that the flag is just an object (perhaps an art object), but not a national banner heavily laden with symbolic significance. For that reason the flag is shown rigid, not rippling in the breeze.

There is a school of thought among some art critics that Johns chose the American flag as a subject for personal reasons: One of the artist's ancestors, Sergeant William Jasper (ca. 1750–1779) of South Carolina, was a hero of the American Revolution. During the British bombardment of Fort Moultrie, the fort's flagstaff was struck by a shell and shattered. Sgt. Jasper snatched up the flag and held it aloft under heavy fire until a new flagstaff was improvised. For his courage and patriotism, the governor of South Carolina presented Sgt. Jasper with a golden sword.

IN THE CAR

By Roy Lichtenstein

One day in 1961, Roy Lichtenstein (1923–1997), an art professor at Douglass College in New Jersey, walked into the Leo Castelli Gallery in New York City and asked for a one-man show. He had with him several of his comic-strip paintings. After looking at Lichtenstein's work, Leo Castelli agreed to give Lichtenstein his own show, passing over another Pop Artist who had wanted to exhibit there, Andy Warhol.

Lichtenstein's trademark technique was forming his images using oversized Ben-Day Dots. In the 1950s and 1960s, comic books were printed using the Ben-Day Dot method in which tiny dots of color were used to create gradations of color in the drawings. Readers of comic books weren't supposed to notice the dots, but Lichtenstein exaggerated them so viewers would be forced to look at this visual device and how it affected the artwork. To make the dots, Lichtenstein applied oil paint using a plastic-bristled dog grooming brush. Later he applied dots to the canvas through a pre-punched metal stencil.

Early on, Lichtenstein's fans thought his comic-strip paintings were a send-up of the twentieth century's mass-produced culture, but Lichtenstein refuted that interpretation. Commercial art (another of his sources of inspiration) convinced people to buy certain products; and people bought a lot of comic books. Clearly, this kind of art enjoyed broad audience appeal. "There are certain things that are usable, forceful and vital about commercial art," Lichtenstein explained.

An art critic for the *New York Times* declared Lichtenstein "one of the worst artists in America," but collectors disagreed. His large-scale, highly polished paintings of comic book panels that depict a moment of crisis in the story (he lifted the panels from the *Girls Romances* and *Secret Hearts* comics published by D.C. Comics) transformed something commonplace into a thing of beauty. At the time that he painted *In the Car*, Lichtenstein's paintings were going for $4,000—about $30,000 today.

TWO WHITE DISKS

By Alexander Calder

Alexander Calder (1898–1976) was a reluctant artist. His father and grandfather were noted sculptors, his mother was a painter, but young Calder was only interested in mechanics. He built his own toys and wanted to be an engineer. In his twenties, when he gave in and took up "the family business," he brought his love for the mechanical to his art. One of his first creations was the *Calder Circus*, a diorama of circus people, animals, and acts made from wire, cork, wood, and fabric. It was easy to make, and very popular, so Calder moved on to the next phase—making portraits with wire bent to represent the sitter's features. The wire portraits had the strong lines of a drawing, but the three-dimensionality of a sculpture. Calder had just invented a new kind of art.

In the 1930s, Calder was still experimenting with the possibilities of wire art when he came up with the idea of creating moving sculptures. Ever the engineer, he attached pieces of aluminum to wire and powered the sculpture with a motor. The movement of the finished piece dissatisfied him—it was unnatural and predictable. He began again. This time he hung the aluminum-and-wire sculpture from a string. A light breeze or a touch of a finger was all it took to put the sculpture in motion—and it never moved in exactly the same way twice. When Marcel Duchamp saw Calder's hanging sculptures he called them mobiles, from the French for "to move." Just as he had invented a new type of portraiture, now Calder had revolutionized sculpture. It was no longer immobile and rock solid; a sculpture could be fluid, moving in surprising ways. (Of course, the fact that a sculpture moved at all was the real surprise.)

The demand for Calder's mobiles was enormous—not just from the art community, but from toy companies, too.

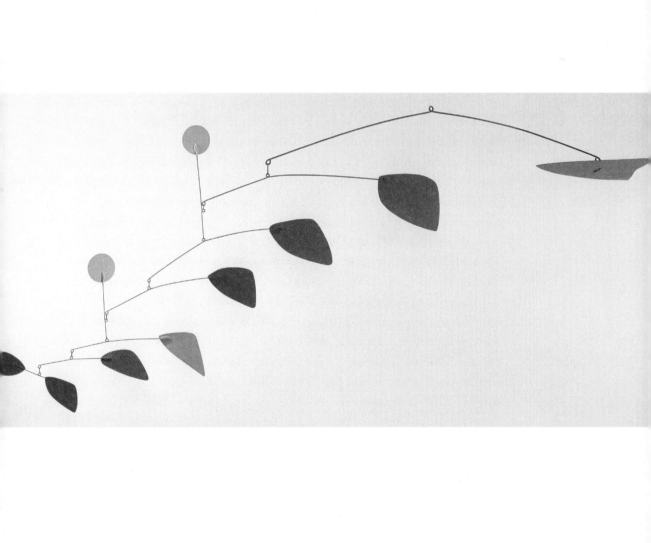

CAMPBELL'S SOUP

By Andy Warhol

The oddball guru of the Pop Art scene of the 1960s, Andy Warhol (1928-1987) regarded his paintings as merchandise, not much different from a can of soup. He had started his artistic career as a graphic artist whose illustrations appeared in glossy fashion magazines, and like any savvy advertising executive, Warhol learned how to create a demand for his product.

He began with instantly recognizable objects and people: a can of Campbell's tomato soup, a box of Brillo pads, a glamour shot of Marilyn Monroe or Elizabeth Taylor. And like a major manufacturer, he produced not one, but many copies and versions of his "products." He called his studio The Factory, and he took up silk-screening because he could put his assistants and interns to work on an assembly line, churning out art the same way Ford turned out automobiles. In so doing he skewered one of the primary principles of art—that each piece was unique. Warhol, responding to the throwaway culture of post–World War II America, mass-produced his art. You could buy a single canvas of *Campbell's Soup* (just like in the supermarket), or you could buy a silkscreen of many cans of soup (again, just like in the supermarket).

Warhol liked the idea that, in America, iconic products were the same for everyone. "You can be watching TV and see Coca-Cola, and you know that the President drinks Coca Cola, Liz Taylor drinks Coca Cola, and just think, you can drink Coca Cola, too," Warhol explained. "A coke is a coke and no amount of money can get you a better coke than the one the bum on the corner is drinking. All the cokes are the same and all the cokes are good."

Since Warhol's death in 1987 his fans have made the pilgrimage to his grave in St. John the Baptist Byzantine Catholic Cemetery outside Pittsburgh. It has become a tradition to leave a can of Campbell's soup on the gravestone.

PORTRAIT OF CHRISTOPHER ISHERWOOD AND DON BACHARDY

By David Hockney

One of the most versatile painters of the 20th century, David Hockney (1937-) has spent his entire life mastering new techniques, experimenting with new styles, and creating an enormous body of exceptional work.

In his early years he adopted a *faux-naif,* or false amateurism, using sophisticated methods of painting for crudely drawn images. His sources of inspiration included the art of Pablo Picasso and the poetry of Walt Whitman. And he was not shy about revealing his homosexuality in his work, for example in the painting *We Two Boys Together Clinging* (the title is taken from one of Whitman's poems).

In the 1960s, Hockney moved from England to California. In an interview with a French journalist Hockney said, "I was drawn towards California . . . because I sensed the place would excite me. No doubt it had a lot to do with sex." Hockney wasn't the only Englishman who went to California in search of bronzed surfer boys; the English novelist Christopher Isherwood had moved there years earlier. It was here that Hockney developed his "California style"—strong light, bright colors, handsome men, and sharp lines.

And it was in California that Hockney began painting portraits of his friends, including this double portrait of Isherwood and his lover, American artist Don Bachardy. Hockney worked on it for six months, experimenting with various props and having the men in various forms of attire. This sketch for the final painting shows Bachardy looking straight out at the viewer while Isherwood looks at Bachardy with what some believe is a trace of anxiety. The painting has become one of Hockney's most popular works: It is not only an affectionate portrait of two of the artist's friends, it is also a snapshot of a relationship.

Girl Putting on Mascara

By George Segal

In the late 1940s and early 1950s, art took third place in George Segal's (1924–2000) life. He and his wife, Helen, operated a chicken farm in New Jersey. To boost their income he taught English and art at a local high school, and sometimes gave classes at Rutgers University. He made some plaster sculptures, but his breakthrough came in 1961 when a student gave him a box of dry plaster bandages. That night he and Helen experimented with the bandages, applying them to Segal's body. Once he got the hang of how the bandages worked, he was able to make plaster casts of various body parts, then assemble them into a complete, life-size human figure. His first such sculpture was a seated figure of a man. He decided to give his sculpture an environment so he added a chair, a table, and a window frame—now he had more than a solitary statue; he had a tableau. *Man Sitting at a Table* was the first of the sculptures that became Segal's trademark.

Segal is often listed among the Pop Artists of the 1960s; this is a mistake. He was not interested in mass-produced objects or logos or commercial art; Segal wanted to create sculptures that expressed the human experience.

Sometimes he painted his figures, but typically he kept them stark white. Given that the figures' facial expressions and posture often suggest melancholy, the all-white sculptures have a spectral, or ghostly quality.

Some of Segal's sculptures are public art. *Gay Liberation,* which shows lesbian and gay male couples, was installed in Sheridan Square in New York's Greenwich Village.

In 1978, Segal was commissioned to design a sculpture, in bronze rather than plaster, to commemorate the Kent State University shootings of 1971 in which National Guardsmen opened fire on student demonstrators, killing four college students and wounding nine. Taking his inspiration from the biblical account of Abraham's sacrifice of his son Isaac, Segal sculpted an angry middle-aged man poised to stab a young man, bound, almost naked, and on his knees. The piece disturbed the university's administrators and they refused to accept it. Today, Segal's sculpture is displayed on the campus of Princeton University.

Installation Art

Installation Art can be bewildering, which makes defining it very tricky. Typically the artist takes a large room, gallery, or other indoor space with lots of square footage and fills it with a variety of objects that, generally speaking, are unrelated to one another, but that will evoke a gamut of reactions, emotions, and associations from the viewers. For example, Tony Cragg's *New Stones—Newton's Tones* is a haphazard array of plastic objects—from children's toys to household utensils to disposable lighters—scattered on the floor. But look again and they have been arranged in segments that echo the colors of the spectrum.

Another example is Klaus Rinke's *Water Sculpture,* a tangle of yards and yards of opaque whitish hose with a tall steel tube sticking out at one end and leaning against the wall. It looks like an enormous serving of spaghetti with a single chopstick. And perhaps that is what Rinke wants his viewers to think when they see *Water Sculpture.* It is hard to say, because Installation artists tend to be cryptic or noncommittal when asked about their work.

Arrangements of objects leads one to conclude that Installation Art is a type of sculpture, but the artists often confound that assumption by incorporating sound or video or live performance in their work.

Installation Art grew out of Marcel Duchamp's use of ready-made objects and mounting them or assembling them in a style that is reminiscent of (or pokes fun at) traditional works of art.

New Stones-Newton's Tones by Tony Cragg, 1978

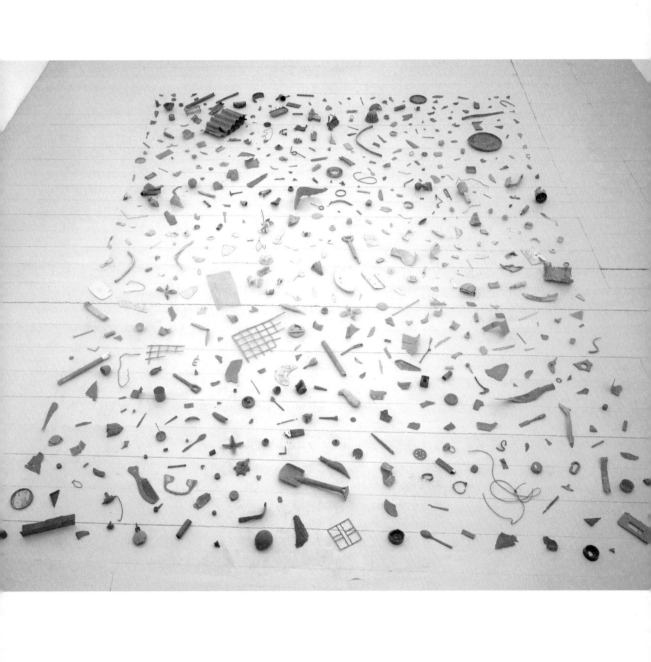

ICE BAG

By Claes Oldenburg

In the late 1950s and early 1960s, artist Allan Kaprow sponsored what we would call performance art (his term for these spontaneous performances was "happenings") at sculptor George Segal's chicken farm in New Jersey. Claes Oldenburg, the son of a Swedish diplomat, participated in these radical theater pieces. He recalled later the point of the happenings was to break down "barriers between the arts and [create] something close to an actual experience." Kaprow, Segal, and Oldenburg were among a new breed of artists who rejected Abstract Expressionism because they considered it removed from human experience and meaningless to the vast majority of people. Oldenburg's solution to the problem presented by Expressionism was to create art that everyone would recognize, but on an enormous scale.

His *Ice Bag* is big, but it will fit inside most museum and art galleries. It is not a readymade in the tradition of Marcel Duchamp because, in real life, there is no such thing as an ice bag of this size, but it is not Pop Art since Oldenburg took a commonplace, mass-produced object and hand-crafted it into a monumental sculpture. And the *Ice Bag* is a sculpture. The folds of the bag are beautiful, comparable to the drapery in a painting by the Renaissance master Andrea Mantegna.

Many of Oldenburg's sculptures, however, could only work outdoors as public art. His first commission for such a large-scale work came from the Yale School of Architecture. In 1969 he installed *Lipstick (Ascending) on Caterpillar Tracks* in Beinecke Plaza at Yale. There is nothing random about the sculpture; Oldenburg had visited the plaza where his sculpture would be displayed. There is a World War I memorial in the plaza, so Oldenburg's tube of lipstick echoes the classical columns of the monument. The caterpillar tracks refer back to the war, since the tank was first used in combat during World War I.

Colonization, from the History of Labor Murals

By Jack Beal

When twenty-five-year-old Jack Beal (1931–) finished his studies at the Chicago Art Institute, he was an Abstract Expressionist—just like all the other art students of that time. By the 1970s, however, Beal had allied himself with the New Realists, artists whose paintings of people looked like real people. Beal identifies himself as a "life painter." He paints still lifes, portraits, allegorical works, and that genre of painting modern artists have been deriding since the nineteenth century, historical narratives.

His *History of Labor* murals are four large oil paintings on canvas (each measures 146 inches by 150 inches) that trace the story of labor in America from the seventeenth century to the 1970s. The murals were commissioned by the U.S. Department of Labor and installed in the Frances Perkins Building in Washington, D.C. Beal's fee for this commission was $150,000. The paintings show a progression from the colonial period, when the first settlers had to cooperate with one another to survive in the American wilderness; to the eighteenth century, when work was a communal activity involving the whole family as well as helpful neighbors; to the Industrial Revolution, when work became impersonal and even menacing; to the high-tech world of the late twentieth century, when labor is performed by licensed specialists.

Beal's paintings are a return to artists' classic concerns: drawing, composition, color, and light. The scene is set on an upward-running diagonal, starting with the leg of the buckskin-clad frontiersman on the lower left and ending with the thick tree trunk at the upper right. Visual tension is supplied by the clouds, which run along the opposite diagonal, the woman carrying the bucket of water, and the settler poised to swing his axe. The dominant colors of purple, blue, gray, and black, along with the rugged mountains in the background, convey the total isolation and precarious situation of this tiny band of pioneers.

Peasant Wedding

By Philome Obin

The paintings from the first half of Philome Obin's (1892–1986) life are gone, lost or destroyed or possibly even thrown away by people who did not value them. Middle- and upper-class Haitians did not care for traditional Haitian-style paintings such as Obin created; they wanted to hang French paintings in their homes. Occasionally, he got work doing a decorative mural for a store, or a Masonic temple, or a Protestant chapel, but the fees were not enough to support the artist.

Obin's watershed moment came in 1944. That year an American Quaker, Dewitt Peters, opened the Centre d'Art in Port au Prince, the Haitian capital, to encourage Haitian artists and help them find a market for their work. Obin sent a painting of President Franklin D. Roosevelt to Peters, and Peters sent Obin cash. It was the start of a friendship between the two men and also of a financially successful art career for Obin. Peters's Centre d'Art became a gallery for Haitian artists, with Peters often acting as a distributor, getting the artwork to shops, collectors, and foreign tourists who found the naïve, colorful style of Haitian artists enchanting. Obin's fees rose steadily—in the 1970s he could command $3,000 for a painting.

Peasant Wedding, one of Obin's last paintings, shows a Haitian bride and groom on horseback, accompanied presumably by their families, wading across a stream en route to or from the wedding ceremony. There is undeniably a naïve quality to the painting—the blocks of color, the stance of the people and the horses, and the tree that looks like a cardboard cutout. And the view of bare feet and horse hooves in the water is a delightful touch. Compared to other Haitian artists, however, Obin's palette is much more subdued. There is nothing garish here. Obin tries to capture a real-life event in a realistic way, but filtered through the classic naïve Haitian style.

Un mariage de Paysans.

Still Life in Ostia

By William Bailey

For at least forty years, William Bailey (1930–) has spent his summers in Italy—and it shows, not only in the titles of his paintings, which often refer to places such as Arezzo, Urbino, and Citta di Castello, but also in his palette of colors, which imitate the rich shades of rose and ochre Italians use to paint the stucco walls of their houses.

Bailey paints still lifes, giving them a cool, pristine, otherworldly quality. His arrangements include bowls, vases, jugs, and eggs—simple things you find in every kitchen. Each piece is perfectly placed, so perfect that it would be criminal to touch them and disturb the arrangement. In some respects, they look more like sacred objects that ought not to be handled rather than household objects people use every day.

Bailey's paintings are a break from the still life tradition. The Dutch and French still lifes of the seventeenth and eighteenth centuries were overflowing with stuff—fruit and vegetables spilling out of their bowls, puddles of wine and olive oil on the table, a haunch of meat too large for its platter. You will not find such a riot of colors, textures, and activity in a Bailey still life. His paintings are not about excess; they are about precision.

In this quest for perfection, Bailey's work borrows from abstract art. In real life, jugs and bowls don't really look like this. And Bailey is aware of that, of course. He has said of his still life paintings, "I'm trying to paint a world that's not around us."

1661

SMALL VASE OF FLOWERS

By Jeff Koons

With Jeff Koons (1955-), Pop Art has made a comeback in a big way. Make that a HUGE way. Like Andy Warhol, Koons has made himself into a celebrity inside and outside the art world. But Koons is so careful about his public persona that at one point he hired an image consultant—something Warhol never did.

In the art world, reaction to his work largely falls into two camps—adoration or vitriol. His *Balloon Dog*, for example, a monumental metal sculpture shaped and painted to look exactly like balloons twisted into animal forms at children's parties, left art critic Jerry Saltz "wowed by the technical virtuosity and eye-popping visual blast." Mark Stevens of the *New Republic*, on the other hand, believes Koons is fundamentally a cynical artist who serves up meaningless, overpriced work to people who don't know any better, specifically, "the tacky rich." Yet the connoisseurs buy Koons's work, too. In November 2007, the Gagosian Gallery bought Koons's *Hanging Heart* sculpture for $23.6 million—the highest price ever paid at auction for a work by a living artist.

Koons's work comes out of the anti-art philosophy of the Dadaists, Duchamp's readymades, Pop Art's fascination with the mundane, and Claes Oldenburg's monumental sculptures of everyday objects. For Koons's critics, *Small Vase of Flowers* is overdone kitsch, while Koons's defenders would say he is overturning traditional standards of good taste with this overdone polychromed wooden sculpture of spring flowers.

It is hard, perhaps impossible, to find meaning in Koons's work, yet he insists his balloon art and giant flowered puppy sculptures are rich in meaning. And it is true that the world is filled with much more kitsch than fine art. Is it proper to love the kitsch as much as we love a da Vinci or a Monet? That's what Koons asks, and the question refers back to a debate that has raged for thousands of years—what is art, and who gets to define it?

Index

Special thanks to Charles Merullo and Ali Khoja at Endeavour.

The Book of Art was created by Black Dog and Leventhal in conjunction with Endeavour London Limited.

Monuments Francais, Paris, France/Giraudon 136; Church of Sveti Kliment, Ohrid, Macedonia 138; Scrovegni (Arena) Chapel, Padua, Italy, Alinari 140; British Library, London, UK 142; Worcester Art Museum, Massachusetts, USA 144; Tretyakov Gallery, Moscow, Russia 146; Galleria degli Uffizi, Florence, Italy 148; Alte Pinakothek, Munich, Germany/Interfoto 150; National Gallery, London, UK 152; Chartreuse de Champmol, Dijon, France/Lauros /Giraudon 154; Galleria dell' Accademia, Venice, Italy/Giraudon 156; Museo Nazionale del Bargello, Florence, Italy 158 top; Baptistery, Florence, Italy 158 bottom; Musee Conde, Chantilly, France/Giraudon 160; Brancacci Chapel, Santa Maria del Carmine, Florence, Italy 162; Museo dell'Opera del Duomo, Florence, Italy 164; National Gallery, London, UK 166; Museo Diocesano, Cortona, Italy 168; National Gallery of Art, Washington DC, USA 174; Galleria Nazionale delle Marche, Urbino, Italy 176; National Gallery of Art, Washington DC, USA 178; Graphische Sammlung Albertina, Vienna, Austria 180; Orsanmichele, Florence, Italy 184; Memling Museum, Bruges, Belgium 186; Pinacoteca di Brera, Milan, Italy, Alinari 188; Musee National du Moyen Age et des Thermes de Cluny, Paris 190; British Museum, London, UK 192; Louvre, Paris, France/Giraudon 194; Prado, Madrid, Spain 196; Galleria dell' Accademia, Venice, Italy/Cameraphoto Arte Venezia 198; British Museum, London, UK 206; Galleria Degli Uffizi, Florence, Italy/Alinari 208; British Museum, London, UK 210; Private Collection 212; Private Collection/ © Agnew's, London, UK 214; Galleria degli Uffizi, Florence, Italy 216; Loggia dei Lanzi, Piazza della Signoria, Florence, Italy 218; Musee d'Art et Histoire, Geneva, Switzerland/Photo © Held Collection 220; © Isabella Stewart Gardner Museum, Boston, MA, USA 222; Scuola Grande di San Rocco, Venice, Italy 224; Kunsthistorisches Museum, Vienna, Austria 226; Private Collection/Giraudon 228; Musee Nat. des Arts d'Afrique et d'Oceanie, Paris, France/Giraudon 230; Toledo, S.Tome, Spain/Giraudon 232; Victoria & Albert Museum, London, UK 234; Museo e Gallerie Nazionali di Capodimonte, Naples, Italy 236; Contarelli Chapel, S. Luigi dei Francesi, Rome, Italy 238; Louvre, Paris, France/Giraudon 242; Louvre, Paris, France/Lauros /Giraudon 244; © Isabella Stewart Gardner Museum, Boston, MA, USA 248; Metropolitan Museum of Art, New York, USA 254; Louvre, Paris, France/Giraudon 256; Mauritshuis, The Hague, The Netherlands 260; Aldo Crespi Collection, Milan, Italy 262; © Ashmolean Museum, University of Oxford, UK 264; Yale Center for British Art, Paul Mellon Collection, USA 266; American Museum of Natural History, New York, USA/Photo © Boltin Picture Library 268; National Gallery, London, UK 270; Musee Cognacq-Jay, Paris, France/Giraudon 272; Residenz, Wurzburg, Germany/Bildarchiv Steffens 274; Musee des Beaux-Arts, Rennes, France/Giraudon 276; Musee Lambinet, Versailles, France/Lauros/Giraudon 278; National Gallery, London, UK 280; Private Collection/Phillips, Fine Art Auctioneers, New York, USA 282; The Detroit Institute of Arts, USA/Founders Society purchase, Dexter M. Ferry Jr. Fund 284; National Gallery, London, UK 286; © Collection of the New-York Historical Society, USA 288; Nottingham City Museums and Galleries (Nottingham Castle) 290; Chateau de Versailles, France/Giraudon 292; Private Collection/Photo © Bonhams, London, UK 296; Louvre, Paris, France/Giraudon 298; Musees Royaux des Beaux-Arts de Belgique, Brussels, Belgium 300; Hermitage, St. Petersburg, Russia 304; Brooklyn Museum of Art, New York, USA 306; Prado, Madrid, Spain 308; The Detroit Institute of Arts, USA 310; Hamburger Kunsthalle, Hamburg, Germany 312; Victoria & Albert Museum, London, UK 314; Louvre, Paris, France/Giraudon 316; Worcester Art